DESIGN AS
FUTURE-MAKING

Bloomsbury Academic
An imprint of Bloomsbury Publishing Plc

50 Bedford Square
London
WC1B 3DP
UK

1385 Broadway
New York
NY 10018
USA

www.bloomsbury.com

Bloomsbury is a registered trademark of Bloomsbury Publishing Plc
First published 2014

British Library Cataloguing-in-Publication Data
A catalogue record for this book is available from the British Library.

ISBN:
HB: 978-0-8578-5838-2
PB: 978-0-8578-5839-9

Library of Congress Cataloging-in-Publication data is available for this book.

Design by Evelin Kasikov
Printed and bound in India

Edited by
Susan Yelavich and
Barbara Adams

DESIGN AS
FUTURE-MAKING

BLOOMSBURY
LONDON · NEW DELHI · NEW YORK · SYDNEY

Table of Contents

UP-ENDING SYSTEMS

ACKNOWLEDGMENTS

We wish to express our gratitude and appreciation to our colleagues, friends, and families, without whose encouragement, patience, and support this book would not have been possible. *Design as Future-Making* grew out of a significant Parsons initiative begun in the fall of 2005—a course titled Global Issues in Design and Visuality in the 21st Century: Culture. With the support of Tim Marshall, in his capacity then as dean of Parsons, and of Hazel Clark, former dean of Parsons' School of Art and Design History, scholars and practitioners from around the globe came to New York to share the ways in which their practices reflect and intervene in the complex changes brought on by this particular moment of globalization. Collectively, their work amounted to nothing less than a reconsideration of design's capacities to change social and cultural value systems in a world increasingly dominated by one value system, namely that of the marketplace.

Out of those multifarious conversations emerged a groundswell of voices calling for a more expansive and relevant role for design and designers—one that is more fully situated in the social, political, and environmental contexts of the people with whom they work. So our first debt of gratitude is to the contributors to this volume: Arjun Appadurai, Anna Barbara, Elio Caccavale,

Stephen Talasnik, *Cluster*, 2013, detail, pencil. Courtesy Stephen Talasnik.

Hazel Clark, Teddy Cruz, Clive Dilnot, Sean Donahue, Jamer Hunt, Ivan Kucina, Sze Tsung Leong, Tim Marshall, William Morrish, Tom Shakespeare, Mette Ramsgard Thomsen, Bruce Sterling, Cameron Tonkinwise, Jilly Traganou, Grace Vetrocq Tuttle, and Otto von Busch. Hazel Clark, in particular, receives our special thanks for her encouragement to pursue this project as a book. At the time she suggested the idea, Parsons' Masters of Arts in Design Studies was in the process of inception. Now that the MA Design Studies is a reality, this project has immediate relevancy to a new and growing body of scholars of design at Parsons and around the world. Another early supporter, and briefly a collaborator as well, was Julia Dault. A treasured friend and colleague, Julia has since left Parsons to devote her energies to her highly successful career as an artist. We thank her specifically for her help during the critical stage of framing the book's thematic structure.

Of course, translating this collection into a cohesive volume in such a way that it will appeal to an audience as diverse as its contributors requires conscientious and meticulous attention to language. In this, we were especially fortunate to be able to rely on the considerable editing talents of Thomas F. Reynolds, a long-time colleague of Susan's. We thank him for his patience, his eye and ear for locution on the page, and his camaraderie throughout. Thanks are also due to Parsons MA Design Studies student Komal Sharma for her expeditious photo research and technical support in the final stages of manuscript preparation.

For making it possible to present their ideas as a publication, we want to extend deep and sincere thanks to Rebecca Barden, our editor at Bloomsbury in London, as well as to her assistant, Abbie Sharman. We recognize that publications such as this one require a faith in ideas as much as a faith in their ability to be taken up and read. Bloomsbury is that rare publisher that is fearless.

Lastly, we would be remiss in neglecting to cite our main sources of fortification: Susan's husband, Michael Casey, and her son, Henry T. Casey, and Barbara's husband, Xavi Acarín. They are the embodiment of the values we cherish.

FOREWORD

Arjun Appadurai

This important collection of essays marks a new moment in design studies in which design is fully conceived as a practice that continuously reimagines its own conditions of possibility.

Designers and design scholars have always understood that there is an obvious kinship between design, innovation, and newness and, thus, that design is a natural ally of futurity. The essays in this collection take this insight out of the domain of common sense and move it into the space of creative and critical reflection.

One way in which this space is created is by reopening such issues as ephemerality, artifice, and innovation to deeper scrutiny. Several of the authors use these lenses to suggest that the relationship between fashion and time is not necessarily smooth or coherent but can be asymptotic and critical. In these perspectives, design and temporality can be seen as co-productive, and design can reopen the dialogue between memory, futurity, and newness, rather than serving as a mere mirror of commodified duration.

In a similar manner, several essays in this volume invite us to rethink the problem of materials and materiality by suggesting that design is not a mere operation upon preexisting materials of an ideal (or idealized) series of creative operations. Rather, whether in the matter of clothing, architecture, or digital design, materiality can be viewed as a design context, and design can be treated as a form of vibration (in the sense of Jane Bennett's idea of "vibrant matter")

Barbara Kruger, *Past/Present/Future*, 2010, Stedelijk Museum, Amsterdam.

that disturbs and creatively animates the material world and adds new forms of movement to already moving and dynamic materials.

It follows too that the thinking behind this volume unsettles the ways in which space and time have been segregated in prior design thinking. By looking at the future less as an abstract topology and more as an embedded property of the life of things, space appears in this volume as a "fold" within time, as a medium that shapes, and is shaped by, temporal processes. Design thus emerges as a mediator of the relationship between space and time and not just as a manipulator of the temporality of things.

Photograph Hanny Breunese. Courtesy Hanny Breunese.

Finally, reading these essays together produces in the reader a deep sense of the potential liberation of design thinking from the short-term tyranny of the cycles of fashion. While those cycles, no doubt, are an unavoidable part of the logic of late industrial consumerism, the authors in this volume, by reanimating the ideas of sustainability, materiality, and context, show us how design can begin to realize its most interesting potential, which is to mediate the relationship between long-term logics of sustainability and the short-term logics of fashion. Looking both ways at once, design can open up a new ethics of thingness, which might make social life both more exuberant and more just.

INTRODUCTION

Susan Yelavich

Design is always future-making. Present and powerful, it is the economic stimulus *du jour*. Silent and ubiquitous, it is perpetually underestimated as a social, political force. We live in a culture that waits for the next name-brand designers to lend their names to big-box retail, yet few people think about the pervasive conditions—the openings and barriers, physical and virtual—that shape and inhibit their lives. Which, of course, are their futures.

This paradox of visibility and invisibility is not just a reflection of the differences between design understood as commodity and design as social practice; it is inherent in the ways of acting *in* and *on* the world that are peculiar to design. Designers deploy knowledge derived from actions that literally change things and, therefore, behaviors. At the same time, they are never solely observers; they are interventionists who never act alone.

Design as Future-Making is a testament to the breadth and scope of design's social nature or, better put, the social relationships embedded in and mediated by the spaces, places, messages, and things encountered everyday. This collection of essays from designers and theorists hailing from various practices and places in the world is less concerned with design per se than with how and where design can contribute to conversations larger than itself.

The previous century listened patiently to the perennial complaint of the adolescent design field that no one understood what it was. Finally recognized—often under the glare of celebrity floodlights—design finds itself

Alex S. MacLean, Landslides Aerial Photography. Film capture, Pivot Irrigators in the Desert, Strauss Area, New Mexico, 1994. Courtesy Alex S. MacLean.

in an identity crisis. This is something of an ironic state of affairs, considering that branding is now one of design's core specialties. Perceived as a holistic makeover, design has become a panacea for whatever ails. Politically neutral, never demanding, the popular perception of design threatens to override its criticality and obscure its capacity to engender *agency*, in the best sense of that word. We are at risk of losing sight of design's part in enabling us to live well with each other and to live wisely with finite resources.

Design as Future-Making offers emergent models of design that are much needed today. It positions contemporary practice within a pan-disciplinary framework. This is especially critical now that virtually every object, place, and phenomenon is understood to exist in an ecology of forces and counterforces. Of course, it was always so, but the situation is far more complicated today. Networks are no longer metaphors but a vast agglomeration of cables, extruding untold billions of electronic exchanges that can and do alter the world at breakneck speed.

The resulting convergences, frequently blamed for accelerating market-driven conformity, have also had another effect. From the torrents of information, certain lively new tributaries can be identified. Anthropologist Arjun Appadurai, whose work was a critical catalyst for this book, calls these new "sodalities." [1] Designers of conscience are seeing their concerns echoed across the particularities of culture and traditional measures of distance. The same global flows that accelerate consumption are also creating a climate that supports the reinvigoration of design as a fundamentally ethical activity. [2] I deliberately write "reinvigorated," since so much of the history of design is a history of reform.

However, the ideas and the work represented in Design as Future-Making differ from the past in two important respects: they reject the idea of proselytizing in favor of conversation and healthy dissent, and they eschew the idea of a yet another unified design movement to attend more closely to the social interactions that occur within the microcosms of context. The risks of fragmentation and isolation are increasingly mooted by the growing presence and exposure of these projects to one another, a welcome, if backhanded, gift of globalization. If this portrait of a groundswell sounds utopian, it is, but only in the sense of what architect and critic Michael Sorkin calls "eutopian." In choosing *eu*, the Greek prefix for "better" over *u*, meaning "best," Sorkin calls for a plurality of visions for *topos*, or "place." [3] However, where Sorkin locates *topos* in architecture and urbanism, Design as Future-Making also includes all that is implicit in those spaces: the messages, objects, images, and conversations that reverberate and crisscross within them. They are all sites of potential.

Certainly, the authors included in Design as Future-Making view the fusions and collisions of networked culture as a source of new understandings and new possibilities. Challenging the limits of professionalization without eschewing their craft, they are opening the field to other voices and other conditions. Masses are understood as publics, practitioners as collaborators. They see issues—social justice, environmental health, political agency, education, and even the right to pleasure and play—not as dematerialized ideas and values but as occasions for design. *Design as Future-Making* demonstrates how each of those realms of daily life is affected by, and indeed determined by, their physical and virtual contexts. But for all its quotidian presence, design is ultimately the art of the possible. If design is to be relevant to the twenty-first century, it must be as multifarious and complex as the challenges ahead.

Organized by three interrelated themes, Crafting Capacities, Shifting Geographies, and Up-Ending Systems, the essays in *Design as Future-Making* show that design can promote individual agency, engage communities, and propose systemic changes within a global framework of mutual obligations. The approaches discussed in each section range from the pragmatic to the poetic, but they are unified by the conviction that design must embrace the immanent nature of its work: never finished, always in progress, open to alterations, and always conscious that making entails destruction.

To that end, the work featured in Crafting Capacities challenges design production that is done out of sight. It augurs direct engagement with the tangible and visceral, maintaining that things have things to teach us. These authors believe that the sensory qualities, physical behaviors, and the cultural connotations of materials should be considered in tandem with the virtual technologies that increasingly govern daily life. Otherwise, design risks encouraging the kind of social amnesia that comes with uncritical consumption.

Product designer Elio Caccavale and bioethicist and sociologist Tom Shakespeare use provocative objects to pose thought experiments that enable the public to reflect on the merits and risks of a new medical device, practice, or system before it becomes a fait accompli. Media designer Sean Donahue shares design techniques and strategies with marginalized communities so they can fully engage in civic life, not merely respond to civil laws. Instead of perpetuating the idea that new fashion design is sui generis, hactivist Otto von Busch taps into its gene pool. He breaks its codes—the signs, structures, and strategies that come to define a label—to give people the means to make themselves "fashion-*able*" and to introduce injections of micropolitical will into the channels regulated by industry. Architect and computer scientist Mette Ramsgard Thomsen focuses her research on material intelligence to explore how structures might *behave* (as opposed to how they might *appear*) as part of her long-term investigations into more sustainable ways of building. My own essay on the relation of textiles and architecture questions whether the digital algorithms that now allow buildings to be woven and knitted risk producing a sterile virtuosity if the culture of cloth and its history in architecture is overlooked.

The contributors to Shifting Geographies recognize that, even with the flattening of distances and time zones that has come to define twenty-first-century life, the human psyche is not quite prepared to dispense with geography and the associations attached to it over time. The reality is that notions of national identity, cultural habit, and all manner of political claims are being transported and reconfigured, sometimes hybridized and sometimes hardened. This condition presents designers, in concert with communities, opportunities to critique the discriminatory role of borders, to question the difference between human rights and legal rights, and to recognize the pleasures of difference and foster conditions for cosmopolitan hybridity.

When we hear the word "geography," we tend to imagine it as "topography." Urbanist and architect William Morrish reminds us that underneath our increasingly artificial landscapes is a largely invisible infrastructure, which is becoming the critical determinant of the health of our towns and cities as they are buffeted by the affects of climate change. Here, he discusses the urgency of making infrastructure and its affects not just visible to, but also actionable by, communities. Inextricable from structures, geography becomes political. Architect Ivan Kucina is likewise committed to the emergence of the citizen-designer and the designer-citizen; however, instead of directing attention to the unseen, he is concerned with the visible but overlooked. Informed by his experience of informal (and too often dismissed) building initiatives during the Balkan conflicts of the 1990s, Kucina writes of a new self-regulated urbanity. He looks to what can be gleaned from the informal strategies with which everyday people customize their cities and the services and events they offer. Architect and spatial studies scholar Jilly Traganou and design researcher and strategist Grace Vetrocq Tuttle look at the opportunities afforded by the design of the Olympic Games to draw attention to unsupportable and deeply problematic claims by nations to monolithic cultures in a globalized world and the protests designed to contest them. Teddy Cruz is an architect who works in geographies of conflict, in particular the border region between San Diego and Tijuana. He explores and initiates ways in which each side of this artificially bifurcated geography can *constructively* contaminate each other's dwellings and cities. In her essay on Peruvian fashion designer and activist Lucia Cuba, fashion studies scholar Hazel Clark offers a case study of conflict of another type altogether: a program of forced sterilization, which became the impetus for a critical line of clothing. Concluding the section is a series of urban portraits by and an interview with photographer Sze Tsung Leong, whose work centers on global cities past and present, reminding us that our moment of globalization is hardly unique in both its devastations and its achievements.

We spend our days negotiating systems—commuting, working, shopping, following the news—that seem locked in place. That is, until they are not, and we find ourselves locked out. The contributors to Up-Ending Systems echo the philosopher Nelson Goodman's succinct, but powerful, observation that "... worlds are as much made as found," [4] and offer a counterpoint to the social inertia that prompted Goodman's caveat that the future will be made without us unless we act otherwise. These authors demonstrate that world-making is not only possible but is also the very essence of what design does. Design acts otherwise.

Taking that assertion as a given, design studies scholar Clive Dilnot asks if design is making a just world. Since design opens and closes opportunities through its imbrication of goods and services into the economy, he argues that we need to understand its actions and consequences as fundamentally political. As fairness and justice boil down to equitable access to ever-shrinking resources—resources deployed to make the world as we know it—design studies scholar Cameron Tonkinwise writes that design is in fact a "de-futuring" enterprise. He argues that designers urgently need to develop proficiency in subtracting things, before those very same things light the bonfire of our present-future. Science fiction writer and design critic Bruce Sterling has made a life's work out of imagining worlds. Here he considers design's frailties and strengths in a multisystemic universe where changes are a constant and the challenge is in detecting the variable speeds with which they occur. Designer Anna Barbara thinks less about speed than about time, not as an abstraction but as a quality of space. Now that technology has rendered time seamless, she observes that architecture has followed suit, generating experiences like indoor skiing that are at odds with the seasons and surreal lighting affects that counter the workings of clocks. She asks designers to consider the destabilizing consequences of upending time. Anthropologist and transdisciplinary designer Jamer Hunt introduces yet another dynamic: scale. Playing David to the Goliath of gigantisms, from the Internet to political systems, Hunt points to subtle design decisions that reintroduce humanist values, if not human scale, to systems that seem to elude understanding, much less participation.

Cumulatively, these writers' perspectives contribute to the critical trajectory coalescing around the field of design studies. They assert design's role in developing active capabilities to negotiate our material, natural, political, and social entanglements. They ask us to be aware of how we choose to live in the world and what that world might be. They remind us that design's greatest possibility, its primary responsibility, is the reduction of suffering and the maximization of potential.

CRAFTING

CAPACITIES

CRAFTING CAPACITIES

Barbara Adams

In 1958, the sociologist C. Wright Mills addressed the International Design Conference in Aspen, Colorado. Mills encouraged designers to act not as adjuncts to the commercial apparatus but to understand themselves as agents of change and as critics who craft the physical frame of private and public life.[1] Mills was prescient in recognizing the central values that have emerged in design practice—the virtue of dialogue across fields, the significance of social collaboration, and the importance of craft in shaping the future. This understanding of craft is echoed in the essays that follow. Here, craft is understood expansively to mean a fundamentally social way of working with people through the medium and intelligence of materiality. With the arrival of smart materials that fuse artificial intelligence with the native intelligence of metals, fibers, and synthetics via sensors, microprocessors, and photovoltaics, materiality also includes composites of pixels and bytes and the flows of electrical current. The line between the ephemeral and the solid, between the natural and the artificial, has long since disappeared. As media scholar Anne Balsamo puts it, "Designers work the scene of technological emergence: they hack the present to create the conditions of the future."[2]

Richard Barnes, Nest #13 *Gabula Singularis*, 2000. Courtesy Richard Barnes.

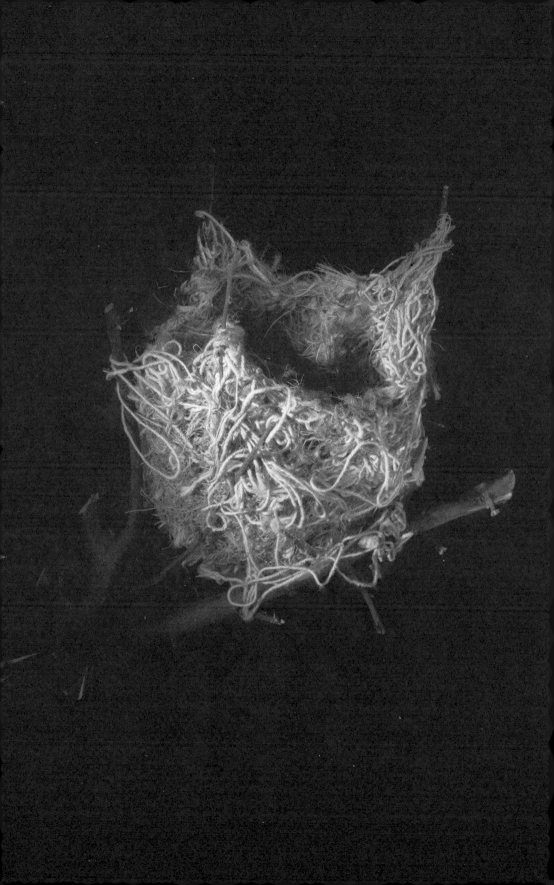

Craftsmanship, Mills maintained, is deeply tied to the sociological imagination that considers the ways in which individual biographies are related to larger histories, the ways in which personal concerns are related to broader social issues. Those who engage the sociological imagination (and Mills encouraged designers to do so) place their society historically and look at how it moves in its particular period.[3] Moreover, they seek possibilities for change by cultivating images of what society might become.[4] Craft is a way of activating our knowledge of social behaviors and desires, in the context of time and place, through work. For the craftsman, plan and performance are unified through an experience of working that is characterized by iteration, exchange, and continuous learning. The work of the craftsman is poetic in the sense that people cooperate with materials to prompt processes that are both expressive and productive, opening other ways of knowing and engaging the world. As such, craft harbors the capacity to create aesthetic experiences that allow us to comprehend more than just our present condition. Encompassing both process and product, this way of working allows us to imagine and initiate that which has not yet taken shape.

The practices and projects discussed in this section of *Design as Future-Making* embrace similar understandings of craft. They illuminate craft's capacities to create networked ways of working, to engage a range of publics, and to foster critical temperaments and disciplinary reflexivity. They generate novel forms of social relations—coproduced by and with spatial, material, and digital resources. Most vitally, they nurture opportunities for agency. Hierarchies are eschewed in favor of shared space in which mentoring, skill transference, and mutual discovery are the a priori values of the workshop. The negotiative and performative capacities of design are explored through systems that enable creativity and foster skill, through digital crafting that underscores the material logics of making, and through the use of design to raise and address troubling ethical and philosophical questions. Design in these instances is entrusted as a way to think and construct knowledge through fabrication. More than that, it opens forums for meaningful action.

The projects and provocations discussed in Crafting Capacities assert that design may be less about creating objects for subjects and more about crafting subjectivities themselves, without forgetting that those subjects interact with things that either inhibit or evoke possibilities for them on a daily basis. Designed and made things are understood as densities of cultural values and historical memories. They communicate and are endowed with the capacity to perform as animate agents imbued with the values of their makers. There is a mutuality of creation in which materials have as much affect as people do. Where architect

Louis Kahn famously asked "what the brick wants to be," now designers and architects ask how the proverbial brick might behave.[5] Today, designers have the capacity to collaborate not only with a wide range of constituencies and communities but also with things in all their vitality, with things in different social and material contexts. These alliances, as Deleuze argues, nurture the movement of thought that can lead to action:

> Mediators are fundamental. Creation is all about mediators. Without them, nothing happens. They can be people—artists or scientists for a philosopher; philosophers or artists for a scientist—but things as well, even plants and animals. . . . Whether they're real or imaginary, animate or inanimate, one must form one's mediators. It's a series: if you don't belong to a series, even a completely imaginary one, you're lost . . . one is always working in a group, even when it doesn't appear to be the case.[6]

The authors in Crafting Capacities see mediation as fundamental and think seriously about the redistribution of knowledge and how we might develop new vocabularies for thinking via design processes. This section of the book asks how design might traverse the capacities of work and action. Hannah Arendt maintains that work is worldliness and involves the capabilities necessary to negotiate with nature in order to design and produce the artificial things that house our lives and legacies. Action, she avers, is the activity between the plurality of people that constitutes the public and political realm. When we act and speak, we set in motion an "agent-revealing capacity" that allows us to see who people are (versus simply what people are) and to negotiate, yet maintain, our differences to establish a shared reality from which we might actualize our capacity for freedom.

In order to recognize the identities of people or to establish shared histories or to experience togetherness, Arendt argues that we need storytellers. In the essays that follow, we see how design engages the narrative and performative qualities that might create public realms where people act and speak together. As Arendt notes, these spaces are fragile and ephemeral, dissolving each time people disperse. Thus, the public realm is an ongoing project where the forum for dialogue is created and recreated each time people assemble to establish relations and create new realities.[7] This process is based in action, yet it does not render making insignificant. Although Arendt claims that action goes on "directly between men without the intermediary of things or matter,"[8] she also notes that *homo faber* (for our purposes, the designer who adopts the ethos of craft) has the ability to create a durable world of things that connect those who have it in common.[9] Human affairs need human artifice to house them:

> [A]cting and speaking men need the help of *homo faber* in his highest capacity, that is, the help of the artist, of poets and historiographers, of monument builders or writers, because without them the only product of their activity, the story they enact and tell, would not survive at all. In order to be what the world is always meant to be, a home for men during their life on earth, the human artifice must be a place fit for action and speech.[10]

One of the capacities of craft is to create a home not only for the world in which we live but also to consider how to house the yet-to-come. This raises overwhelming and recalcitrant questions about of how we inhabit the world, questions that need to be considered relationally. Whereas Arendt saw *homo faber* working in isolation, the authors in this section imagine the work of making differently. Here, design is initiated outside conventional contexts in an expanded field of new alignments—with people, with nature, with things, with technologies—that open new possibilities for what can be made and done. This quality is characteristic of the boundlessness and natality of action. In blending artifice and action—in construing making as another form of action—the authors in this section redefine users as actors and recognize vitality in the material. In doing so, they create new platforms for mediation that not only accommodate the future but cultivate active, public participation in how the future takes shape.

THINKING DIFFERENTLY ABOUT LIFE: DESIGN, BIOMEDICINE, AND "NEGATIVE CAPABILITY"

Elio Caccavale and Tom Shakespeare

What is design for? Most people would say that its overall purpose is to optimize the function, value, and appearance of products and services for the mutual benefit of consumers (or citizens, to use a better and less obsolete term), clients, manufacturers, and other stakeholders. But recently, we have also seen how designers have moved from products and services to designing systems, organizations, and citizenship.

To us, this is hardly new. Design has always had multiple roles. Almost a century ago, László Moholy-Nagy wrote, "We need to bring many types of knowledge into design." The role of design continued to evolve during the last decade, which has seen a proliferation of products and services that are intended to enable philosophical reflections. The traditional roles of design, designer, and designed object are redefined through new understandings of the relationship between the material and immaterial aspects of design, where the product or service is an embodiment of food for thought.

We know that design can help people to live better lives, but here we are particularly interested in using design as a tool for philosophical inquiry by creating design objects that do not just promote social innovation, or functional or stylistic enhancement, but that prompt the viewer to see things differently or to ask questions. We propose that certain products and services can function like extended philosophical thought experiments: "What if we could talk to our beloved pet dogs or cats?"[1] (Fig. 1). "What if we could clone our pet—would

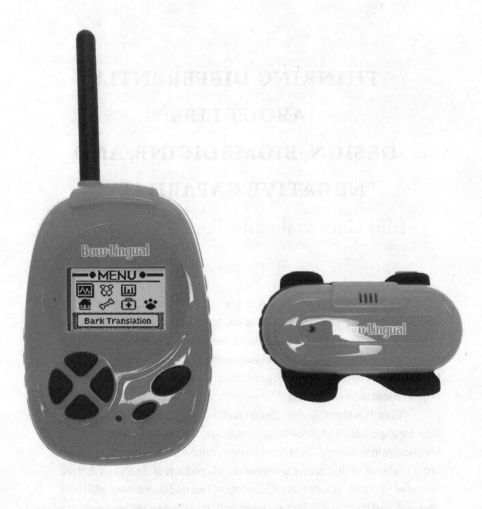

Fig. 1 Bow-Lingual, Glasgow, 2013. Photograph Elio Caccavale. Courtesy Elio Caccavale Design Studio.

26

we want to do that?"[2] In this essay, we are particularly interested in the clash between technological innovation and human concerns—for example, between ethics and social conduct—and in the role of design in the face of emerging needs, such as the need for innovations introduced by technology.

The poet John Keats proposed the concept of negative capability, defined in an 1817 letter as the state "when man is capable of being in uncertainties, mysteries, doubts without any irritable reaching after fact & reason." To us, this highlights how there are experiences and problems in life that are irresolvable. We may have access to all the empirical evidence, from the social sciences, and all the normative arguments, from philosophy, but still we lack clear answers. For example, in our own academic research, we have found the dilemma of prenatal diagnosis and selective abortion, crossover species, and assisted conception to be a few such conundrums. Another example of this issue of complexity is the predicament of disability, simultaneously medical and social, individual and structural. Faced by these lived realities for which there are no simple explanations or solutions, there is a need to grasp the nuance and the complexity of a particular situation. We think design can help us reach this state of negative capability, to rest with the mysteries and doubts and thus take the time to better understand.

We would like to borrow from the world of design to create thought experiments that enable an exploration of these dilemmas and possibilities. Thoughts are windows into the fundamental nature of things. A philosophical thought experiment is a hypothetical situation in the mind that often exceeds the bounds of current technology, or is even incompatible with the laws of nature, but reveals something philosophically enlightening or fundamental about the topic in question. Thought experiments can make abstract issues tangible and demonstrate a point, entertain, illustrate a puzzle, lay bare a contradiction in thought, and move us to provide further clarification.

Indeed, design thought experiments have a distinguished history. Consider, for instance, Archigram's Walking City, which constituted huge apartment blocks, including shops and services that could walk around on robotic legs. They suggested that this dynamic urban form would be better suited to the lifestyle of urban dwellers who were frequently forced to change jobs and find new apartments due to the fluctuations of the modern economy. Archigram's task was not to revolutionize architecture but rather to present a way of thinking (philosophizing) about it.

Intriguingly, if you are familiar with the work of Memphis, Superstudio, and, more recently, Dunne & Raby, you are likely already aware that some of their projects might be understood as a sort of materialized form of philosophical discourse. Groups like these sometimes work at a university and sometimes as independent designers. They also mix these worlds in various ways, especially in the ways in which they communicate their work through exhibitions and books.

Many designers today work with scientists, social scientists, and philosophers, opening up alternative ways to scrutinize science. Projects have explored biotechnology, robotics, and nanotechnology. In this world, designers have learned to articulate their aims and methods with new types of arguments.

Arguing about Science

Designers have also become involved in two debates that have raged in the world of social and cultural studies over recent decades as to the status and role of science. The first, often labelled the Science Wars, represents the collision between relativist critical theory and realist science. Thomas Kuhn demonstrated that science does not progress in a smooth line toward greater knowledge. Instead, development occurs via paradigm shifts, prior to which scientists are unwilling or unable to contemplate possible new interpretations, despite problems with contradictory data.

Post-Kuhn social scientists began to deconstruct science's positivist assumptions. Post-structuralists and post-modernists challenged the truth claims of objective science, claiming that knowledge depends on the observer and is socially constructed. Such shifts triggered a tidal wave of esoteric theory and open season for those who were skeptical of science's self-confidence and impact, not to say envious of all that funding.

Those scientists who noticed that their assumptions had been radically questioned by other sections of the academy began to fight back. Their main tactic was to show that all this challenging theory was no more than fashionable nonsense. Physicist Alan Sokal submitted his now-notorious paper "Transgressing the Boundaries: Towards a Transformative Hermeneutics of Quantum Gravity" to the leading critical theory journal *Social Text* and gleefully revealed it to be a hoax, once it had been published.

The second debate was a more British affair. Faced with a series of crises in the legitimacy and public acceptance of science, including the bovine spongiform encephalopathy (mad cow disease) disaster, the MMR vaccination controversy (the now-discredited claim by Andrew Wakefield that MMR led to autism), the disruption of Monsanto's genetically modified crop trials, and the Alder Hay scandal (in which a pathologist retained the organs of dead infants for research without seeking appropriate permission from parents), the scientific establishment decided that something had to be done.

Back in 1985, the Royal Society—the advisory body to the British government on matters of science—issued the Bodmer Report on the public's understanding of science. The report, which is now credited with the birth of the Public Understanding of Science movement in Britain, suggested that there was a serious problem in the perception and acceptance of science because most members of the public were so ignorant about basic matters of scientific fact and methodology. This left lay people vulnerable to misinformation and scare-mongering, and it also fueled suspicion and hostility to science. A commonly cited phrase was the "yuck factor," signifying the process whereby lay people who were unfamiliar with or disconcerted by scientific breakthroughs then rejected new advances on the basis of knee-jerk emotional responses rather than evidence or reason.

The scientific establishment decided that the answer to the crisis was to fund initiatives in the Public Understanding of Science, which would inform people of the true nature of research and put their minds at rest. The Royal Society, the Wellcome Trust, the Medical Research Council, and other funders began to support a range of work on the social, ethical aspects of science and in science communications.

Social scientists reacted negatively to this top-down, and somewhat naïve, approach. They argued that the deficit model on which the Public Understanding of Science assumption depended was mistaken. The public were experts on their own lives, not ignorant dupes. It was not necessary for them to be lectured on the facts of science. Scientists were members of the public themselves and should be held to account. They had responsibilities for the application and implications of their work. True dialogue was needed between science and the public, in which both sides had equal status.

In both of these often-contentious debates, it seemed to us necessary to reach a third position. As even proponents of science studies such as Bruno Latour have argued, it is important to accept the scientific method and the validity of research findings in an era when global warming threatens to undermine safety, security, and well-being across the planet. Bent Flyvbjerg calls for "phronesis," or practical wisdom, in which it is accepted that both science and social science have their separate roles and areas of expertise.

In terms of public responses to science, again, a balanced approach is needed. Improving scientific literacy is a priority. While the public does not need to know the details of research, it is important that people understand basic principles. Many young people find science difficult and daunting and give it up at the earliest opportunity. Ways to continue some level of awareness and involvement in debates about science can be found through science engagement activities. At the same time, scientists should accept that they have obligations to society and that deliberative dialogue on questions of safety, ethics, and funding priorities can be an effective way of increasing the legitimacy of research without blocking progress. Emotions may appear irrational, but they influence both scientists and lay people alike. Making a space to explore feelings is important, alongside the gathering of evidence and the development of argument.

The Contribution from Design

Thanks mainly to the work of the Royal Society, the Wellcome Trust, the National Endowment for Science, Technology, and the Arts (NESTA), the Engineering and Physical Science Research Council (EPSRC), the Art and Humanities Research Council (AHRC), and the Gulbenkian Foundation, design and science collaborations have become both fashionable and ubiquitous. In this world, designers have learned to articulate their aims and methods with new types of arguments. It began as part of the broader Public Understanding of Science agenda and as a belated response to C.P. Snow's claim that the "Two Cultures" of science and the humanities had become dangerously polarized and out of contact. Under the aegis of design and science collaboration, many initiatives and projects have been funded that bring designers, social scientists, philosophers, and scientists together to collaborate or that enable designers to have visiting research fellowships and residencies in research institutions. Designers have found the imagery and technology of contemporary science instructive and fascinating, making work that reflects on science or illustrates science.

An example of a design and science collaboration is Material Beliefs, a two-year research project, based at the Interaction Research Studio in the Department of Design at Goldsmiths, University of London, and funded by EPSRC. The project brought together a network of designers, engineers, scientists, and social scientists to explore potential implications of emerging biomedical and cybernetic technologies. The ambition was to produce design objects, exhibitions, and public discussions that would move scientific research out of laboratories and into public spaces. Four designers were responsible for the production of collaborative projects. They developed relationships with biomedical and cybernetic researchers at UK labs and institutes, guiding a design process in which scientific research became embodied in design objects. By responding to ethical, social, and cultural questions about our expectations of emerging technology, these productions acted as suggestions, not for potential products, but for alternative and often provocative roles for biotechnology in everyday life.

Fig. 2 Neuroscope in use, London, 2008. Photograph Robin Turner. Courtesy Elio Caccavale Design Studio.

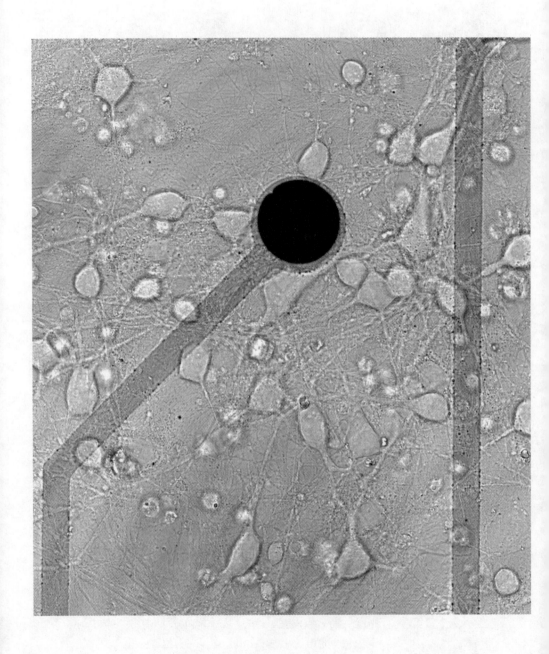

Fig. 3 Detail, Multi-Electrode Array, Reading, 2008. Cells grown on a Multi-Electrode Array (MEA) dish with a carpet of connections between them. Photograph Mark Hammond. Courtesy Elio Caccavale Design Studio and University of Reading/Cybernetics/School of System Engineering.

An example of a design object produced for the Material Beliefs project is the Neuroscope (Fig. 2). The project is a collaboration of Victor Becerra, Julia Downes, Mark Hammond, Slawomir Jaroslaw Nasuto, Kevin Warwick, Ben Whalley, and Dimitris Xydas—researchers and doctoral students at the Schools of Pharmacy and Systems Engineering at Reading University—and designers Elio Caccavale and David Muth.

The Neuroscope is an interactive toy that employs wireless technology to connect an interface to a culture of rat neurons living on electrodes (Fig. 3). Each electrode can detect neural activity and stimulate the culture based on user input. When the neuronal network displays suitable activity, the device reveals a virtual environment that provides a window into the life of the cells. Neuronal activity is displayed using animated graphics, and the user can directly interact with the culture using the control interface. This enables the virtual cells to be "touched," resulting in electrical signals sent to the actual neurons in the laboratory. The cells then respond with changes in activity that may result in the formation of new connections. The user experiences this visually in real time, enabling interaction between the user and cell culture as part of a closed loop of exchanges through the Neuroscope.

The Neuroscope exemplifies one possible future relationship with an emergent class of entities or living assemblages that can be categorized neither as organism nor as object—a hybrid, to use Latour's term. In this context, we can define the Neuroscope as a new generation of product that exists between object and biological systems, categorized as body and object. The device can be seen as a tool for philosophical investigation within a new emerging category that Latour defines at the intersection of the living and non-living, where a non-living thing in this context refers to a technology assembly. The result can be interesting and even disturbing, but at the same time makes us think about how this could become, one day, part of our daily life.

Another example of design and science collaboration is the Future Families project, which was developed during a residency at the Policy, Ethics, and Life Sciences Research Centre (PEALS). The project was initiated by the Arts Council's Artists Insights program and managed by Dr. Simon Woods, the co-director of PEALS. The project investigates IVF, donor conception, and surrogacy and the effects they might have on our notions of identity, self, and family. The structure of the traditional family has greatly shifted. A baby today can have up to five people responsible for its birth: a sperm donor, an egg donor, a surrogate mother, and a couple of any gender combination, or a single mother or father who will raise the child. The project is centered around the social relationships emerging between gamete donors, surrogates, recipients, commissioning parents, and children who are growing or could grow in families with other parents or progenitors who do not have a social connection.

Two examples of design objects produced for the Future Families project are Dummy Tummy and Fertilitoys. The first object is designed for surrogate pregnancies and consists of a rubber balloon attached to an electronic device. The balloon inflates in proportion to the surrogate's growing abdomen, making it possible for the commissioning parent or parents to remotely participate in the pregnancy while psychologically preparing themselves for the birth. The Dummy Tummy also includes a small celebrative pin that can be used to burst the inflatable tummy once birth takes place. The second example is a collection of soft dolls designed to support and guide would-be and current parents in the issues they will face being open with children about donor conception and surrogacy, thereby avoiding secrets. The Fertilitoys dolls consist of child-friendly sperm, egg, and womb dolls available in both donor and non-donor versions. Each doll or a combination of them can be used to explain to children how they were conceived using donor eggs, donor sperm, or a surrogate.

The Future Family project engaged with different audiences through interdisciplinary workshops, exhibitions, and public presentations. By presenting these issues through design objects, the debate was shifted from the merely speculative to practical questions of how and why these products would be used in daily life.

Final Thoughts

Designers have had access to the world of academic and scientific research, and have used this to interpret science for wider audiences. None of the work cited is didactic, let alone propagandist. But in each case the designer has enabled others to make connections or see different aspects of the biomedical issue under investigation. These designers are not offering easy answers, but neither are they ducking the significance and relevance of the phenomena they explore. The work presents problems and helps viewers think through their responses, and it humanizes the science and medicine that underlay the designs. We think these designers are concerned about revealing the emotional and relational as they explore questions about ethics and responsibility, difference and identity.

To us, design interventions of this kind answer the queries we raised earlier about the added value of design and science collaborations, showing how designers can provide their own distinctive take on the world of scientist, social researcher, and philosopher, offering something beyond and often deeper than these other disciplines. Each project has engaged philosophically and socially with scientific research and emerged with thoughtful responses that we can now share. But the skeptic in us would not finish this discussion without raising doubts that have occurred to us, not just about these particular projects, but about the field in general.

For example, it is certainly a cliché but maybe also a cop-out to be always asking questions rather than giving answers. Perhaps where there are such different experiences and opinions, and where issues are so complicated and personal, it is difficult or even dangerous to make work that gives a single explanation or response. But sometimes we yearn for designers to produce a work of advocacy, judgment, or polemic to show that they have views of their own. Illustration and clarification are both useful, but we also need solutions.

Second, the argument of this essay is that design can be accessible, bringing issues in science and medicine to wider audiences that are enabled to engage with complexity and think through what these developments mean for their lives. But this process assumes that lay people are willing to engage with design and are capable of doing the work of interpretation and imagination. It also depends on designers making work that can speak directly to the widest possible public. We believe that the valuable design and science collaborations discussed in this essay manage to make that connection, not sacrificing complexity but achieving impact. Yet, in general, design and science projects can also be as esoteric and exclusive as any science. Designers often create projects for other designers or for curators rather than for the general public. We do not think these provisos or concerns invalidate the premise that design engagement with science and medicine can be of both instrumental and intrinsic benefit. However, the reservations perhaps serve as warnings, promoting necessary reflexivity and self-questioning. Design and science collaborations provide responsibilities, as well as opportunities.

One thing is certain: science will continue to develop in ways we cannot predict. Human beings will continue to be excited, alarmed, and confused by the choices that scientific research offers them. For explanation and illumination, society can turn to the careful arguments of philosophers or to the empirical evidence of social scientists. But the conversation will be incomplete if it does not also include the contribution of designers. We hope that this essay is an attempt to demonstrate the different qualities and questions that designers can bring to contemporary and historical scientific research and how, at its best, design can open up a space for philosophical inquiry that adds an important dimension to contemporary debates on science. After all, the point of linking design and philosophy is that you do not have to agree with the particular conclusion that a certain designer draws; what is interesting is when it makes you think in a different way about your own life.

UNMAPPING

Sean Donahue

It takes a surprising amount of strength to open a rolling gate. You make that first tug on its chain with your arms, and the rest of your body quickly realizes it's going to have to lean into it if it is going to move. I do so with the second tug, which simultaneously gets the gate rolling upward and lifts me off the ground with its momentum. Clinking rapidly, the gate rolls all the way to the top with the last few pulls. With both hands, I wrap the chain around the inside hook, once, twice, then free a hand to grab the worn bolt that's been hanging there since before my residency—I wonder how long it's been hanging here. Who hung it? What was this space to them? I quickly return my focus to the gate and put the bolt through a link to keep the chain from unwrapping and letting the gate roll back down.

Only now can I reach the front door. I find the key amongst my now growing set of keys, but only after stopping at several others first. I push the key, teeth facing up, into the lock, and it takes its ride across the tumblers, bouncing ever so slightly over each one. This particular key requires that I ease it back just a hair for it to settle in before I turn it clockwise two times, returning the latch back to its home in the lock. The door now relaxes and opens just a bit by itself. I open it the rest of the way and step into the space. I walk immediately to the light switch and turn on the lights; it's a side step really, and only two steps, at best. Once the switch is up, I hear the rushing buzz of electricity first, then see the fluorescents flash several times before settling in. Now the conversations may begin.

This description of a seemingly ordinary routine is not a fiction or a speculation or a metaphor for a series of notions toward reconsidering community, the civic, the urban. It is a narrative of things, of experiences, and of interactions—tangible engagements that collectively launch the possibility or impossibility of the day. It is in these material and experiential manifestations that meaning is constructed; it is here, for me, that *design* exists. Within the reciprocity between things and actions lies the ability to see, to recognize the value, the potential, the usual and the unusual that these built and material environments hold for those who engage them. My ability to push and pull these qualities using the language of design in order to construct other types of engagements, exchanges, and understanding—this is where the speculation lies, where the ability to unmap the usual orientations and expectations proposes a different possibility, relationship—the future.

The mutuality of action and response involved in the daily ritual of opening a space is a process that became my own during a project I led called LA Has Faults (Fig. 1). The project is part of an ongoing investigation into how design can be used as a catalyst to initiate, facilitate, and support new kinds of conversations—conversations conducted at different scales, led by different and differing agendas, from the individual to the household to the neighborhood to the city and beyond. This particular "conversation space" was designed to reside in the district of Westlake, located in Los Angeles, California, and act as a hub for building community and support systems for emergency preparedness.

An Ontological Preface

Before I go too far, I should disclose my relationship to the discipline of design; it is based on a very specific set of orientations. It's important to recognize and share these orientations because they shape how I see my role as a designer and what I am able to contribute. I thrive on these orientations; they provide me with a platform to untether from the isolating canons of discipline and focus instead on the unique qualities that designing can bring to an expanded field of issues, contexts, and interrogations. There are a number of them, but I will focus on three.

First, design and its contributions are not predefined by how others have applied them in the past. That is, as applications of the language of design, prior examples certainly inform our practice and are absorbed into the craft of design. They do not, however, predetermine how or to what the discipline is able to contribute.

Second, designers use the elements of design along with an understanding of context and materiality to construct meaning, value, and use. This is a very different orientation than saying that designers make logos or

Fig. 1 LA Has Faults, 2008. View of the introduction event at MacArthur Park. Photograph Yee Chan. Courtesy Sean Donahue.

Fig. 2 LA Has Faults, 2008. Creating letters to encourage conversation with and among neighborhood residents. Photograph Yee Chan. Courtesy Sean Donahue.

books or consumer products (all outcomes from the application of the elements of design in the past).

Third, design itself is a mode of knowledge production, and "designing" is an act of inquiry and synthesis. This requires methodologies and approaches that support both the specific needs unique to design and its inquiries, as well as the context of its intervention. This means not simply adopting preexisting methodologies from associative disciplines; after all, they have been created to support their own unique requirements and methods of knowledge production, not design's.

Together, these three specific beliefs provide the platform from which designers are able to move beyond simply repeating the formats of past ideas of practice and instead support the construction of new questions in new contexts with new contributions.

LA Has Faults

With these principles in mind, we can now return to LA Has Faults. This project focused on the near-downtown district of Westlake, home to a densely populated, predominantly Latino community. Encompassing a range of social and cultural institutions and economic scenarios, Westlake provided an ideal opportunity to address the largest demographic in Los Angeles as well as the convergence of issues associated with urban residential living.

Introductions

To introduce the initiative, a team of collaborators and students from Art Center College of Design in Pasadena and I conducted a large-scale design intervention in MacArthur Park, the social, cultural, and transportation hub of Westlake. The event ran for a full day, during which we constructed 20-foot-high letters that spelled five different words that could be associated with earthquakes and earthquake response. Built one at a time—each was left standing for 30 minutes to one hour—these words, in English and Spanish, were intended to reflect familiar earthquake rhetoric while piquing the curiosity of passersby (Fig. 2). "Shake," "Shift," "Aware," "Alerta," and "Alto" were used as prompts to start conversations with and among park visitors, passing commuters, and local residents. Recognizing that preparedness for an emergency disaster is not solely the responsibility of an individual or family unit, the letters were designed to be read from the top and at an angle, not just the side. This allowed the words to also be seen by the office workers, government officials, and service agency employees who worked in the high-rise buildings that surround the park. This attempt to engage a more holistic recognition of the range of actors with agency in this space helped support what "community" would need to come together to facilitate multiple scales of response. This was central to the design work done that day and to the entire initiative.

Although the words were left in place from 30 to 60 minutes, it took between one and two hours to build them. The lengthy time it took to produce each word was not an accident of process. It was not considered down time but rather an essential design element of the project. As we built the letters, public curiosity about the production of each word proved to be the greatest facilitator of conversation. Seeing the scale of the production and not knowing what was going on—let alone what word or thing was going to come out of it—became an ongoing source of questions, interest, and opportunity for involvement. This became the project's introduction.

As the center of many types of activities, including religious services, child-care outings, and people simply taking a break from the day and stretching their legs, the park enabled exchanges that would become central to LA Has Faults. Throughout the day, children would play between the boxes and in the tunnels of the letters' interiors. They would lend a hand to stack the "blocks" while the adults—who had stories of their own experiences in Southern California, Mexico, El Salvador, and Guatemala—took time to share their experiences. A conversation was built not just between the proverbial "us" and "them" (in this case, design facilitators and neighborhood participants) but also between "them" and "others" (local residents and passersby). This expanded series of exchanges was essential to the growth of the conversation and to forming a community to lead it.

Community, the Rhetoric of Good, and Working with People: An Interlude

Before sharing the second part of the project, it is important to describe the framework that this project was built on by looking at the ideologies and platforms that modeled and shaped the larger relationships and engagements advanced by the project. I'll start by discussing our particular use of the notion of community. In design, "community" is almost exclusively invoked to suggest a positive connotation of cohesion, to refer to a geographically close group of people (and by extension places and things in those places), or to characterize a practice where a designer works directly with people, as in community-driven design. But, in fact, communities as social structures host a multitude of formal and informal relationships and mechanisms that often limit participation, access, and resources, advancing certain members and subjugating others.

Design's role in situations like this, particularly those operating outside of the commoditized realm of exchange, more often than not relies on an unquestioned rhetoric of good to describe its intent without critically engaging the actual mechanisms of community as a social organizing structure. Misguided Victorian notions of philanthropy and missionary proselytizing, which have often permeated so-called social design, actively work against any nuanced understanding of the agendas, relationships, material infrastructures, and ecologies that could or do support "change" in any specific "community." Designers need to move beyond the framework of benevolence and explore the apparatus of these issues. "Good" is not simply a belief or value to be invoked. When good intentions are exercised, they activate a series of mechanisms, interactions, and exchanges that are supported and motivated by a multitude of agendas, not all of which are universally invested in "helping." When you interrogate spaces where there is a perceived lack of resources and services, you find that helping is often not the best framework to achieve a supportive role. In fact, there are often situations where help is invoked as a motivation, while the mechanisms of the engagement are not meant to help at all—at least in the way that the rhetoric of good as a concept is often promoted.

Instead of thinking of community as a token way to describe a neighborhood and viewing community-centered design as a default reference for good work, we might consider the notion of community through one of several possible qualities it could facilitate, for example a unity of will. We can then begin to parse how design's formal qualities advance or break down the effort to contribute to this intent. Rather than "creating community," which, we could argue, is less dependent on design than people, we can then focus on how what we design helps initiate or support a unity of will. This at least acknowledges specific agendas, interests, concerns, as well as our own positions. It also opens the door to engaging and acknowledging the range of design opportunities that come with issues of scale, participation, trust, ownership, systems, and evaluation, as well as the political ramifications of these issues and others. These issues tend not to follow the timeline usually allotted to, and by, designers to produce a scalable or market-based contribution. We need to recognize these characteristics and develop an expanded formal language and repertoire of tools that provide makers with a vocabulary to consider and build from so they can contribute to these spaces of engagement.

When the effort is made to engage people directly, it is often supplemented with methods that focus on examining and reinforcing the consumer-product orientation emphasized by the West's cultural emphasis on the individual. I believe that, as typically exercised, "people-centered" approaches—codified in design variously as human-centered design, user-

(213) 388-8812

2126

L.A.
Has
Faults

GUEST EXPERTS

TODAY

centered design, participatory design, co-creation, critical design, or design ethnography—do not properly support designers who want to address expanded social relationships. This is particularly true for those directly confronting issues and relationships of power, access, authority, gender, race, socio-economics, and the multitude of agendas and affiliations in a global context of policy or systemic engagement.

Each of the aforementioned approaches promotes an individual-centric position that isolates the individual (and on occasion those in immediate relationship to the individual) in order to study insights, habits, preferences, aspirations, and values either directly around consumer-product relationships or, more generally, at the level of individual-to-artifact exchange. All of them are orientations (accompanied by ideologies) that fall well short in many of the contexts of practice that engage actual community dynamics, systems, multiplicity, and policy. Approaches to engaging people and community need to move beyond a product or service orientation and develop a language and understanding of how to participate in and contribute to the politics, scale, and sustainability of power, authority, and access across multiple social agendas and positions. This requires methods and methodologies that directly confront these issues—methods and methodologies that acknowledge their actors' position and the position of others.

Conversation Space

Back again to LA Has Faults. Central to the second part of the initiative was being able to tell people we would be residing in this neighborhood, not just putting up unusual signs in the park. The next step was to create a space for additional and ongoing resources that would be able to host an ongoing conversation with the multitude of actors that influence, and are influenced by, the topic of earthquakes, all with the goal of defining and articulating the considerations unique to this neighborhood and its various communities (Fig. 3). We created our conversation space by converting a former retail space across from MacArthur Park into a dialogue center for advancing community conversations around the issue of emergency preparedness. The space was designed to provide an environment that facilitated dialogue and fostered communication among civic leaders, residents, and service providers. The space we ultimately chose acted as a conduit to identify and directly address the

Fig. 3 LA Has Faults, 2008. Converted conversation space located in Westlake, Los Angeles, along Seventh Avenue. Photograph Yee Chan. Courtesy Sean Donahue.

unique preparedness issues of this neighborhood and the community formed in the process.

     To do this, we designed everything from the signage to outreach, to multiple modes and scales of participation that allowed different and differing levels of engagement. Our goal was to flatten the hierarchies that usually characterize meetings between residents and local authorities. We focused on using design to create vehicles that would allow the people who are more often than not excluded from the outreach process to participate and contribute in ways meaningful to them. The design of the furniture was particularly central to this effort. The furniture oriented people to directly confront the explicit and implicit power and authority that representatives from different institutions bring with them when they attend outreach events. Each piece of seating was designed to hold at least two people. These variously sized benches all fit along a 40-foot-long table, which was made of smaller tables that could separate to support smaller groups when needed. The family-style seating required individuals to negotiate and share from the first act of sitting down. The benches were also designed to sit a little lower then usual. This was done so as to defuse any undue confidence that may come with simply wearing certain types of clothing, such as a suit. When you wear a suit and your knees are raised just slightly higher than usual, the pant legs rise and tighten around the back of the knee, exposing an unusually large amount of calf and sock. This not only makes most suit wearers a bit self-conscious, even uncomfortable, it also makes them look a little awkward or silly to those who notice. This attempt to displace or defuse dimensions of soft power, which are either exercised or implicit, is meant to create a platform for a more equitable exchange in a situation where, fairly or unfairly, suits embody an inhibiting hierarchy.

     The design of the space also worked toward moving conversations out of preexisting arguments and entrenched positions, and toward supporting the emergent concerns of the various communities coexisting within this neighborhood. Events of the week included regular luncheons that were open to all. There were also meetings with select groups of guests, who were invited by participants on prior days. Guests would range from representatives from the city of Los Angeles' Office of Emergency Management to the pastors of local churches, to principals and teachers of neighborhood schools, to newscasters, and to doctors in local clinics. All the food served at these lunchtime

Fig. 4 La Has Faults, 2008. Designer Vera Valentine waiting pensively to know what her lunch contains. Photograph Yee Chan. Courtesy Sean Donahue.

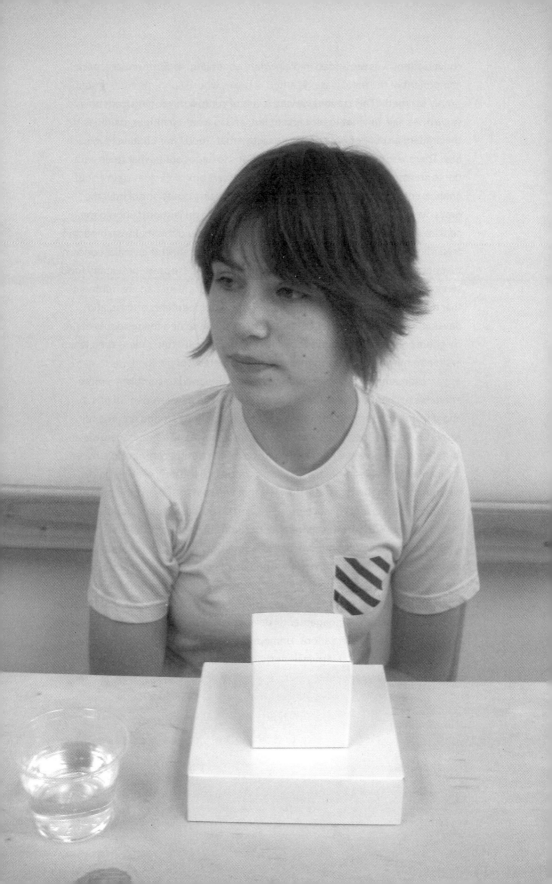

conversations was presented in plain white boxes **(Fig. 4)**. Furthermore, each component of the meal was presented in boxes whose contents were described simply as "food." This created varying levels of confusion, ranging from how to serve one's self, to what to pick first or last, and in what quantities, paired with the primary anxiety of not knowing exactly what "food" was contained in each box. There was an additional set of conditions to negotiate—what to do with the contents themselves. For example, the dessert box of cookies didn't hold enough cookies to feed everyone at the table, raising questions of how the group would navigate this: Would someone have to go without? Should the cookies be broken in half to serve everyone? How would this make each person feel? These questions were deliberately conceived to reflect the similar concerns that people encounter when negotiating emergency response shelter and food services. These personalized and shared experiences created an environment that enabled participants with differing agendas to negotiate, discuss, and develop collective responses that supported and benefited the residents of the neighborhood as a community coming together around this issue—even when at times it may be contrary to their individual interests or position.

Ultimately, this conversation space was designed to stimulate a more equitable exchange—one that in fact resulted in the development of plans and resources to support the community's expectations around emergency response. To that end, it was a success. The project was also simultaneously an investigation of possible roles and contexts for the design contribution. As we are increasingly able to see the changing conditions the new century holds, we contend with this question: How is it that we want to support the human condition in the twenty-first century? Relying on outdated frameworks and ideologies that support the agendas of positions blatantly antithetical to, or in conflict with, your own, your practice's, or your discipline's, while sticking to old approaches will not get us there. Recognition of issues such as access, power, authority, and equity is a start. However, expanding the definition of design and opening expressions of its capabilities to intervene in new contexts that question each point of possible engagement, I believe, will at a minimum serve as a way to unmap our existing orientations. Unmapping will allow design to develop new languages, definitions and questions that respond to the question in a twenty-first-century way.

FASHION HACKING

Otto von Busch

Fashion System and Passivity

Over the last decades, there has been a tendency to describe fashion as going through a process of democratization. With fast and relatively accessible fashion and collaborations between cheap brands and high-profile designers, there seems to be a more fair distribution of fashion goods throughout western societies. Yet the term "democratization" makes us believe we now have access to the decision-making processes of fashion, while we are simultaneously, and quite bluntly, locked out of any control or having a mandate to influence the brand. Clothes are still designed far from us, and the goods come to us ready-made on the hanger. We are steeped in a system of pacification and total control of what is deemed worthy and what is right, even if we feel we can pick from an endless amount of choices. All sensibilities of dress are funneled through the enormous, but narrow, fashion economy.

Fashion may be the perfect example of the activity substitution philosopher Slavoy Žižek and psychologist Robert Pfaller both call "interpassivity."[1] Throughout history, this mechanism of substitution has manifested itself in historical wailers—women hired to cry at funerals—and can today be found in the canned laughter on television. For Žižek and Pfaller, interpassivity is a type of surrogate ritual that displaces or delegates agency. We trade one type of agency for another in what we consider a better deal. Fashion may also be an example of interpassivity. The designer garment expresses some of my identity, as a complement to my own behavior. I submit to fashion in order to gain a claim to the zeitgeist, symbolic agency, or a sense of popularity. But at the same time, I position myself in an unreflected situation of submission. Through interpassivity, we give up our field of activity to a prepackaged one. In fashion this takes the everyday form of ready-to-wear.

One immediate response could be to start making things ourselves, a common practice of perceived independence. Making clothes at home has been an occupation since the beginning of textiles, so this is nothing new, but the motivation for these engagements has changed over time. The objectives of home sewing in the West were just a few decades ago still primarily those of economy or fit. Today, however, as with many other do-it-yourself (DIY) activities, the objective has changed to address instead questions of individual accomplishment, creativity, self-confidence, independence, self-reliance, development of skills and, not the least, lifestyle.[2]

As I will argue, there are DIY practices that deal not only with the hands-on activities of being frugal or repairing and making things, but with systematic and strategic application and repurposing, where these practices are inserted back into existing operating systems of society. These activities are dynamic design interventions, which insert new practices on a systemic and strategic level (Fig. 1). They are thus not isolated events, but interconnected with other actors, forces, and practices, forming new intersecting or complementary ecologies of practice. To get a clearer example of this we could look to the methods of hacking.

Hacking the Fashion System

Hacking is a contested concept. In popular media it connotes everything from dangerous cyber criminals and anarchic file-sharing pirates to obsessive programming geeks and car-tuning enthusiasts and usually some sort of countercultural rebels. Within hacker communities the term is also much disputed, not least the distinction between hacking as constructive or destructive. Programming guru Eric Raymond put the distinction simply as: "hackers build things, crackers break them,"[3] while media theorist William J. Mitchell paints a more nuanced description: "The best hacks are cleverly engineered, site-specific, guerrilla interventions that make a provocative point but aren't destructive or dangerous."[4]

Anthropologist Christopher Kelty suggests that hacking or, as he puts it, the practice of "geeks," introduces new entities into the world and is, in this

Fig. 1 Openwear Workshop, 2011. Photograph Zoe Romano. Courtesy Zoe Romano.

sense, constructive. Yet these new entities often overturn existing concepts and modes of representation, and can thus be seen as destructive. As Kelty notices, geeks are "involved in the creation of new things that change the meaning of our constituted political categories."[5] It is this constructive act—which in turn mobilizes a mix of entities, such as software or hardware, law, people, and practices—that makes the distinction too hard to draw. What from one producer seems like trespassing can, from the perspective of the newly introduced entity, seem as a rightful appropriation of everyday culture as exposed in the motto of the DIY magazine *Make*: "If you can't open it, you don't own it."[6]

This makes hacking a practice that highlights conflict and dissent simultaneously as it circumvents defenses and borders. When hackers build their own systems, even if the basic act is not in itself confrontational, it draws new borders, displaces power, and re-circuits established chains of command. When building a new system, it may become an incompatible counter-system and thus challenge consensus. In this way, hacking is similar to the "adversarial design" examined by interaction designer Carl DiSalvo, in which design exposes inconsistencies and disagreements and becomes a type of political design based on agonism and contestation.[7] With such an approach, design becomes a tool to provide, recognize, and express dissensus, and also construct paths for change. As DiSalvo notes, "adversarial design can identify new terms and themes for contestation and new trajectories for action."[8]

This political aspect of design also relates to a common misconception that hacking somehow dissolves power and is democratic, usually through examples of open-source software, the Linux operating system, or the online encyclopedia Wikipedia. But as highlighted by media theorist Alexander Galloway, the architecture of flat network structures and open protocols only shifts control from a highly visible, top-down command structure to a mode of control that is hidden inside the collaborative protocols themselves. Under the umbrella of collaboration, a systematic execution of power may reside that is just as effective as hierarchical oppression. As Galloway puts it, concerning the protocols for collaboration, "The contradiction at the heart of protocol is that it has to standardize in order to liberate. It has to be fascistic and unilateral in order to be utopian."[9] It is the interoperability between components of open systems that makes them dynamic and ready for change, thus encouraging interventions and contestation. But as mentioned, as hackers reorder the world, they are themselves forming new political arenas of dissensus.

To understand hacking as a practice, it must be examined on a systemic, strategic level. According to the Jargon File, the lexicon for hacker slang, the entry for hacker suggests that it is: "A person who enjoys exploring the details of programmable systems and how to stretch their capabilities, as opposed to most users, who prefer to learn the minimum necessary."[10]

The programmable systems could be operating systems in general, various forms of apparatus, or more soft systems, such as the structural arrangement of culture, capital, or communication. Thus, from my perspective hacking is an activity to improve things by acquiring and disseminating knowledge of the inner workings of systems and a mastery of the techniques that modify these systems. Hacking means to open black boxes, reverse-engineer their circuitry, and build a new plug-in to the system, challenging it and releasing new capabilities from it.

Furthermore, I would suggest there is a distinct difference between the 1968 counterculture movement or other forms of popular protest, in which the key tactic has been to drop out of the system, subvert it, or make it stop by sabotage. Hacking is not about sabotage but keeping the power on. Not dropping out, but plugging in. This means that hacking does not aim to destroy, take, or overthrow power, but rather to tune and disseminate power, bending the system in a more desirable direction through hands-on interventions and constructive acts. Hacking a system advances it because you love it, not because you hate it.[11]

To take a hacker perspective on fashion would mean to reverse-engineer, modulate, and plug into its inner workings on a strategic level. Just as a software operating system involves not only code but also people, law, and practices, the fashion operating system involves not only a technical system of production, fabric, and seams, but also a cultural belief system, full of icons, rituals, cultural signifiers, and, not least, the everyday practices of people involved in the consumption and display of fashionable goods. Fashion hacking means to start applying a hacking mentality to the fashion operating system, challenging it, and contesting its influences in a systemic way. This could mean breaking the interpassive logic of consumerism as well as organizing DIY efforts with the aim of self-determination. Ultimately, hacking produces hands-on tools and engagements for self-reflection, challenging the interpassive imperative of consumption.

Some Examples of Fashion Hacking

Fashion hacking is a strategic and empowered endeavor that reverse-engineers the inner functions, practices, and rituals of fashion in order to build a plug-in practice. I will highlight three examples that trace different levels of hacking: Hacking-Couture by Giana González, Counterfeit Crochet by Stephanie Syjuco, and the OpenWear platform of Milan.

New York-based interaction designer Giana González runs the project Hacking-Couture. As a mix of programming practice, fashion education, and civic engagement, she organizes workshops in which participants reverse-engineer fashion brands, deprogram their visual language or code, and map this source code into charts. These charts are used to trace how a brand's components are constituted and identified in order to build further on the code. The participants later use old garments to reinterpret the code and render visible their own versions and executions of the code. They are, in turn, photographed and turned into new codes of the brand. As the participants "Chanelify" their old garments into new Chanel-like fashions, they use the same code as the brand, and their own creations can thus be regarded as authentic as the originals. To González, great fashion designers are masters of similar coding skills. A fashion programmer, like Karl Lagerfeld, may fully grasp the source code of his brand, explicitly read its historic code, and parse strong new codes in order to produce new programs or patches, but he does not share the process as open source. The Hacking-Couture workshops thus make the hidden designer source code available to amateurs as they engage in fashion code hacking.

This aspect of González's practice resonates well with the media ecologist Alexander Galloway's ideas about code being a stronger text: "code is the only language that is executable."[12] Code is thus not only a text or message, but also an actualizer. Code transmits an impetus or a force of execution. It wants to run, to control operations. "Code has a semantic meaning, but it also has an enactment of meaning."[13] For González, this means fashion code is not only in the shape and proportion of garments, but it is also executed by the wearer through posture and movement. In the end, González's workshops are a total code-recycling that renders the full hack visible, where visual code is first reverse-engineered and tuned by the participants and then re-executed in front of the camera in order to become open and authentic code again. It is a recycling activity that happens on two levels, material as well as visual. It also includes skill building on several levels, decoding brands and activities, as well as reverse engineering and appropriating in addition to the basic skill of sewing.

San Francisco-based artist Stephanie Syjuco's Counterfeit Crochet Project uses similar techniques of engagement (Fig. 2). Syjuco encourages participants to print out their desired "it-bags" as low-resolution images from the Web and enlarge them into full-scale pixelated patterns. These abstract depictions of online desire then become crochet patterns for the bags in which each pixel is translated into a crochet stitch. As amateur crafters reproduce their objects of desire, they turn their passion for upmarket handbags into basic crafting skills as they are "crafting their hearts' desires, and both laughing at and paying homage

Fig. 2 Counterfeit Crochet Gucci Bag, 2007. Photograph Otto von Busch. Courtesy Otto von Busch.

to the 'high-end' fashion world!"[14] If you squint your eyes, the counterfeit may even look like the real thing.

Just as the technical drawings of fine craft goods are outsourced for production, Syjuco also distributes her counterfeiting practice among pirate peers and global collaborators. Through this process, the counterfeits explore the limits of craft as technique and as a systemic political act in which questions are raised about the borders between copy and original, revaluing the worth of desire, labor, and exchange. To facilitate this process, Syjuco shares patterns and instructions online for knock-off production and encourages free-forming and a "healthy sense of experimentation on the maker's part."[15] Instead of using a small needle and thin yarn for high resolution and good finish, she promotes the use of thick yarn to make the process faster and easier. It is not a question of making a perfect copy with exclusive threads but instead to debase the original using common materials.[16]

Where Hacking-Couture has a more direct relation to hacking techniques and puts emphasis on tracing, deciphering, and reproducing once-exclusive brand codes, Counterfeit Crochet examines the modes of production and everyday craft dissemination through objects of desire. Syjuco negotiates a design dialogue between amateur craft, traditional skillfulness, and glamorously exclusive fashion through a systematic use of crocheting.

The Italian OpenWear project is a platform for open-source fashion (Fig. 3). The loosely organized initiative grew out of a series of media activism campaigns, such as the Euro May Day demonstrations against precarious work and a network of fashion designers mobilized for an activist fashion hoax during the Milan fashion week in February 2005. In this hoax, a group of activists created a fake brand called Serpica Naro (an anagram of San Precario, the patron saint of precarious workers) and staged a protest on the catwalk in front of the international fashion press. The participants shared an interest in emerging ideas of open-source software, self-organization, and new models of collaboration. The media campaigns formed a point of attraction for many young creative individuals wanting to network their practices into a sustainable alternative to the large-scale fashion industry.

The OpenWear platform has a digital presence focused on sharing patterns and production methods and is manifested physically through workshops and an emerging production lab. It follows the model of the popular hacklabs and fablabs (fabrication labs). These environments for making are spaces for sharing technical, small-scale production equipment for prototypes, and are scenes for local exchange of ideas and techniques. The OpenWear production space is called "WeFab," with the slogan "make the right thing," emphasizing the micro-ethics of sharing ideas and patterns and the

Fig. 3 Openwear Collaborative Clothing, 2011. Photograph Zoe Romano. Courtesy Zoe Romano.

community aspects of networked local production. The platform also acts as a ground for experimenting in new forms economies to support independent and small-scale entrepreneurs, for example, by buying bulk and pooling orders to get better prices or by sharing expensive equipment. The platform supports the local ecology of designers by facilitating the digital dissemination of ideas and patterns and the physical spaces and techniques of production. In this sense, OpenWear is a strategic assemblage of makers, exploring how to organize independent makers into larger networks on both digital and physical levels.

In an apparent paradox of DIY activities, Karl Lagerfeld, Chanel's famous designer, made a pattern for Burda Style, the online pattern-sharing site, in 2010. In a similar vein, for the spring/summer 2010 line, he also released a small crocheted clutch bag in an amateur style common on the online craft bazaar Etsy. Lagerfeld, who is very trend sensitive and often an early adopter of street culture for the catwalk, thus manifested a re-appropriation of styles very similar to those practiced by DIY fashion producers or Syjuco's distributed crocheters.

On the surface there seems to be little difference between the material outcomes of these two camps: you make a Chanel yourself through a Lagerfeld-designed pattern or you buy a real Chanel that looks homemade. Lagerfeld may even be educating some home sewers by sharing his patterns, so even Lagerfeld may be "empowering users." So what is the difference between the DIY hacking and Lagerfeld's version?

First, we could draw a distinction between what I call "executables" and "instructables."[17] Executables are DIY techniques in which the act of production is intended to replicate an original plan, a double-click directive of action. Typical examples could be the assembly of plastic airplane models or IKEA furniture. The executable action does not take the user any closer to becoming an aviation engineer or cabinetmaker. Instructables, on the other hand, have the purpose of educating the user, like cookbooks. For every recipe you cook, you reclaim a part of the kitchen, and soon enough you can improvise and cook on instinct. Much of the hacker or open-source movement has a similar pedagogical imperative. Code is shared and commented upon by the programmer in order to make sure those who build on it further can understand how it works or how hardware is made. While Lagerfeld may be sharing his patterns, his aim is not explicitly to educate users or facilitate their advancement toward independent fashion producers, and it is not to build platforms upon which these skills can create new collaborations.

Second, and perhaps more important, when examining DIY practices, we must ask how these actions change our capabilities beyond what is offered within the narrow funnel of consumerism. How does hacking in a systematic manner distribute competence and increase capabilities to act and be free in the world? It is from such perspective of capabilities that fashion hacking becomes most apparent.

The Capabilities of Fashion Hacking

DIY craft projects, and especially hacking, reassemble the competence of design in new ways. Tasks once delegated to professionals are reclaimed and redistributed. All technologies and tools are agents "that rearrange the distribution of competence within the entire network of entities that have to be brought together to complete the job in hand."[18] Hacking highlights this distribution and opens it for collaborative intervention.

We could draw parallels between automation in industry and the action spaces offered to us through consumerism. As stressed by design researcher Sir Christopher Frayling, early anti-industrialism movements such as the Luddites were not anti-progress per se. Instead, their protests were concerned with how industrialism caused the fragmentation of working communities and changed the distribution of capacities and control of labor.[19] Automation in industry means attending the machine, not working with it.[20] Likewise, craftsmen were "fighting for the status of a way of life: that is, retaining control at the point of production."[21] Being capable or able means to have influence or control.

According to economist Amartya Sen, one fundamental mistake we make when examining societal development is to focus merely on economy and access to commodities.[22] As Sen argues, possessing a commodity does not mean it can be actualized to one's advantage. It is easy to only judge commodities by their characteristics, as we believe that "[s]ecuring amounts of . . . commodities gives the person command over the corresponding characteristics. . . . However, the characteristics of the goods do not tell us what the person will be able to do with those properties."[23] Sen instead argues that we must look at "what the person succeeds in doing with the commodities and characteristics at his or her command."[24] We need to look at capabilities rather than commodities. Philosopher Martha Nussbaum, a collaborator of Sen's, suggests that capabilities "are not just abilities residing inside a person but also freedoms and opportunities created by a combination of personal abilities and the political, social, and economic environment."[25] Frayling approaches the notion of skill in a similar vein, in which it is not only a matter of internal ability but of control of "the circumstances [that] make possible any skilled activity."[26]

We usually believe that owning a fashionable garment immediately transfers its characteristics onto us, making us fashionable. But in this transaction, we are not in any sense in control of the capabilities of being fashionable. Instead, we have only dressed in an ephemeral incarnation of the zeitgeist and left all control of production to the brand or designer. Fashion hacking actualizes the skills, control, and systemic capabilities of fashion, that is, the ability to engage in fashion. As seen in the examples here, fashion hacking and, in the end, "fashion-ability," would mean a socially engaged participation in the fashion ecology beyond the mere act of choosing one garment over another. It instead resonates well with Nussbaum's idea that "[t]he notion of freedom to choose is thus built into the notion of capability. . . . To promote capabilities is to promote areas of freedom."[27] Fashion hacking realizes new, grounded freedoms in the realm of fashion beyond the parameters of the fashion industry's operating system. It happens on individual as well as on a systematic level as skills are networked into strategic capabilities for self-determination. To be "fashion-able" means having the ability and the freedom to choose beyond the current commodity interfaces of fashion consumerism.

DIGITAL CRAFTING AND THE CHALLENGE TO MATERIAL PRACTICES

Mette Ramsgard Thomsen

Shadow Play is an architectural prototype made as a site-specific installation for the entry space of the Architecture House in Copenhagen. The installation is part curtain, part *mashrabiya*—the carved wood latticework found in the Arab world to screen for light and sight; it is a soft structure filtering light. Placed between two glass sections, the pine construction of loose loops colors the direct sunlight, adding a new warmth. Copper ties reflect the light, creating a shifting pattern changing throughout the day. The structure is both dominant and subtle. Large in scale, it fills the entry, but because the loops are constructed perpendicular to the space, they vanish with the light, becoming hard to see and, at the same time, distinctly noticeable in the way they affect the quality of the environment.

Shadow Play is an experiment in implementing textile structures for architectural-scale constructions. It uses 0.6-mm pine veneer as a base material, which is bent to continuous interconnected loops. As a three-dimensional textile, Shadow Play weaves layers of loop stitches together, creating a thick mass in which each member is inherently weak, but the structural whole is strong. The structure makes use of the inherent flexibility of the pine veneer. At the scale of the stitch, each loop bends the material into varying levels of tension.

Fig. 1 *Shadow Play*, the installation, 2012, Center for Information Technology and Architecture (CITA), Copenhagen. Mette Ramsgard Thomsen, Karin Bech. Photograph Anders Ingvartsen. Courtesy Mette Ramsgard Thomsen.

At the scale of the structure, these pre-tensioned loops are then tied together creating interdependencies that further tighten the structure, in effect creating a new material.

Questioning Our Material Practice

As an installation at the Architecture House, Shadow Play explores its environmental effects and its ability to create a dynamic flow of light and pattern. But as an experiment, the installation probes how digital design tools and their ability to control geometric variation can be used to create new structures that exploit material behavior. By creating new structural interconnections, Shadow Play examines textile principles usually employed at small scale, seeking to understand how, when used at large scale, they can help designers reconceive the way we understand material and structure in architectural design practice. Textiles are interesting structural models because they are strong, lightweight, adaptable, and enable great formal freedom.[1] They challenge the traditional hierarchical thinking in building construction, in which primary, secondary, and tertiary structures carry each other. Instead, they propose structural systems in which the textile membrane consists of distributed networks of parallel material connections. Furthermore, textiles build from the weak to the strong. The network of interweaves, loops, or stitches relies on the integral flexibility of the base yarns to create structural integrity at higher level. As such, textiles embody a complexity of performance operating across the scales of the fiber, the yarn, and the textile structure itself **(Fig. 1)**.

In Shadow Play, the material system is organized as a series of interconnected loops. Each loop stitch binds two members together and passes the fibers forward in the structural weave. The installation is tied in a three-dimensional weave system. Using copper ties, each member is interconnected in a series of looping stitches that gathers the material and interconnects in three dimensions.

It is by means of these inherently complex performances that Shadow Play examines the profound challenges that designing for and with material performance presents to architectural design. Instead of thinking of material as static or inanimate, textiles propose a new thinking of multiscale performances relying on the inherent softness, flexibility, and bending of the material. This fuses the architectural design space with a new set of ideas. When materials are conceived as active, as flexible, compressible, or stretchable, how can we as designers make use of their inherent performances to optimize the way we think about structural design? How does this impact the way we industrialize material fabrication to challenge mass production and instead open up for the emergence of a new practice designing site- or use-specific materials? Can this affect the way we understand the connections between environment, building, and user? And how do we invent a new design space that can embed and control this new dimension of inter-scale, performative dynamics?

Inventing a Digital Craft: New Tools for Material Design

The term *digital crafting* suggests the intersection between digital design tools and the capacity for precision, variation, and control within the craft tradition. Designing for digital fabrication necessitates an embedded understanding of the craft tradition. Whether working with the milling machine, the laser cutter, robots, or the vast array of other computer numeric controlled tools, it is essential to understand the way the tools address the material and what happens as material tensions are augmented or released. There is, therefore, an inherent tension between the static understanding of materials in representation, where material variation is denoted only through a difference in notation, and the reality of working with live materials. As exemplified in Shadow Play, materials such as pine veneer are full of potentials for actively deforming under the stress of structural loads and gravity (**Fig. 2**).

To design the system, we used simple parametric design tools incorporating an empirical evaluation of the performance of pine veneer. The three-dimensional model draws the relationships between each member, allowing for mapping the looping. Minimum, the breaking point, and maximum, lack of tension, parameters are defined through empirical testing. The model exists as a programmed design space in which the shadow space of the installation can be tested and designed. Finally, the design model is interfaced with a second-tier fabrication model in which the lengths of each member and the position of the loops are detailed.

By understanding materials not as static or inanimate but as engaged by complex behaviors and performances, new dimensions of design potential have unleashed innovative structural thinking.[2] Architects, engineers, and designers are creating a new generation of prototypes that challenge the way we think about materials in the built environment.[3,4,5] These examples harness digital design and fabrication tools' capacity to increase complexity through variation, interconnectivity, and the sheer number of elements, while at the same time reconsidering the ways in which the material itself actively adds to the design intent and the structural performance. As such, they point toward new ways by which we can understand structural performance and create better, less materially intense and, therefore, more sustainable structures.

This is leading to the emergence of a new digital-material practice in which the design and detailing of materials are directly linked to the design and detailing of buildings.[6] These new material practices rely on the ability to model force and flow, parametrize, and calculate low-scale material properties, and compute complex interscalar dependencies. Expanding the digital chain, the aim here is to interface CNC manufacturing tools to design bespoke materials whose particular detailing and specification becomes a central part of a project's overall solution. Learning from advances in material science and engineering, and the ability to model materials at micro- and meso-scales,[7] the aim for this emergent digital-material field is to achieve a performative understanding of materials at a micro level that can lead to an understanding of buildings at the macro level. Currently, these research questions are addressed through a series of efforts looking at specific material practices that allow for high degrees of specification, including textiles, 3D printing, and polymer-based composites.[8] Rather than understanding the digitization of the building industry as merely a measure of optimization, the ability to create site- and use-specific materials is radically changing the ways in which we understand the interrelations between the built environment and its occupation.

Conclusion

In Shadow Play, digital design tools are used to invent a new material craft (**Fig. 3**). Digital tools are used to parametrize the geometry and thereby control variation in the structure. The variation has spatial as well as structural impacts, in effect changing the performance locally. In our work, Shadow Play is understood as a sketch. By enlarging the textile principles from the scale of fabric to the scale of the interior, the prototype proposes that these structural principles can be imagined at building scale. The design of Shadow Play relied on hands-on experience in working with pine veneer. By understanding the performance of the pliable veneer and engaging in its crafting, we were able to define the minimum and maximum stitch sizes for the loop structure, which in turn were encoded into the digital model. These parameters control the digital model, allowing an interface between material performance and design intent.

However, if we are to understand the full potential of working with material performance, we need to develop better tools by which this parametrization can take place. In addition to relying on the intuitive learning processes that working a material embodies, we need to understand how

Fig. 2 *Shadow Play*, interior, 2012, CITA. Mette Ramsgard Thomsen, Karin Bech. Photograph Anders Ingvartsen. Courtesy Mette Ramsgard Thomsen.

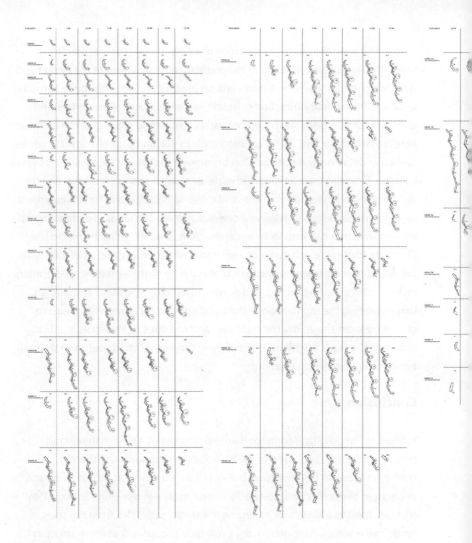

Fig. 3 Detail, *Shadow Play* with material diagram, 2012. Mette Ramsgard Thomsen, Karin Bech.

more formalized knowledge of material behavior can be embedded. Learning from the field of material science and the ability to model materials at micro- and macro-scale, the aim for this emergent field is to understand how the performative potential of materials at a micro level can lead to a performative understanding of buildings at the macro level. This has profound impact on the practice of architectural design. Building practice has traditionally been organized hierarchically as a sequenced set of subsystems, each with its own scale of engagement and team of specialized professions. From the master plan to the detail, each scale drawing revolves around its own problem set. But understanding design as a progression through the scales limits the potential for design innovation, as it excludes our ability to understand how the small

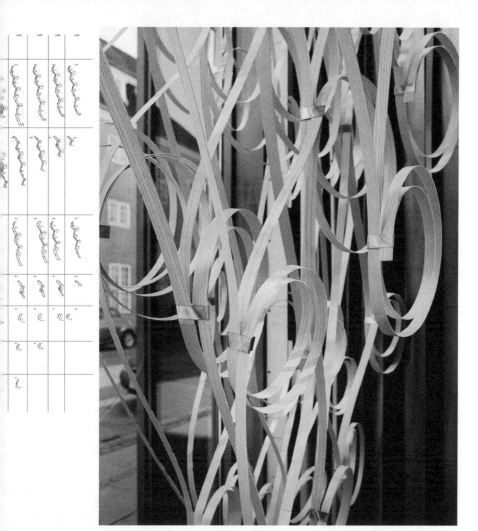

Photograph Anders Ingvartsen. Courtesy Mette Ramsgard Thomsen.

scales—material or detail—can affect large scales—environment or structure. We therefore need to develop a new set of representations or models that support feedback between the different scales of engagement. As active models, they need to calculate the low scale material performances and calibrate how these affect high-scale structural performance.

Shadow Play develops the conceptual thinking of this new design space. It creates a new representation that calibrates the material, but more importantly, it suggests a new structural principle that actively uses the material performance. In learning from textiles, it presents architecture with a non-hierarchical, densely stranded model existing somewhere between structure and the making of a new material.

PETRIFIED CURTAINS, ANIMATE ARCHITEXTILES

Susan Yelavich

The essentially structural principles that relate the work of building and weaving could form the basis of a new understanding . . . and textiles, so often no more than an after-thought in planning, might take place again as a contributing thought.
—Anni Albers, "The Pliable Plane: Textiles in Architecture," *Perspecta*, Vol 4., 1957

Anni Albers turns out to have been remarkably prescient. Today it is possible to speak not only of weaving but also of knitting, knotting, and twining a new kind of hybrid architecture. The tectonic capacities of textiles have been amplified and expanded by technologies barely imaginable in 1957. When Albers wrote "The Pliable Plane: Textiles in Architecture," the operative word in the essay's title was "in." Now it is "of." It is increasingly feasible to conceive and make an architecture of textiles and textile tectonics (Fig. 1). Infusing buildings with the behaviors and properties of cloth is not, however, a radical break from the past.

For millennia, the union of textiles and architecture has enjoyed periods of fertility, suffered separation, and endured various forms of compromise. The twenty-first century opens in the midst of a reconciliation, a reunion of material and conceptual opposites, of ephemeral cloth and enduring tectonics. Motivated by the urgent need for more sustainable models of building, architecture is re-embracing the virtues of textiles—their lightness, flexibility, and adaptability. Yet without an understanding of the cultural qualities of cloth and its relationship to building over time, the algorithms that make rigid walls malleable run the risk

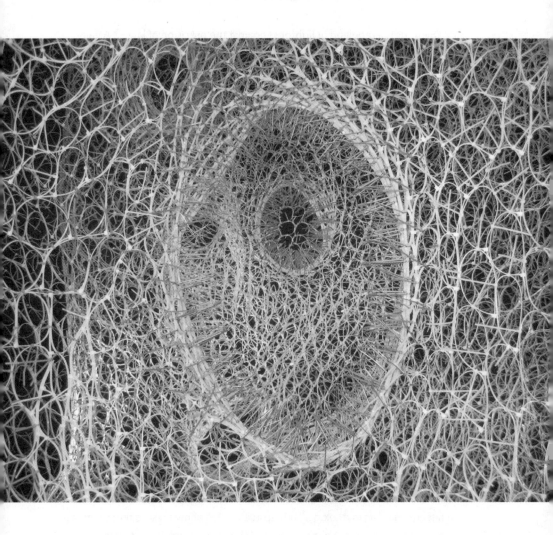

Fig. 1 Detail, *Branching Morphogenesis*, LabStudio, 2008, Jenny E. Sabin, Andrew Lucia, Peter Lloyd Jones. Photograph Jenny Sabin. Courtesy Jenny Sabin.

of producing stillborn offspring, lifeless buildings uninhabited by memory. This essay is an attempt to reconstruct that memory, and given that memory is never precise or perfect, this recollection begins with a myth.

In his poetic reconstruction of the philosophical foundations of Western culture, *The Marriage of Cadmus and Harmony*, Roberto Calasso writes:

> Olympus is a rebellion of lightness against the precision of law ... A vain rebellion, but divine. The gods know that the two imprisoning nets are the same: what has changed is the aesthetic appearance. And it is on this that life on Olympus is based. Of the two they prefer to submit to Eros rather than Ananke, Necessity, even though they know that Eros is just a dazzling cover for Ananke."[1]

Cover in the literal sense. Ananke's inflexible bond, which tightens in a great circle around the world, is covered by a speckled belt, which we see in the sky as the Milky Way. But we can also see it, in perfect miniature, on the body of Aphrodite when the goddess wears her "many-hued, embroidered girdle in which all charms and spells reside. . . ."[2]

But even Ananke, the goddess of Necessity, takes the form of a textile under Eros's speckled belt. Calasso tells us: "Necessity is a bond that curves back on itself, a knotted rope (*peirar*) that holds everything within its limits (*péras*)."[3] These primal forces—need and desire—are materialized in dwellings. Both forces are first characterized as textiles. But Calasso also notes, "If Ananke commands alone, life becomes rigid and ritualistic."[4]

Similarly, the necessity for shelter is paramount, but without Eros, that shelter is not a work of architecture, merely building. All architecture is an articulation of being in the world; architecture that integrates textiles into its fabric projects a particular way of being in the world. There is an ethos of cooperation intrinsic to textiles: They are made of individual threads embodied within a collective.

Just as Calasso argues for the affect of myth on the shaping of human consciousness, I argue that the memory of cloth is deeply embedded in architecture and its mythology. The capsule version of my thesis is this: When we were nomadic, we took shelter in textiles. When we settled down, textiles were variously embedded in our buildings. Now, as we become more nomadic again, textiles are resurfacing in architecture again, not as furnishing but as its very fabric.

Taking the position that textile-based technologies are never separate from the values and bodily experiences that have accrued to textiles themselves, this investigation looks at how meaning and the culture of cloth have been carried forward in architecture. However, what follows is not a linear progression but rather a sequence of recursive loops between the past and the present. The narrative begins with the overarching theme of the nomadic condition that links contemporary use of textiles in architecture with practices in the past. It delves into the ways, during years of settlement, that textiles were made solid in ceilings, walls, and floors and emerges with the reanimation of the textile in architecture via sensors, photovoltaics, robotics, and adaptations from biological systems. A coda concludes this story (and much of what follows is precisely that: projections of what might have been and could well be) with a discussion of the values long associated with the feminine in hybrid architextile structures.

The Nomadic Condition, or Why Textiles Now?

In these early years of the twenty-first century, we hear time and again that the nomadic condition is our condition. The immigrant, the exile, the tourist, and the urban wanderer populate the global social imaginary. While I don't disagree, words like "exile" and "wanderer" imply a near universal dispossession, an implication that is contradicted by our ongoing, albeit fraught, relationship to things. We are certainly more mobile than previous generations but never entirely rootless or devoid of things. We are caught betwixt and between our desires for rootedness and the reality of our hypermobility, a condition the art critic and curator Nicolas Bourriaud describes when he writes: ". . . the contemporary subject is caught between the need for a connection with [the] . . . environment and the forces of uprooting, between globalization and singularity, between identity and opening to the other."[5]

Searching for the kinds of connections that might be satisfying, but not paralyzing, in negotiating between globalization and singularity has led me to spaces and things, which, no matter how new, carry muscle memories of the past—muscles that are exercised when designers recognize what sociologist Richard Sennett calls "the intimate connection of the hand to the head."[6] This is the kind of attentive making that renders the material and virtual worlds we live in meaningful. As Sennett observes: "Friendly to the senses, the cultural materialist wants to map out where pleasure is to be found and how it is organized. Curious about things in themselves, he or she wants to understand how they might generate, religious, social, or political values."[7]

Contrary to the puritanical idea that things and materials corrupt, closer attention to materiality and the knowledge it embodies has the potential to make us more alert to the world and perhaps also more caring. Things that evoke memory provoke a deeper understanding of time. They connect us to other past-presents, to our own past-present. This is important for two reasons. We cannot have much of a sense of responsibility to humans and nature without remembering what we have done to the world. And also for the reason Bourriaud cited: the need for connection. There is a distinct pleasure and reassurance that comes when we recognize a glimmer of continuity with those who came before us, and, arguably, one of the most continuous links to the past lies within the textile. Roughly 9,000 years old, textiles predate the history of agriculture and production of ceramics. Present before the development of architecture, textiles would become central to its history, which may explain certain semantic commonalities.

Urban fabric, curtain wall, canopy, and solar veil are not just literary conceits. The shared vocabulary of architecture and textiles tells a story of material and aesthetic migrations, beginning with the earliest shelters and the most essential elements of their making, the string. According to legend, string has a particular history in building. Seshat, the Egyptian goddess of writing, is said to have ruled over a ceremony of "stretching the cord."[8] In the ritual, string was stretched between posts in order to lay out a temple in alignment with the stars, making string the architect's first drafting tool and part of its calligraphic language.

Today, in Los Angeles, Benjamin Ball and Gaston Nogues of Ball-Nogues Studio are pursuing the potency of fibers to create ethereal volumes that also reorient the movement of bodies in space (Fig. 2). Their deployment of string may not be sacred, but it does construct another "world within a world" by delimiting a space within a space. They create their structures with string that has been dyed in staggered striations that collectively create a kind of three-dimensional ikat. The result is an exploded veil. Neither solids nor voids, their pieces are closer to colloids, whose parts and particles float in suspension.

Beyond the gestural possibilities of single threads massed, draped, or stretched are a multitude of structural possibilities and virtually limitless distances that can be covered when those threads are braided, twined, and woven. Some of the earliest domestic dwellings were made of woven reeds, plaited palms provided roofs and, even now, the tradition of weaving houses lives on in wattle and daub huts.

Today, this elemental form of weaving takes on new life in the work of HouMinn Practice. In 2009, HouMinn partners Marc Swackhamer and Blair Satterfield designed OSWall (Open Source Wall) as an alternative to post and lintel construction, which had gone unquestioned for centuries. OSWall, an armature that the architects compare to a bird's nest, can host a variety of customized elements or "apps," ranging from felted pockets to vacu-formed storage containers. A prime example of Sennett's notion of social craft, this open-source construction platform invites others—designers and laymen—to create their own applications and plug them into the wall.

Fig. 2 Detail, *Unseen Current*, 2008, Ball-Nogues Studio. Photograph Michelle Litvin. Courtesy Michelle Litvin.

This would be yet another gratuitous form of DIY were it not for HouMinn's larger ambition. They have created a system of construction that uses a universal joint system. It can be woven of almost any kind of wood, virtually anywhere, recalling the primal wickerwork that the nineteenth-century architectural historian Gottfried Semper claimed to be the *"essence of the wall."*[9]

Any discussion of architecture and textiles is indebted to Semper's writing on the role and form of enclosure in early architecture. He theorized that the enclosure is one of the four elements of architecture, which also included the hearth, the mound, and the roof. The wall-fitters, or *Wandbereiter* who made the enclosures were, he argued, weavers of mats and carpets.[10] Woven of wood, then covered with carpets, the wall, for Semper, was fundamentally a textile. He claimed that, "Even where building solid walls became necessary, the latter were only the inner, invisible structure hidden behind the true and legitimate representatives of the wall. The wall retained this meaning when materials other than the original were used. . . ."[11] "Meaning" here being the meaning of a textile as a product of both technique and aesthetics, of need and desire: The textile was so fundamental as to never entirely disappear in architecture.

Petrified Curtains

After the widespread abandonment of nomadic tents and fragile woven shelters for more stable, solid dwellings, the textile would find a new role in architecture, variously transcribed onto and into buildings and objects of stone, metal, brick, and stucco. The motivations for this have been various, from an expression of pride in local talent to a declaration of cultural identity to the pleasure of a visual pun. The anecdotal examples that follow are not meant to be taken as proofs of the textile's imprint on building; they are meant to provoke a different way of reading architecture.

I've often sensed that medieval Italian churches were painted to give the sense of being enveloped in cloth. This was particularly acute in the *basilica inferiore*, the lower portion of the church of San Francesco, in Assisi, where the dark brown frescoes seemed, to me, not dissimilar to the Franciscan robe. However fanciful the thought may have been, the idea that cloth would assume such a presence found support, if not absolute confirmation, in the Duomo in Erice, Sicily, which has a striking stucco ceiling patterned like a lace coverlet and is, in fact, described as *stucchi merletto*. While the ceiling is most likely a nineteenth-century embellishment and not contemporaneous with the church's late medieval origins, it raises the possibility that it might be connected to Sicilian craft work, which is in fact true for the church of the Badia Nuova in Alcamo, just 20 miles east of Erice. There, behind the main altar, is another stucco design, this one from the early eighteenth century. Decorated in gold leaf, the wall honors the needlework of the local Benedictine nuns, making it conceivable that the ceiling in Erice was also so inspired.[12] Either way, it is arguable that in both cases textiles were sublimated into the interior as a matter of provincial pride.

A more explicit, and far more elaborate, form of tribute appears in the interior of Santa Maria Assunta dei Gesuiti, in Venice, of 1729, which was designed by Domenico Rossi. The Gesuiti's green-and-white marble interior has been documented as a detailed simulation of the brocaded textiles used in the liturgy of the Forty Hours Devotion, in the Jesuit's main church of Il Gesù in Rome.[13] Calculating in its theatricality, the textile was sublimated as a strategy of the Counter-Reformation, part of a larger spectacle of persuasion designed to reinforce the Church's power, then under threat from ascetic Protestantism.

With the circulation of pattern books, beginning around the start of the sixteenth century, the textile would also find its way into grates, grilles, altar screens, and window borders, crossing borders of every conceivable kind. The ubiquitous openwork pattern of rococo ornament can be seen as a more delicate iteration of fishing nets. The fretwork of northern Russian peasant architecture has been referred to as "wooden lace."[14] Mozarabic pavilions like the Court of the Lions, sometimes described as a valance, in the Alhambra in Granada, Spain, are thought to be derived from the textile geometries and patterns of earlier, less permanent tents.[15]

These acts of transference continue today in the work of architects like Los Angeles-based Elena Manferdini. Atelier Manferdini's Villa Ascona of 2010, in Switzerland, builds on a growing body of projects that draw on the principles and appearance of lace. At the Villa Ascona, the form of lace is used not just to soften the coldness of concrete but also to draw attention to the sense of lightness and domesticity that are intrinsic to the geometry of open work.

One of the most psychologically complex and, at the same time, one of the most familiar textile adaptations involves the veil. Here we move from material exchanges to exchanges between belief systems articulated by cloth. Tectonic screens and veils are perhaps the clearest physical embodiment of ancient dualisms: we/they, male/female, permitted/prohibited, sacred/profane. Historian Joan Branham writes that the lattice railing that separated the Gentiles and Jews in the Second Temple of Herod the Great of 19 BCE in Jerusalem was called the *soreg*, which comes from the Hebrew word to gird and to weave. Transgression of the soreg was punishable by death.[16] Deeper inside, cloth veils further separated the heart of the temple, the Holy of Holies. These same veils also embody a contradictory dynamic, the ability to link. To that point, another historian, Nicholas Constas, writes that the veil of the tabernacle was seen in

Christian writings as prefiguring the veil of Christ's flesh woven from the body of the Virgin Mary. To wit, Mary is portrayed holding a spindle in Byzantine icons.[17] Ironically, in early Christian and Byzantine churches, the veil became the *matronium,* a gallery designed to conceal and segregate women.

Far more pervasive was, and remains, the matronium's Arabic counterpart, the *mashrabiya.* A latticed screen used both on exterior and interior projections of buildings, the mashrabiya dates to the twelfth century and is thought to have originated in Baghdad. Its longevity stems from the fact that, apart from being a means of keeping women out of view, yet giving them a view, it also served as a means of shade and ventilation in intensely hot places. Centuries later, the modernist *brise-soleil* would seemingly purge the perforated sheath of ritual and default to the realm and rhetoric of climate control; the notable exception being Jean Nouvel's adaptation of the mashrabiya in his 2005 Arab World Institute in Paris.

However, even buildings less explicitly charged by cultural identity, such as Herzog & de Meuron's de Young Museum of 2005, in San Francisco, and Morphosis's academic building of 2009 at Cooper Union, in New York, to name just two, continue to thrive on the tease of screens that obscure the body of the building while hinting at its silhouette. Their secular veils continue to evoke memories of the sacred strictures and taboos that invested them with power in the first place.

Animated Architextiles

Moving beyond the imagistic power of textiles, a growing number of architects are testing their performative possibilities, their relationship to life itself. Outside of conventional practice, and certainly beyond the scriptural apocrypha of soregs and wombs, analogies to the body are thriving today in textile tectonics, most especially, in the work of architect Jenny Sabin. Her first foray into the realm of architextiles came in a project called the Body Blanket, which translated a body's binary pulse into a continuous woven network of white and black threads. Significantly, it wasn't an anonymous pulse that inspired the blanket; it was her brother's. She wanted to probe how much personalization can be produced from the biology of the body to offset the clinical neutrality of hospital care.

Sabin has since developed a partnership with biologist Peter Lloyd Jones. Lloyd Jones is a matrix biologist who believes that DNA contains only half the secret to life. The other half lies outside the cell, which is continually changed by the bio-neural-chemical environment around it. Likewise, Sabin believes that buildings are not, or should not be, immune to their environments. The collaboration supports Sabin's interest in creating three-dimensional models of responsive surfaces, while also affording Lloyd Jones and other scientists three-dimensional models of cellular interactions that would otherwise only be visible under a microscope or on computer screen. Spatial structures like Branching Morphogenesis of 2008 visualize not cells but the interface of their force networks (Fig. 3). Completely hand assembled, it is made up of 75,000 zip ties that can be drawn tighter or looser to reflect the strength of those networks. The laborious process of building the piece was meant to slow down the process of designing in the rapid digital environment of the computer screen and to mitigate the detachment of virtual data with a more haptic design development process. Sabin believes in developing a bodily intuition from a practiced hand and then making decisions about adjusting the computer codes. She wants to animate architecture with the essential processes that support our everyday existence.

Where work like Sabin's is largely schematic, a growing body of work is beginning to integrate energy systems and sources into textile structures to develop an architecture more closely attuned to its environs. To that end, the London-based partners of Loop.pH, Rachel Wingfield and Mathias Gmachl, have been exploring the capacities of traditional lacemaking in concert with solar technology. Their best known work, the Sonumbra column of 2006, was designed for use in an African marketplace or wherever the sun is very intense. This high-tech extrapolation of the traditional umbrella is a filigree column threaded with fiber optics; it offers shade during the day and lights up at night. The advantage of large-scale lacemaking, where each strand is held on a bobbin and inter-laced according to pattern, is both material and structural: The strands can be intertwined with vegetal, optical, or other synthetic fibers, and they can easily turn corners, enabling the rapid construction of more complex environments.

Where Loop.pH's explorations are conducted in temporary installations, the work of Sheila Kennedy of Kennedy & Violich Architecture (KVA) is being realized in habitable structures. Instead of using textile construction techniques, she deploys the textile itself in the form and role of a curtain, into and onto which micro-energy sources can be easily grafted. In her 2007 prototype for the Soft House, which would ultimately evolve into the prize-winning entry in the Internationale Bauausstellung Hamburg (IBA) competition, the curtain is integral both as a domestic feature and infrastructure. Made of photovoltaic cloth, the drapery, which also serves as a room divider, is designed to store enough energy to charge cell phones and appliances, making it the equivalent of a lamp. In KVA's fully realized IBA project, Soft House of 2013, the curtain moves outdoors. The awning-like textile cladding is made of flexible solar nano-materials and bends to respond to the sun or to open views. It is also embedded with LEDs that visualize wind and climate conditions and heighten residents' relationship to their immediate environment.

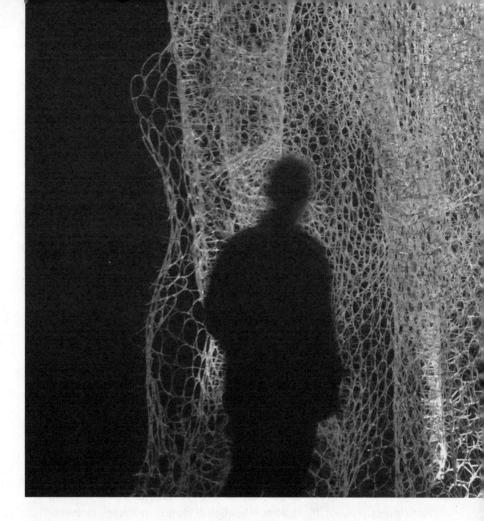

Fig. 3 *Branching Morphogenesis*, LabStudio, 2008, Jenny E. Sabin, Andrew Lucia, Peter Lloyd Jones.

Working with a longer research and development horizon of twenty years or more, architects such as Mette Ramsgard Thomsen, in Copenhagen, and Philip Beesley, in Toronto, are exploring the structural possibilities of artificially intelligent textiles, using combinations of robotic, sensor, and material technologies. Thomsen, who has also contributed an essay to this volume, exploits the porousness of the knitted or woven textile; Beesley animates synthetic geotextiles, which to all appearances are solid but in fact are permeable in soil. Their work is informed by the most advanced computational technologies, albeit in respective ways. However, the infrastructure of mathematical abstraction neither diminishes nor neuters the poetics of their speculations as they look ahead to an architecture less susceptible to wasteful behaviors.

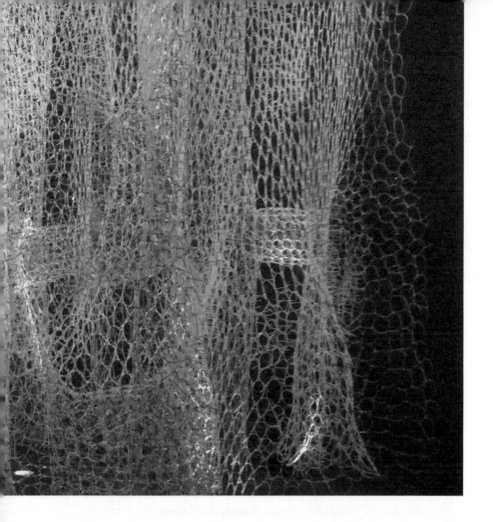

Photograph Jenny Sabin. Courtesy Jenny Sabin.

Thomsen wants to develop an architecture of time. Instead of using smart technologies to satisfy predefined needs, she's more interested in developing a robotic architectural membrane with its own behaviors and metabolisms. For example, Vivisection, which she designed with Simon Løvind in 2006, is a three-chambered structure skinned in a conductive organza affixed with sensor chips that register changes in its electromagnetic field. Anything that touches or passes underneath the structure activates its fabric chambers to behave like lungs. In other projects, such as Slow Furl (2008) and Thaw (2010), Thomsen does not attempt to make the textile structural; instead, she uses it in conjunction with slender, mobile wood armatures, taking advantage of the textile's ability to accommodate their movement. Such self-regulating structures may be more efficient since they have no internal representation of the world; they use their environments directly for all their decisions.[18]

Where Thomsen envisions an architecture in which humans are just one of the catalysts for its behavior, Philip Beesley has been exploring the possibility of an architecture that would live alongside us. He has designed a series of installations, variously titled Hylozoics, named after the concept of hylozoism, which holds that life is inseparable from matter. Beesley's laser-cut geotextiles are like artificial forests suspended in space. Their ghost-like clusters of synthetic petals and tentacles are nourished by microprocessors and, most recently, by biological materials such as vegetable oil. They move and respond to their surroundings, developing more intelligence with each interaction. One might view his structures as empathetic to their environs or think of them as indifferent and post-human. Beesley says he doesn't feel the need to choose one option over another.[19]

Such inquiries into the behavior of cloth and its abilities to reflect and influence our behavior, through its own behaviors, may seem radically future-forward. However, like most things casually labeled "new," these investigations, can be viewed in a different light. Here, I return to Calasso and his claim that "myth is the precedent behind every action, its invisible ever-present lining,"[20] to make the case that these investigations, in fact, share an ancient pedigree.

Fated Feminine

In Greek mythology, human destiny was imagined to be woven from cloth by three Fates, all daughters of Zeus. Klotho spun the thread at the beginning of ones life, Atropos wove the thread into the fabric of ones actions, and Lachesis snipped the thread at the conclusion of ones life. They and other mythological figures offer a useful point of departure to another critical dimension of the architextile, that is, the issue of the feminine.

Of course, the Greeks were hardly the only people to conjoin textile production with women's work. In North America, the Anasazi and Navaho peoples believed that a spider woman was the creator of the world. The Norse peoples, too, had their three Fates, the Norns, who spun the thread of life. All three represent destiny. The exact origin of the name *norn* is uncertain. It may derive from the verb "to twine" and refer to twining the thread of fate.

Not all depictions of twining, weaving women have been so positive, as we know from the myth of Arachne, the young woman who Minerva turned into an ugly silk-secreting spider because she dared to boast of her prowess as a weaver. The lesson that virtuosity is not synonymous with virtue is no less relevant today when the facility of parametric software is just as likely to default to gratuitous references to textiles patterns. Nonetheless, I find it interesting that the story of Arachne is narrated in Ovid's *Metamorphoses*, since architextiles come out of their own metamorphoses.

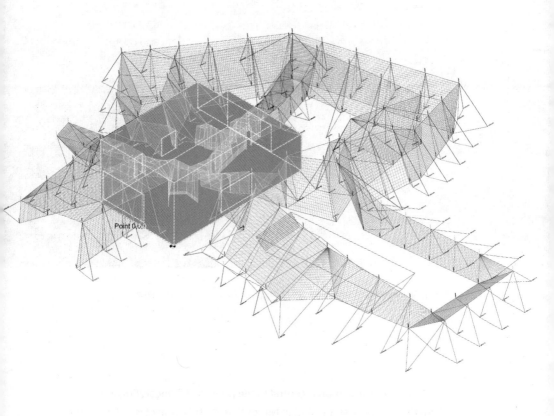

Point 0.0.0

Fig. 4 Drawing, *Spidernethewood*, 2007, François Roche. Courtesy François Roche.

Fig. 5 *Spidernethewood*, Nîmes, France, 2007, François Roche. Courtesy François Roche.

Such a transmutation is central to the poetics of François Roche's Spidernethewood house, of 2007, in Nîmes **(Fig. 4)**. This project is not a matter of mimesis for its own sake or an illustration of the tale of Arachne or the three conniving Fates. Instead, Roche's work is a protest against, "the architectural object, which having claimed authority for four centuries has the power of unparalleled destruction."[21] He wants to "territorialize" architecture so that, "... 'place' gains a social, cultural, and aesthetic link means inserting it back into what it might have been on the verge of destroying."[22] Roche wants to implode the binary relationships that dominated the last century's modernity **(Fig. 5)**. Arguably, masculinity and femininity are perhaps the most notorious of them all.

However, I caution against discounting the ascendance of the feminine in architecture, particularly as it moves from a model of compression to tension, from being thrust into the ground to being wrapped over and around it. It also may be premature to applaud the collapse of binary relationships, especially if they devolve into some kind of oneness not inflected by difference. As the philosopher Luce Irigaray argues, such oneness could be skewed as predominantly, and dominantly, masculine. In fact, it is arguable that Roche preserves the culturally feminine by weaving the house and its netted walls into the landscape by accepting the intrusion of branches and other natural matter.

The question remains: Is it possible to preserve the sense and meaning of female in the feminine, while still recognizing feminine as a cultural adjective that is not exclusive to women? In *Luce Irigaray and the Philosophy of Sexual Difference*, Alison Stone offers an approach that may be helpful in her attempt to reconcile Judith Butler's privilege of gender over sex, with Irigaray's conviction that dually sexuated bodies shape our being. Stone's compromise, to paraphrase, views sexual duality as only one manifestation of a continuously self-differentiated nature.[23] In this view, sexual duality exists, but it is not stagnant.

When ideas are embodied in design—and architecture is an embodied idea—it does not happen in isolation from our bodily natures, which at least in part are sexual. The alternative view, that sexual differentiation is purely cultural, only leads to another false split, one between body and mind. So it behooves us to consider how and what is the feminine in the realm of architextiles and to take the role of myth as seriously as we take ideology and biology. Virtually all of the experimental work discussed here operates in the realm of projection; one could even say, of fairy tale. Wishing our buildings could shrink and swell, that they could be alert to us and the weather is perhaps not so distant from the myth of Icarus, the myth of flight that came into being through design.

However, it's not enough to identify origins; more important is how we interpret and act on them. To wit, the textile, for this purpose the mythically feminine web, offers the tantalizing possibility of a design of an inter-subjective nature. One that oscillates between poles of feminine and masculine, an oscillation that might further enhance the dynamic between interior and exterior, between our need for shelter that consumes resources and our need to conserve and produce the selfsame resources.

Instead of viewing the web as a trap, we need to understand it as a source of energy and nourishment. It certainly is for the spiders that build them. So perhaps these delicate, permeable structures can be seen not only as a model of acceptance for the unstable, bipolar nature of gender, but also as a way to model a new kind of architecture of textiles.

SHIFTING

GEOGRAPHIES

Fig. 1 (top): Eagle from German coat of arms; **Fig. 2** (bottom) Eagle from Polish coat of arms. Shutterstock.

SHIFTING GEOGRAPHIES

Susan Yelavich

There is an apocryphal tale about a beguiling garden city set amidst a borderland in Central Europe. Designed by Paul Heim, Hermann Wahlich, and Albert Kempter and built between 1919 and 1935, the town was called Zimpel. The story goes that the streets of this town were laid out in the shape of the heraldic German eagle, as would befit a suburb of Breslau, which was then a major city in Germany (**Fig. 1**). After World War II, when the Allies awarded an eastern swath of Germany to Poland, Breslau became Wrocław, and neighboring Zimpel became Sępólno. Likewise, the eagle changed its feathers. Today, it is thought that the town plan cannot possibly refer to the German coat of arms because the Teutonic eagle's feathers are always arranged parallel to its trunk, while the Silesian eagle's feathers reach out laterally, as do the streets of Sępólno, at least in the eye of one beholder[1] (**Fig. 2**). All by way of saying the town is Polish, not German.

This feather-splitting lore of regional identification is fascinating on at least two counts. In the first place, what seems to be a trivial claim based on local allegiances masks shifting geographies that entailed two ethnic cleansings: the Nazi's expulsion of Poles and Jews from its eastern lands and the postwar expulsion of Germans from the very same region. Secondly, given that this is a twenty-first-century fabrication—there is absolutely no evidence to support it— we might also construe it to be a rehearsal of lingering resentments, hurts, and slights. A volatile mix of history and memory, the anecdote is not just a provincial phenomenon but part of pervasive pattern. Witness the series of crises in recent decades that have resulted from perceived and real threats to national, regional, and religious identities in the face of globalization.

A more hopeful response to the kind of folklore coming out of Sępólno comes from designers whose own lives and practices have been shaped by the mobility and multiple allegiances implied in this section's title: Shifting Geographies. Instead of dismissing this tale of two eagles (and others like it) as a xenophobic fabulation, they see it as an opening for serious conversation. This section of *Design as Future-Making* is about those kinds of conversations, conducted through design practices of a different order and with different priorities. Instead of trying to invent fixes for social problems—be it in Sępólno or San Diego—designers are increasingly using their capacities to identify community initiatives that they can strengthen and amplify. Ezio Manzini, one of the most eloquent advocates of design as the co-production of social experiments, points out: "the planet is very rich with potential intelligent operators."[2] The scale of the social and environmental challenges that face us (and that designers now take into their remit) begs for the activation of that potential.

This is why growing numbers of architects, urbanists, and designers see their roles not as prescriptive but as catalytic. They run workshops, form NGOs, join city councils, and otherwise become involved in order to help create space (and sometimes spaces) for communities to exercise ideas about how they want to live. These are practitioners who give visibility and agency to those painted out of official narratives.

The impetus for such collaborations is especially clear in this excerpt from a call for entries to a project called Insiders: folklore coming:[3] "The exercise of power, shrinking all the time under the influence of the constantly expanding processes of the capitalist economic system, leaves vacant spaces for those who wish to appropriate them. . . . [F]olklore allows people to connect with their past, with their collective history, what is at stake here is actually a central part of life in the present: something ultralocal at the heart of the global whole."[4]

Recognizing the ultra-local at the heart of the global whole need not valorize only the parochial; it certainly doesn't mean that there is no place at the table for the designer and her experience. In fact, it would be an abrogation of ethics for the designer to become so self-effacing as to be mute. Designers who worry that the inventiveness to be found in the everyday might be polluted by their interference might want to reconsider those interactions as cosmopolitan contamination—the constructive shifts in thought and action that come from engagement with others different from ourselves.[5] After all, design is not a meditation; it is a conversation that, by definition, must be at least a two-sided exchange. Conducted in good faith, the conversation welcomes the unforeseen, a kind of experiment too often taken for granted. By extension, design is an experiment in giving presence to voices.

However, as the curators of Insiders note, "[this] will require the awakening of unfinished experiments that lie dormant in the folds of the present."[6] Future-making cannot be done in a historical vacuum. Therefore, it is worth remembering that many of those unfinished experiments can be located in early modernism's flawed but sincere efforts to flatten the hierarchies that perpetuate inequity.

Sępólno was just such an experiment. It also happens to be a ten-minute walk from the Housing and Workplace Exhibition (Wohnung und Werkraumausstellung, or WuWA), organized in 1929 by the Deutsche Werkbund. Both estates were a product of the Weimar era's pressing need for housing after World War I. Both embodied utopian ideals of socially progressive living. Sępólno provided attached and single housing, a school, and two churches (but no synagogue; this in a city that had the third largest Jewish population in Europe). Key, however, was the inclusion of small private front yards and nearby garden allotments, which are still worked today. These amenities provided a transitional space and activity for residents who may have found garden city urbanism unfamiliar and alienating.

WuWA did not offer gardens, but it did offer variations on the ideal of communal space. Some residences featured common entrances, communal dining and recreation rooms; many came equipped with built-in furniture, in keeping with the social economies of *Existenzminimum*.[7] Most striking was the attempt to design housing typologies to suit the specific needs of different demographics, such as Hans Scharoun's hostel for newlyweds and singles, Adolf Rading's apartment block for families with children, and Paul Heim and Albert Kempter's kindergarten, built not just for the benefit of young children but also to give mothers more time for their own pursuits. (While hardly feminist by today's standards, the architects of WuWA consciously addressed ways in which their designs could free women from some of the drudgery of housework.)

However, where Sępólno was designed on the model of the English garden city, the WuWA estate was emphatically modernist. The young universal style was meant to transcend locality and, by extension, promote a pacific way of living untainted by nationalist allegiances and styles. (No matter that architects Heim and Kempter were involved in the design of both Sępólno and WuWA.)

That Sępólno and its street plan raise questions of identity today, and the WuWA estate does not, probably has more to do with the fact that the former still operates as a community, while the latter is unevenly occupied by disparate individuals and institutions. Still, it must be noted that the modernist architecture and spaces of WuWA have yet to trigger any open speculations about its German-ness. Regardless, the microcosm of "identitarianism" encapsulated in these two compromised utopias raises questions larger than their geography would suggest. Namely, can an architectural program, its internal massing, and its external appearance (its form-function) engender a social imaginary? Which begs the larger question, can design engender agency?

Today, as in the Weimar era, designers from all areas of practice (not just architecture) aspire to reduce isolation, whether the political isolation of the marginalized or the social isolation that permeates a culture of self-actualization via consumption. These designers are also aware that, for every obstacle they might remove toward the larger aim of affording agency beyond the typical confines of class, gender, or race, new issues will surface over time. More than being aware, they embrace the inevitability of shifting socio-cultural geographies and, to the extent possible, make room and rooms (virtual and analog) to account for the unforeseen.

Nonetheless, as architectural historian Antoine Picon has observed, there is a particular challenge for these alternative design practices because they espouse the same values promoted by twenty-first-century capitalism—creativity, emergence, and indeterminacy—using the same networked strategies, albeit toward different bottom lines.[8] Perhaps one thing that global capital cannot afford, though, is a close attentiveness to, and recognition of, the truly specific conditions and variables that make up the ways people live and wish to live. This is where the intimacy of folklore may have an advantage.

Design projects like those discussed in this section of *Design as Future-Making* are not blueprints with minor variations, like those that fast-food companies use to adjust menus and décor to nationality and region. Working under a different set of pressures, designers committed to a social praxis have the liberty to work small. However, they also have the responsibility to explore when, where, and how that work can be extrapolated, reinterpreted, and shared. Designers need to be able to contend with shifting geographies and navigate the layered temporalities with tremendous humility.

URBAN ECOLOGIES: QUATRE SYSTÈMES DE CONCEPTION POUR LA FABRICATION DE "LA CITÉ"

William Morrish

Envelope of Regularity

Over the last ten years, an interdisciplinary team of earth scientists and researchers has been assembling a detailed global history of the interactions between humans and the rest of nature. The research team, comprising ecologists, natural historians, anthropologists, geographers, climate scientists, and environmental systems analysts, is using advanced digital tools and modeling techniques to organize an extraordinary volume of data on the 100,000-year-old relationship between human societies and earth systems. Mapping the historical, archeological, and paleo-environmental record has revealed that patterns of stability and collapse reverberate through the *longue durée* of human history. Thousands of observations and measurements of the earth's biophysical processes—made over time, conducted from diverse geographical sites, and aggregated—make up the dimensions of a so-called predictable environment, an "envelope of regularities," a relatively stable ecological and climatic space within which cities and civilizations have grown and prospered for millennia. But a century of dynamic, unprecedented change— population growth, rapid economic expansion, globalization, war, disease, climate change, mass migrations, and the rise of megacities—has thrown ecological rhythms and processes so wildly out of sync that we have moved into

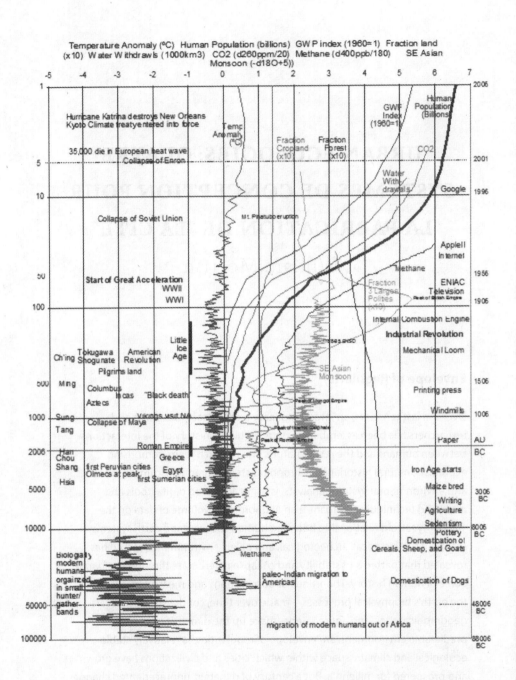

Fig. 1 Envelope of Regularity: selected indicators of environmental and human history. Lisa Graumlich, Robert Costanza, Will Steffen, Carole Crumley, John Dearing, Kathy Hibbrad, Rik Leemans, Charles Redman, David Schimil, 2007. Creative Commons License.

a wholly new envelope of regularity whose dimensions are historically different and still unfolding.

The lines in the middle of the diagram (Fig. 1), which sharply break out of the envelope of regularity, indicate massive environmental change on a global scale. We have entered a period of radical, successional redirection. Our urban theories and practices are based upon an ecological context that no longer exists. Simply tinkering with technology and markets, social systems, and urban form won't do much to address how "the current global system will adapt and survive the accumulating, highly interconnected problems that it now faces."[1] Having crossed into this turbulent landscape of intense co-evolution, we need a new framework for thinking about city-building and living well within the unsettled environmental and social currents of our time, our inescapable, urbanizing ecologies. There is no going back.

This chart is composed of selected indicators of environmental and human history. While this depiction of past events is integrative and suggestive of major patterns and developments in the human-environment interaction, it plots only coincidence. In this graph, time is plotted on the vertical axis on a log scale running from 100,000 years before present (BP) until now. Technological events are listed on the right side and cultural, political events are listed on the left.

La Cité

Houses make a city, but citizens make la cité.[2]
—Andy Merrifield, "Citizens' Agora"

I felt that Istanbul was my home, and Taksim Square my sitting room. And I felt that someone came in and bulldozed my sitting room.[3]
—Birkan Isim, a forty-year-old lawyer who blocked the first bulldozer approaching Taksim Square

Andy Merrifield's reworking of Rousseau's famous affirmation of citizenship translates *la cité* into a contemporary urban ideal, a new "citizens' agora." In ancient Greece, the agora was the heartbeat of the city, an open, highly valued public space that hosted civic assemblies, markets and libraries, schools and scholars, theater and discourse. A place of public action and imagination, an idea that encompassed a setting and the people gathered there, the agora supported a panoply of dialogues and encounters that sustained urban life. To be sure, the agora was hardly a perfect, wholly just civic space, but the ideal, expressed in urban form and the art of citizenship, created a lively, generative public realm.

Today, everywhere, the public realm is contested terrain. As cities increasingly rely on strategies of dispossession and enclosure to develop and brand the metropolis as a luxury product, the public realm, writes Merrifield, "hasn't so much fallen from grace as gone into wholesale tailspin."[4] The demolition of informal markets and neighborhoods in Lagos and Rio de Janeiro, the rise of private eco-cities in Kenya and China, the tragic collapse of infrastructure and civil society in New Orleans in the aftermath of Hurricane Katrina, the economic gulf between central Paris and its poorest banlieues, and the appropriation of public space for private gain, as in Istanbul's Taksim Square, all signal a politics of exclusion. These mechanisms segregate wealth and poverty, limit public dialogue, and enclose or control what should rightly be the commonwealth of all citizens: the cosmopolitan street; clean water, fresh air, and good food; work and safety; rivers, parks, and forests; and the messy, noisy, joyous, profane, productive, beautiful encounters that come with full citizenship and full access to city life. La cité.

At the same time, the uprisings at Tahrir Square, Taksim Square, and other public spaces around the world suggest, as Merrifield does, an abiding, irrepressible, "passionate desire for equality" and, indeed, a hunger for "a new social contract around which citizenship might cohere."[5] This growing call for justice demands a new urban form, a citizens' agora: a public realm, both real and ideal, physical and virtual—an urban landscape and an imaginative commons—in which people might come together, actively encounter one another in dialogue and debate, and discover "an affinity of urban citizenship."[6] In la cité, Birkan Isim's Taksim Square "sitting room" becomes "a living space of modern democracy in the making,"[7] an agora operating as an urbanizing ecology.

It is inaccurate to call this la cité activity an informal action or space. Rather, it is a democratic process working to become a public realm, co-creative and co-producing missing middle systems of la cité. Actions such as public square occupations, communal construction in urban barrios, and digital hackers fighting for data freedom and public access are just a few signs of an active sea of la cité connective flows and upwelling creative forces designing new urban la cité systems that seek to break away from the confinement of conventional urban planning concepts, such as a city being composed of distinctly formal and informal spaces.

Let's explore this new sea of la cité systems by starting with the so-called informal sector of the city (**Fig. 2**).

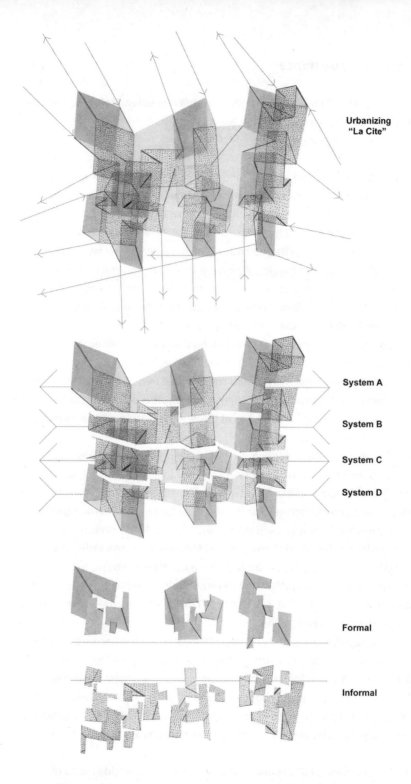

Fig. 2 Urbanizing "La Cité," William Morrish, 2013. Courtesy William Morrish.

System D Coexistence

Ecology includes all the ways we imagine how we live together. Ecology is profoundly about coexistence. Existence is always about coexistence.[8]
—Timothy Morton, *The Ecological Thought*

What is the living space of modern democracy in the new envelope of regularity? If informal, sprawling slums and formal grade-A enclaves define the extremes of our polarized urban landscape, what is the civil terrain in between? How do the two billion people who live in megacity favelas, which are often declared illegitimate and denied basic services, sustain their lives and creatively participate in the life of the city? With great determination and perseverance, argues the noted journalist Robert Neuwirth. In his essential *Stealth of Nations: The Global Rise of the Informal Economy*, Neuwirth argues that slum dwellers not only have the right and the capacity to fully participate in the economic and social life of the city, they are in fact creating their own vibrant economies. In a collection of case studies on thriving street markets in Lagos, Guangzhou, and São Paulo, he notes that markets and communities frequently labeled informal are in fact complex, productive systems that express civic values and contribute to the commonwealth.[9] Indeed, half of the workers in the world are working in the informal economy.

Along with other economic scholars, Neuwirth calls the informal economy System D, shorthand for *des brouillards*, which the French use to describe "particularly effective and motivated people," the "inventive, self-starting, entrepreneurial merchants" who make System D so extraordinarily productive.[10] In Dharavi, a slum in Bombay, the annual economic output of thousands of leather workshops, garment factories, food processing plants, and other small, unlicensed manufacturers is estimated to be more than $1 billion. In India at large, System D is responsible for as much as 90 percent of all employment. Globally, it is valued at $10 trillion and employs more than one-third of the world's population.

In Lagos, Nigeria, a city of nearly 20 million that has become synonymous with urban nightmare, Neuwirth sees an "economy of aspiration" and celebrates the "irrepressible and kaleidoscopic" trade in the city's largest marketplace, the "chaos, cacophony, and commercial energy" of the kiosks, street markets, bazaars, and improvisational enterprises that make up System D.[11] Critically, amid the unruly chaos, he sees an organized system that makes people's lives better:

What happens in all the unregistered markets and roadside kiosks of the world is not haphazard. It is a product of intelligence, resilience, self-

94

organization, and group solidarity, and it follows a number of well-worn, though unwritten, rules. It is, in that sense, a system. . . . Ruled by the spirit of organized improvisation, [System D] will be crucial for the development of cities in the twenty-first century. . . . By 2020, the OECD [Organization for Economic Cooperation and Development] projects, two-thirds of the workers of the world will be employed in System D. There's no multinational, no Daddy Warbucks or Bill Gates, no government that can rival that level of job creation. Given its size, it makes no sense to talk of development, growth, sustainability, or globalization without reckoning with System D.[12]

System D is indeed crucial to the development of cities in the twenty-first century. Self-reliant, decentralized, flexible, nimble, and quick, it is built for our new, mercurial envelope of regularity. It is also an economic powerhouse, a megacity miracle. As Neuwirth points out, "if System D were an independent nation, united in a single political structure . . . it would be an economic superpower, the second largest economy in the world."[13] No city can survive without System D.

But System D is an economy of unrecognized citizens, not a nation, and if it remains fully ad hoc and improvisational, in perpetual survival mode, its creative social capital may well be wasted or lost in exhaustion and conflict. These hardworking poor seeking a foothold in society and the city remind us that cities and their macro-economies are rooted on a robust and fertile urban landscape of microeconomics, which are typically overlooked in favor of macroeconomic projects and policies or suppressed by political fear and corporate monopolies. In today's global, hypersocial, digital, and interconnected urban reality, System D can be seen as the key signifier for all microeconomic and ecological activities, fundamental not only as a social safety net for the poor and struggling middle classes, but also as a vibrant, active marketplace for technological, economic, and political innovation—one more agile, reflexive, and particular than a major institutional intervention.

Institutions can support and learn from System D, however. The United States Department of Defense and leading information companies sponsor DIY and hacker workshops, which draw from a range of youth across diverse urban classes and ethnic groups, to follow the latest ad hoc electronic crowd-sourcing network tools and techniques. System D represents not only the poorest of the world's efforts to survive, but all microeconomic ventures seeking support and encouragement to take risks, explore, invent, and thrive to increase the city's capacity and resilience.

System D is not merely a Global South, megacity phenomena; it is alive and well worldwide, as productive in New York and Los Angeles as it is in Lagos.

One sees it everywhere in big American cities. New immigrants selling $2 tamales at the tops of subway stairs; umbrella, t-shirt, and cell phone hawkers with their wares arranged on folding street-side tables; day laborers gathered in the Home Depot parking lot.

There is also a new generation of enterprises designed to prosper in System D: adaptive micro-businesses, sharing networks, and open-source platforms built for the uncertainties of the post-recession world, as well as nonprofit institutions, such as Venture for America, designed to support urban start-ups in cities that typically do not draw entrepreneurial talent. Venture for America is an entrepreneurial response to the institutional failures of the Great Recession. The nonprofit recruits the best and the brightest college graduates to work for start-up businesses in Detroit, Las Vegas, Cincinnati, Cleveland, New Orleans, Baltimore, Philadelphia, and Providence—cities that aren't the usual magnets for young business talent. Venture for America connects graduates to e-commerce, bio-tech, media, and clean technology companies through relationships with foundations and local government; it's a job-creating network that supports microeconomic revitalization.

If System D is recognized as a productive microeconomic and ecological system, one designed and developed as a vital social and economic landscape or network in a city's civil terrain, it has the potential to materialize in local urban space, creating new spaces of economic opportunity, citizenship and culture. In effect, System D can restructure the idea of the citizens' agora from a single, central space to a field of unified hubs and points across inhabited terrains where people do the everyday work of city making.

As such a network, System D enacts the persistent human desire for urban habitats that provide well-being for more than a few. Managed and maintained as a creative and open social-economic public network, aligned to local political and urban ecological processes, System D could potentially co-evolve with other city systems into a complex, robust matrix of sub-sheds, patches, and intersections operating as a bundle of urbanizing ecologies, a productive, noisy, multidimensional terrain of operations that sustains and grows the commonwealth of la cité.

The City's Missing Middle: Systems C and B

As shown, the informal is anything but ad hoc and out of the norm. Dividing the city into halves of informal and formal, or micro- and macro-, social, economic, and environmental worlds bypasses a vast hidden mesoscaled hybrid mix of designed city systems. Where System D emerges from the capacity and freedom to participate in the life of the city and create microeconomic and social networks, Systems C and B arise in the fertile middle ground between informal settlements and the luxury city, building the capacity of networks to operate productively and generate social and economic goods. Using natural systems, community operations, and social innovation, they answer the aspirations emerging from System D: Can I build anything from this? Systems C and B represent a rich landscape of urbanizing habitats animated by intermediaries that organize, aggregate, bundle, and enhance resources and connections.

System C projects generate civil society. They support the collective ambitions of the city by tending civil terrain, answering the questions: How do I live and work here safely? Can I be a citizen in la cité? System C social infrastructure creates networks of sociability, exchange, and community governance and connects marginalized communities to city centers. System B projects introduce intermediaries; grow the complexity, connectivity, and productivity of networks; and develop and manage infrastructure as a shared resource. They bundle interests, build partnerships, create markets, and link fragmented urban topographies. Urban food systems and the Internet are System B networks.

System C: Cohabitation

A Constitution is more than a legal document. It is the single most expressive act by which separate, individual people constitute themselves as a people. A people so constituted is, in turn the only genuine source of meaning for the word public, which in Latin meant "of the people." It does not simply mean "of people." People in their separated individuality never become public. They only do that by a deliberate act of constituting themselves as "the people."[14]
—Daniel Kemmis, *Community and the Politics of Place*

Constituting ourselves as "the people" takes a lot of time and hard work, which is a challenge when we all have day jobs that fill our calendars and e-mail boxes every day. Daniel Kemmis is a former two-term mayor of Missoula, Montana, who led a massive restructuring of the city from a working timber, livestock, and farming economy into a city of diversified services: jobs, tourism, and second-homes. Its public realm—the terrain of surrounding forest, mountains, streams, historic buildings, and living patterns—had to be reconstituted. A familiar landscape had to be seen in a different light, with a deeper understanding and acceptance of wider interpretations. The question for the people of Missoula was how to reconfigure their public realm through their everyday living patterns and working processes. They made the idea of reconstitution into an act of cohabitation, which reflected an understanding of what the American cultural landscape historian Jonathan Brinkerhoff Jackson describes as the making of public realms as the integration of a pair of ideal landscapes, the political and the inhabited. In short, these are the two basic types of urban space.

Jackson uses the term landscape, with its implications of "landscaping," as more than cleared forest or cultivated land, or a scenic or artificial garden, park, or preserve. He uses the term landscape to represent the integration of human systems and natural processes into a background landscape or infrastructure that underpins everyday political and habitat cohabitation.

The political landscape might be described as the surrounding environment and systems that define our collective identity, offer access to the larger commonwealth, and provide protection. The word political is used to represent the space "of the polis," the geographic terrain associated with la cité. The inhabited landscape is the space closest to our own bodies or family habitats. This is the edge of the public realm that Merrifield describes as the politics of encounter, where the process of constituting "of the people" needs to address the particularities and differences of human and ecological habitat.

The Political Landscape

System C activities and projects can be seen as a kind of social choreography and collaboration. In Medellín, Colombia, the citywide transformation of public space was conceived as a tool for promoting social inclusion and a new city narrative, a way of rewriting and co-authoring the city. Design laid the groundwork for community and citizenship by "investing the greatest amount of resources, of the highest quality and aesthetic excellence, in the poorest, most violent parts of the city."[15]

Medellín's new social infrastructure enables citizens to become public actors. An innovative public transportation system reduces the distance between the barrios and the city center with a system of cable cars and feeders, giving people access to jobs and the city center. New cable car stations have become neighborhood hubs, and five library parks in the poorest, most dangerous parts of the city are a budding cultural commons. The libraries are connected to the public transport system and the network of state schools.

Juan Luis Mejía Arango, rector at EAFIT University in Medellín, believes that "the virtue of these buildings is that they are rewriting the city. Places that before had dreadful connotations are now acquiring a new sense: the San Javier Library-Park occupies the 'non-place' that before was stigmatized by the presence of a prison and a cemetery. Where the Belén Library stands, there were once the dreaded prison cells. New meaning has been conferred by books and freedom. The new gateway into the area is a library, or rather, an enormous portal through which access can be gained to the accumulated knowledge of humanity."[16]

This is no ordinary urban infrastructure and architecture project with a superb design. Its beauty is achieved through extensive, inclusive community design processes and strategic placement of public spaces, systems, and buildings with an explicit mandate to reveal the connective social possibilities and political power to overcome division, fragmentation, fear, and immobility.

The cable cars symbolize the need to reach out to the poorest of neighborhoods isolated on surrounding steep hillsides from the common central spine to the valley, its river. The libraries are perched on hillside outcroppings, new prospects from different neighborhoods offering radically different views of their everyday urban landscape. New public pedestrian bridges are inserted at pivotal locations creating a new commons, extracted from an environment of crime and fear operating within the darkness of buried mountain stream ravines.

Together, these lines, spaces, and bridges not only offer spaces of social hope; more importantly, they also transformed the public's cognitive map of itself. Citizens no longer see themselves living on the flat map of the city planner, commercial speculator, or political strategist. Every day they can see that they all live together within the civil terrain of their common valley, facing common issues and differing challenges that cannot be ignored. Walking along neighborhood streets where people are allowed to paint murals on the fronts of their homes, residents have filled their community with images of their newly found landscape of the hills, streams, public prospects, and urban patterns, as well as people performing social activities and having parties on streets and in public spaces.

Inhabited Landscape

In Cairo, against the grain of political unrest, citizens and young architects are recreating their relationship to public space and each other. According to Michael Kimmelman:

> Egyptians are figuring out anew how they relate to one another and to the city they have always occupied without quite fully owning—figuring out how to create that city for themselves, politically and socially, as well as with bricks and mortar. Headlines have naturally focused on the macro-battles, but the bird's-eye view does not always reveal what is happening at street level, on corners and in neighborhoods, where daily life today means navigating new relationships with fellow citizens and the spaces they share. . . . Progressive

young architects and planners may be needed here, but there are already a few who are starting to demand the right things. They are not talking about demolishing informal areas but about learning from those neighborhoods, seeing them as resources and solutions. They are collaborating with residents, tinkering with construction methods and materials to allow for more light and air in apartments, wider streets to accommodate emergency vehicles. These forward-thinking Egyptians view the neighborhoods not as endless slums but complex cities in themselves, home to entrepreneurs, government officials, and many young educated Cairenes; they recognize that the future of Cairo will require grass-roots organization.[17]

System B: Co-Production

The Internet of Things—the moment when things connected to the Internet will exceed the worldwide human population—will change everything, including ourselves. For the Internet of Things to reach its full potential, global organizations must work together. Learn how the Internet of Things will change the world as we know it—for better innovation.[18]

—Cisco Systems

Sustaining the city with food, water, energy, transportation, telecommunications, and all the other utilities of living and working seems almost incomprehensible when the long list of systems, volumes of material, and the length of supply chains are tallied. Yet, despite the enormity and consequences of this vast socio-technical infrastructure, its workings are hidden from view. When Hurricane Katrina swamped New Orleans in 2005, it stripped away the veneer of everyday life, exposing a micro-, meso-, and macro-scaled mesh of economic and ecological activities made up of day-to-day actions by real people and creatures co-producing a life for themselves. The historian William Cronon describes this abstract nature or urban landscape as a city's "second nature."[19]

Second nature is one characteristic of System B that seeks design methodology. Development outcomes need to start with an understanding of modern-day global challenges, such as climate and demographic change, cultural differences, and economic dislocation and disparities. The conventional logic of civil infrastructure engineering, which has emphasized single functions, separate projects, traditional institutional silos, and uniform codes, must now be replaced by integrated design and development processes that increase interconnectedness and adjust to unpredictable risks. Revealing a city's invisible infrastructure to society as a second nature is a radical proposition. It transforms traditional infrastructure economic management and ecological maintenance into la cité's shared resource—a meshwork of systems and networks operating as intermediaries between the various components in the other three systems: D, C, and A. Second nature reveals that the city and nature are co-produced artificial environments in which society is the lead agent of geographic change. Roads, pipes, channels, bridges, smartphones, and plumbing fixtures are all didactic displays of society's desire to exclude or include citizens' creative freedoms, openness, accessibility, and equity to commonwealth resources. They are public realms whose nature has been constructed as an intermediary between human collectives and human to flora and fauna habitats.

Interface

Throughout history infrastructure has defined individual identities and bodies. The urban historian Carl Smith describes these two personas as "the urban body and the body of the city."[20] The individual, public, and political constantly utilize infrastructure forms, spaces, functions, operations, and energies to set inclusive and exclusive boundaries. This is as evident in the ancient Greeks' interest in the independent systems of sports, health, bathing, theater, and academies as it is in the early twentieth century's interest in urban sanitation and immigrant health standards. The same boundary-setting infrastructures appear on today's sidewalks, where people plugged into their smartphones are changing relationships among bodies and fashions. (People not only utilize infrastructural forms, they also are constituative parts of these infrastructural forms.) Driven by active interfaces, System B constructs platforms and multilayered infrastructures, such as urban food systems and other productive networks. An urban food system is a socio-technical ecology; it uses information, the Internet, and other forms of infrastructure to support agriculture in a city or a region, bundling the agendas of farmers, food trucks, restaurants, health agencies, consumers, and communities.

Grassroots efforts across the country have successfully bolstered independent sections of the food system, from small farm incubators to mobile farm stands, but there's one piece that still remains glaringly absent: infrastructure. Without well-developed and well-financed networks and institutions to build upon, advocates of strong local and regional food systems find it difficult to connect from one end of the supply chain to the other. That's where local government can come in. Small business owners, farmers, distributors, restaurateurs, and eaters develop innovative strategies to strengthen their respective segments of the local food chain, and municipalities can support this process by creating links down the line and increasing opportunities for food system purveyors to work together. One small story provides a powerful lesson.

I have many friends and know many families who live in New Orleans. Some of them owned restaurants that were devastated by Katrina. Those who were not flooded struggled in the first few weeks of the recovery period to revive their businesses, support their families, and provide meals to returning residents and relief actors. The problem was that access to standard food supply chains had been flooded and cut off. Across the Mississippi River, many local organic farmers' fields had been spared the storm's wrath. Friends quickly reached out through local channels, and the local food chain began to supply city restaurants. The challenge to local chefs and customers was to rethink their recipes, given the nonstandard ingredients. Prior to the storm, local chefs and musicians were living in a city that was famous for great cooking and music, but the food and music venues had become standard tourism spots. Invention had been forsaken for classic dishes. After the storm, chefs, farmers, and even musicians had to learn how to be more creative. From experience, I can say that many of the restaurants are now profoundly better and the menus more diverse.

Intermediaries

Traditional infrastructure is typically organized systemically and operationally into two categories: benevolent monopolies and autonomous enclaves.[21] The classic benevolent monopoly is the city-owned public water supply and wastewater treatment systems, which in cities like Chicago, Boston, and Philadelphia started as public works in the mid-nineteenth century to wash away disease, clean the poor, and attract wealthy residents. The autonomous enclave can be seen today in the design and development of large-scale, sustainable urban centers for wealthy residences living in separate, contained systems, outside citywide systems. The global realities of a different urban era—defined by the collapse and fragmentation of existing systems, new local and corporate agglomerations, advances in ecological and technical sciences, exponential growth in ambient computing spurring an expanding diversity of cultural and social governance hives—are hybridizing new sets of intermediary structural systems and governing networks stripping the viability of the bifurcated approach, which is still pursued by many. The era of monopolies and enclaves has to give way to open platforms, to systems and networks that can support an open creative commons where users are replaced by active individual contributors adding their energy to la cité's vitality as the urban body becomes hyper-interconnected bodies of the city.

"In a talkative world, what are we to do?"

—Rob Van Kranenberg, in conversation with the author

In 2012, 2.5 quintillion bytes of data (1 followed by 18 zeros) were created every day, with 90 percent of the world's data created in the last two years alone. As a society, we are producing and capturing more data each day than everyone has seen since the beginning of the earth, with little idea of how to turn this mass of information into an urban ecology system.

The ancients used the word "ether" to describe the fifth and highest element after air, earth, fire, and water. It was believed to be the substance composing all heavenly bodies. Today, the word has been conjoined with the word "network" to form the term Ethernet, a family of computer networking technologies for local area networks, or LANs. This union of ancient and present tense terminology is an attempt to describe an environment and atmosphere that we cannot see. The air is filled with microwave data that is generated, captured, and sensed by many with simple devices and "mined" by people with big data harvesting machines, by both corporate and governmental agencies. The air is not clear. It is congested.

Natural systems have been responding in reaction to the growth of the fast systems that are, in turn, activating the growth of more and more urban places and stimulating existing and new production industries. Not immediately apparent in this process is what I call the ether waste stream, otherwise known as ubiquitous computing. This stream is producing an ambient technology in which the space between our bodies and the air becomes an ether crowded with massive volumes of digital data. Rob Van Kranenburg, a Belgian philosopher and Internet activist has been on the frontline for the past ten years working and writing about the forces now threatening to supersede our basic ideas of civil society norms of control and trust. He has chronicled and experienced this change as author, consultant, and community activist.

Kranenburg's "Notebook 2: The Internet of Things"—one of the scariest essays I have read recently—is about who controls the space that defines our freedom to act in public, and how the private world is an open mine to be quarried by anyone with the money and computer capacity to harvest random data at a mega-bit scale. This happens not only at the interface between the keyboard, the mouse, and computer but in our everyday commercial and social transactions via cell phones and cameras. Through the use of RFIDS and other sensors, our information (more pointedly, the ways in which we conduct our lives) is being captured seemingly out of thin air, the ether.

Kranenburg writes, "We are entering a land where the environment has become the interface. We must learn anew how to make sense. Making sense is the ability to read data and not noise. . . . Reading this local slowing down of flowing reality has never been easy, in fact it has never been possible. The challenge we are facing is now reading the flowing reality of our surface when the environment is increasingly the interface."[22]

This is a massive expansion of the public realm, well beyond that of the park, plaza, or sidewalk. It now includes what is spoken on a cell phone while walking down the street, every bit of information channeled through fiber optic cables, credit and debit card transactions, RFID tags embedded in a product, sensors in the ground, and cameras focused on the street.

System A: Co-Construction

When it comes to the circulation of knowledge, three things matter above all in what used to be called the Republic of Letters: laying the ground for democratic self-governance, encouraging creative community, and enabling citizens to become public actors, both civic and creative.[23]
—Lewis Hyde, *Common as Air*

Big projects by corporate tycoons, real estate magnates, political leaders, and religious clerics compose a city's skyline. However, it is the co-construction of institutions for the circulation of knowledge linked to a field of micro-working publics that defines la cité's inclusive operation and sustainable generation. This is System A. It depends on circulating knowledge.

Circulating flows and returns—we want to see them. We want to be in circulation, traveling about, spreading and airing ideas, giving them public exposure. The knowledge that comes from circulation starts as grounded data, becomes experienced information and leads to prototyped applications. What follows is one such prototypical response.

An Incubator for Civic Imagination

The cities of San Diego and Tijuana are located in two different countries, segregated by a heavily guarded international border. Yet every day, 50,000 people cross through security stations to work in resort hotels and restaurants, care for families, and bring their skills to a regional building industry. Meanwhile, the civic identities of both cities are framed by a natural geography, an ecological structure and temperate climate that attract millions of visitors and residents. Those same regional ecological systems weave in and out and across municipal and federal boundaries from the hinterlands and through protective wetlands that provide a habitat for migrating birds flying between North and South

America, delivering scarce water resources. So it should not be surprising that the region's concrete-lined channels cause flooding due to increasing rains from a changing climate, or that these iconic urban systems are accumulating trash and waste, which are channeled into the Pacific Ocean.

At the University of California, San Diego, la cité activists Teddy Cruz, director of the Center for Urban Ecology (and fellow contributor to *Design as Future-Making*), and Fonna Forman, director of the Center for Global Justice, working with a network of local civic and community leaders in San Diego and Tijuana, are constructing a new research center and a public development incubator to redraw the economic, social, and ecological boundaries between these two segregated cities. The Incubator for Civic Imagination that they envision will operate from the city halls of both San Diego and Tijuana through a joint agreement between civic leaders to find creative ways of using local residents and business people's creativity to find ways to build their cities together, despite border patrols and the Department of Homeland Security's steel fence that cuts across the social, cultural, and ecological fabric. Their mission is to provide a space for innovation and collaboration in city management, convening the best urban thinking from local residents and experts from across civic sectors and borders. The goal is to construct new public spaces, new management protocols, and to disseminate knowledge that will integrate the local working public into the process of improving the urban neighborhoods that unite north and south cultures into one la cité.

The Micro-Working Publics of System A

The title of this section is an obvious play of the term public works— government-initiated, -developed, and -operated projects such as sewers, bridges, libraries, administration buildings, and city parks. The origin of the new term is derived from those members of the public who are reviving and enhancing cities and neighborhoods with large social, educational, and recreational buildings and landscapes, often through employment of laid-off workers to increase the health and welfare of the community. Today, we face a different global economic, social, and ecological climate situation. La cité requires public works that will sustain generations by collective commonwealth investments that redress continuing social and ecological inequality, diversify its formal properties, reduce external outflows, and adjust our city's foundations to withstand a more dynamic envelope of regularity.

Our daily lives are filled with high-speed texting, virtual meetings, and other experiences that remove us from the gravity of the terrain underfoot. Slow down and watch the building blocks of the city move in non-linear fashion, operating in time frames and spatial dimensions. New buildings begin to age the day that they are inaugurated. Climate-induced sea level increases begin by seeping through the foundations of neighborhood basements and under roads. Responding to constant economic changes, families adjust their lifestyles. We fail to realize that it takes a lot of work to stay on dry, stable land and operate as actors in the city's commonwealth. So how do we take these changes into account and develop a coordinated way of building so that we can enrich our communities? How can design contribute?

The word design has two basic definitions. The one that we are most familiar with is the process of making objects, buildings, urban spaces, landscapes, and infrastructure. It is the formalization of city functions into spaces that represent the values expressed by various la cité system interests. Design also defines how made objects and constructed environments are not only set within but also draw upon and unite la cité systems D, C, B, and A. Each of the systems represents an urban ideal and generates a characteristic governing ethics, urban practices, and civil terrain, all of which define the dialogue between the city, its envelope of regularity, and its future.

Buildings, landscape, and infrastructure must gain their forms and functions from clear intentions about inclusion, constant creative reflection, and maintenance. In this way, they become more than ways of enhancing a city's form, and they function more sustainably by reducing negative impacts. In this way design connects the working agendas of Systems D, C, B, and A to constructed environments that enrich and sustain the four urbanizing ecologies of la cité: co-existence, co-habitation, co-production and -authorship, and co-evolution. Buildings, urban spaces, landscape, and infrastructure become working zones where the various lines, flows, and activities of each system intersect. Energy, wealth, and ideas are exchanged in a clear quest to make vivid and transparent the shared resources of the urban commonwealth in more than one commons or central square. Of course, la cité is never finished, but if nurtured, its urbanizing ecological systems will operate and generate public imagination to sustain its civil terrain into uncharted seas on the globe we all share.

106

ARCHITECTURE OF INFORMALITY

Ivan Kucina

During the last twenty years of post-socialist transition, more than a million informal buildings have been raised in Serbia. The number produced in all these years equaled the number from the previous socialist period characterized by highly regulated and organized building production. This is an intriguing fact, since these informal buildings were made by people with low architectural skills and capacities but, on the contrary, high building potency. They built their solid shelters by themselves, without architects to design and calculate. They built with no vision or plan of a final whole, by adding sequentially, one part to another, with a high level of emergency. Their buildings were clustered around large urban resources, creating a new informal city layer of a hybrid consistency determined by the reduced building techniques engaged and the cheapest materials applied.

Among the millions of informal buildings constructed to satisfy only private interests, three buildings deviate from the egocentric, post-socialist lifestyle following their owners' intentions to share their hopes and faith with the public. They are new contemporary art centers in the rural outskirts of Belgrade, on the banks of the Danube, one of Europe's largest rivers: Zero One International Test Site in Ritopek, built and owned by the artist Dragan Ilić, who spends most of his time in New York City; the Third Belgrade Association in Krnjaca, built and owned by the artist Selman Trtovac, who was educated in Dusseldorf; and the Museum Macura in Novi Banovci, built and owned by art collector Vladimir Macura, who lives in Vienna (**Figs. 1, 2, 3**).

107

Fig. 1 International Test Site Zero One, Ritopek, Dragan Ilić, Miša Mladenović, 2010. Photograph Vojin Radovanović Voya. Courtesy Vojin Radovanović Voya.

Fig. 2 Lunch on the Grass, part of the *Third Belgrade* artwork, 2011. Photograph Saša Čolić. Courtesy Selman Trtovac on behalf of the IAA Third Belgrade.

Fig. 3 Museum Macura, Novi Banovici, Vladimir Macura,
Ivan Kucina and Nenad Katić, 2008. Photograph Ana Kostić.
Courtesy Ana Kostić.

The opening of these three art centers was an important milestone in the Serbian cultural scene as they were the first private actions dedicated to housing a public good. These altruist moves were followed by changes in the concept of art exposure: presented in a very casual manner, works of high art mingle with everyday things, and original historical documentation with up-to-date events and parties. They create a sense of the intimacy of a home, not least because the owners of these art centers actually use part of the buildings as residences and personally admit visitors and excursions.

The architecture of these centers owed its appearance to the ubiquitous manner of informal building. These buildings are made of the most available materials used in the construction of family houses: concrete slabs and columns, brick blocks, and aluminum-framed windows. However, the ordinariness and the rawness of these materials serve as an ideal backdrop, a blank paper pad, in contrast to the outstanding works of art within. The buildings maintain the sense of imperfect objects that reflect a poetics of unfinishedness and unpretentiousness. All of this underlines the personal sensation of freedom that is essential to immediately experiencing the spirit of the contemporary artists on display.

The three art centers that popped up separately as a result of the unleashed cultural ambitions of their owners also have something in common that makes them significantly different from other informal building: they have been built with the collaboration of architects, although they were not fully respected. Professional relations between the owners and the architects were as informal as the buildings, with no contract obligations or intellectual property insurance. They would not be of much help anyway because twenty years of informal practice had degraded architecture management as redundant activity. Architects involved in the design process were not chosen because of their efficient service; they were chosen mostly because of their enthusiasm to enlarge the public good that they share with owners.

From an architect's point of view, designing and building with amateurs makes for both risk and adventure. Moreover, working together with the owners inevitably reduces architectural values due to the many unexpected deviations directed by the owner and a lack of control from the architect's side. On the other hand, a new value is emerging: released from the order of architecture, the building ceases to become an autonomous object and instead a medium of social interactions. The incomplete and controversial architectural appearance results as a coincidence of the unpredictable process of exchange between owners and architects and reveals an opportunity for architecture to regenerate its cultural influence in today's society. Indeed, contemporary architecture needs to develop a new sense of commonality in order to become a relevant force in creating well-being. These three local initiatives trace a more general anticipation of a new architecture for a society in crisis.

Urban development trends show that more than half of the world's urban population will be living in informal buildings over the next decade. This wasted living space is already becoming a demanding new field for well-intentioned architectural activities. Programming the infrastructure for collaboration between the people and the architects would be the first step in the evolution of the informal building. Within collaborative design and building processes, people consistently create opportunistic and changeable objects that can be expanded at any opportunity. On the other side, architects advocate among many conflicting demands in each situation in order to generate socially integrated and environmentally sustainable living spaces. Working together, people and architects could upgrade their individual ambitions and develop innovative strategies and projects based on critical engagement with public interest and spatial revitalization. Almost as a side effect, by improving local conditions for a better future together with people, architects are also generating a shift toward a new architectural discourse.

In order to get the larger picture, it is helpful to step back into the local past. During socialism in Serbia, the relation between architects and the people granted by the ideals of universal humanity was projected onto architecture production following, at the time, the most progressive concepts of modernism. Modern architecture determined simplified functional divisions and standardized dimensions to control the propagation of space. The rules of abstract geometry were taken as principles in processing the absolute harmony of the objective presence. However, these high ideals were realized in underdeveloped technologies and by a rigid administration, reducing this totalitarian concept to the mass production of collective buildings scattered at the peripheries of cities.

In contrast to these groups of modern monoliths, special status was given to exclusive public buildings that were imagined as landmarks representing the cultural progress of the new society heading into a bright future. Their autonomous identities attracted architects ready to display their personal artistic virtues but, on the other side, were rejected by people who found themselves alienated by the divinity of these buildings' abstract presence. Nevertheless, the idea of the autonomous identity of the architectural object survived within the official architectural system, not only as a socialist contradiction, but also in the unexpected turn toward neoliberal capitalism that occurred instead of the promised collective welfare.

The transition from socialism to capitalism as defined by tendencies toward privatization, market growth, and increased profit has affected massive changes in cultural values, in addition to politics and the economy. A new standard of individuality and orientation towards personal success were proclaimed in place of collectivity, reducing the complexity of social relations to never-ending competition on the global financial market. The result of such a process is a commercialized environment made of scattered, solitary buildings radiating a fake image of luxury.

Caught between the totalitarianism of the socialist past and the consumerism of the capitalist future, the arbitrary ambitions of architecture to preserve its cultural influence by creating an autonomous identity were sidelined in building production overall. Only a small number of buildings were completed following formal architecture procedures, and they did not have any significant meaning for the public. The autonomous identity of the architectural object was reduced to irresistible visual encounters that turned out to be no more than icons of consumption. On the other side, as mentioned, millions of informal building activities took place on the ground and out of the scope of the official architectural ideology.

The informal building boom in Serbia started under the United Nations embargo of 1992 amidst an atmosphere of war trauma, media obsession, and politicization. In this context, as a compensation for the disintegrating state and collapsing institutions, a gray economy evolved from the strategies of survival to the primal instrument of economic resilience and growth. Following the evolution of this gray economy, architecture experienced an abrupt change, becoming a dynamic ground on which the rules for construction have been constantly reinvented. Playing around with outdated regulations, informal buildings began to produce innovation in literally every urban domain, from commerce to housing and public services. Informality flooded public spaces around existing buildings, disintegrating the official architectural logic as a series of mutants plugged into the inherited infrastructure.

This informal building layer occurred between distributed and hierarchical systems; innovation was created through conflict and negotiation between individuals and officials. Different degrees of management in construction and the effect of distinctive blends of nonregulated and regulated building operations uncovered the inherent logic of emergent processes. While their patterns were fairly basic, the complexity that arose from them maintained a time-based character of a relational system. In nearly all informal buildings, pulsating and flexible structures were achieved, resembling profoundly hybrid spaces.

In confrontation with an official architecture ideology that remained rigidly attached to the proposition of the autonomous identity of the designed object, cultivation of informal building toward an architecture of informality offers remarkable possibilities for redefining professional participation in making architecture more responsive to present conditions. It is a widespread belief in today's world that everyone exists far from each other and that they follow only their own interests and pre-calculated benefits. The architecture of informality is a temptation of a different kind. It represents a space that is no longer constructed from the standpoint of one exclusive identity, but from the commitment of many. The power of informality comes from the multiplicity of individuals taking advantage of proclaimed regulations to create dynamic and complex networks. It takes architectural production beyond its official limits, into the regions of collaborative enterprise sustained by social relations among the different participants involved. It goes beyond the impulse to reaffirm identity and speaks to the very being of others, discovering the world from the perspective of a commons of diversity.

Behind this messy and disrespectful architectural appearance, learning informal building offers insights to the immanent concepts that could be taken as milestones for developing the discourse of an architecture of informality. The application of these concepts does not presume the determination of a formal architectural order, but rather an open-ended system of interactions among the architects and others that create everyday space. Architecture of informality seeks to maintain lively coincidences that come from the relationships among different participants in the building process that are, consequently, materialized as heterogeneous and vivid organizations. These concepts are as follows:

- Fragmentation: the reduction of authority and growth of unleashed initiatives
- Frame line: a pronounced appropriation of common territory
- Minimum commons: a bit of coexistence where there is nothing left to lose but a lot to add
- Temporary hierarchy: the ability to take over particular spatial actions for a limited time
- Convertible boundaries: the potential for distorting limitations into a space of exchange
- Concurrency: the spatial implications for various simultaneous states of existence
- Hybridization: inventions resulting from the crossover of multiple influences

- Expandability: the capacity of a hosting body to adapt to uncoordinated external partitions
- Shortcutting: unpredictable paths through congestion
- Compensation: the exchange of an expected service for service from another source
- Para source: drawing residual energy from the distributive network
- Leftover: a free space between fulfilled desires
- Raw end: the unintentional result of the literal application of basic building tools
- Under construction: continuous delays due to undetermined rules of development

Bounded from within by these concepts, the architecture of informality may become a new political paradigm for people seeking to participate in the development framework in which they live. As people act and interact through their environments, their living spaces are considered the places for the expression of personal interests, social relationships, and the reconciliation and confrontation of different private and public features. More than decision-making mechanisms, procedures for collaboration between people and architects create a social infrastructure for permanent discussion on vital questions related to the development of their environment. If run adequately, their collaboration overwhelms prepared plans, generating a continuous flow of interactions that produces the social energy needed for permanent spatial transformations.

The phenomenon of interactivity formulates an inclusive approach to environmental transformation, a collaborative use of space, and a transparent operation throughout the course of a building's life cycle. The sustainability of the course, allowing collaborative efforts in which everyone creates for everyone, addresses the problem of compatibility among participants. Living spaces rely upon amateurs as much as experienced professionals, eroding the binary distinction between architect and the people. Architects recognize the core role of collaborator, instead of users, at every stage of the process. Instead of imposing their vision, architects learn about the immediate relations of living space by listening to people's arguments. They use their interdisciplinary knowledge on the concepts of informal building to mediate different interests toward agreement and to translate narratives into a common spatiality. Forms of engagement with people enable a kind of emergent appropriation of space in which the quality of architecture is optimized in terms set by those who are building and using it in order to be able to change it whenever they want. At its best, the architecture of informality is radically democratic, enshrining principles of open access and freedom.

The discourse of the architecture of informality employs the phenomenon of interactivity to signal the end of the objective world, where subjects are separate from objects of observation, or, in other words, individuals from their environment. It praises a relational mode of thinking that identifies the real with relations, not with substances, in contrast to a substantialist mode of thinking that recognizes objective things only visible through direct observation. In this respect, the production of a living space that is radically incompatible with the idea of object autonomy represents a shift from object-oriented design to a relational space constructed as the domain of communal exchange among its participants. For this reason, living spaces are inseparably related and linked with individuals, communities, and the environment itself.

Understanding the architecture of informality as a consequence of perpetual interactions between architects and people questions whether design and building procedures can be shifted from a top-down, immutable delivery mechanism into a transparent, inclusive, bottom-up, and open-ended approach. The apparent direction for architects is to influence, steer, and shift the process themselves, which means a change of focus from designing objects to designing programs for navigating the process of social exchange and sharing. Thus, a new methodology and practice to identify, visualize, and, to a certain degree, predict architectural changeability must be developed.

The architecture of informality lays claim to designing and building as part of an ongoing process, where classical architectural values, such as purpose, durability, and beauty, are not given in advance but are gained though relationships. It supersedes an architecture of static geometrical objects with the introduction of dynamic and participatory processes and systems. It is distinguished by code over mass, relationships over compositions, networks over structures, adaptation over stasis. It reconstructs architectural relevance, hidden beyond official protocols, by enabling people to control and shape their living space. Design and building become an evolutionary process that can respond to many different initiatives. An open-ended system enables everyone to share and compare knowledge and collectively optimize spatial transformations. Its sustainability is embedded in the construction process; in a world of growth and change, a building is never completed.

THE TRANS/LOCAL GEOGRAPHY
OF OLYMPIC DISSENT:
ACTIVISM, DESIGN, AFFECT

Jilly Traganou and Grace Vetrocq Tuttle

The Olympics are a powerful design actor that reshape both the material qualities and the conceptual perception of their host location. This reshaping is accomplished through a myriad of design operations that range from architecture to fashion design. The vast cost of the Olympics, shouldered by both public and private investors, is rationalized through the promise of urban regeneration, infrastructure improvements, and, most of all, the enhancement of national prestige—all part of the triumphal rhetoric of the Olympics.

But the Olympics also function as a platform for the expression of dissent. Unofficial actors and messages defy the International Olympic Committee's (IOC) charter, which prohibits any protest, unless in designated areas.[1] Acts of Olympic dissent have proliferated in the present era of late capitalism, which has seen an expansion of the Olympics as a project of socio-spatial transformation rather than simply as a sports event. Activists and nongovernmental organizations express concerns for issues that range from environmental and human rights infringements to problems of spatial inequality, such as housing evictions and privatizations of public land.

The rise in dissent is also supported by the proliferation of social media and the multitude of social movements and advocacy groups. As media theorists Monroe Price and Daniel Dayan have observed, the Olympics function as "platforms" to be "hijacked" by various interest groups "as blank slates . . . available for all sorts of new dramaturgies besides their own."[2] Often disenchanted by the Olympics, these actors take advantage of the high visibility of the Olympics as "a global theater of representation"[3] through which they can gain the attention of a global audience for their causes. Nevertheless, counter-Olympic acts often remain relatively invisible to the wider public due to the strong interdependence of the IOC's and the media's interests.

In the literature of the Olympics, it is common to find a dichotomy between the intentions of socially minded, grassroots designer-activists and those of official Olympic designers complicit in the elite ideology of Olympic organizers. If the first serve to awaken, the second serve to obscure. On the one hand, Olympic activists speak out on behalf of those neglected by the Olympic grand narrative, typically those with tenuous rights as citizens, such as the homeless or tenants displaced by Olympic constructions. On the other hand, Olympic designers are criticized for mystifying the meaning of the Olympic products rather than making design accessible to public scrutiny and understanding.[4] Activists, journalists, and academics who critique the design of the Olympics question their scandalous costs, and see them as agents of uneven, neoliberal development to different parts of the globe. They criticize the opaque decision-making processes of planning and awarding design commissions to "starchitects" or multinational corporations that reproduce generic versions of global design that neglect local needs.

This essay complicates this dual perception of rigid roles—informal grassroots dissent on the one hand and acritical professional compliance on the other—by identifying design as a language with the potential of nonconformist possibilities that can cut across both Olympic and counter-Olympic acts. Questions of social engagement, transparency, and justice can be foregrounded and tackled from a variety of subject positions—from the street to the drafting table, from the side of activist organizations with little design expertise to officially endorsed designs submitted by commissioned professionals. In the following, we examine design actions that are at odds with the IOC's principles of operation from *both* non-expert and professional standpoints. Most importantly, this essay tries to discern what is designerly about counter-Olympic acts, even when they are not propositional in nature.

Materialized Dissent

Materialized forms of counter-Olympic dissent are meant to put pressure on organizers and local governments while producing conditions of affect that connect viscerally with audiences and participants alike. In some cases, counter-Olympic activism grappled with exceptionally repressive regimes, leading to violent confrontations with authorities. In the context of the 1968 Mexico

Fig. 1 Torch relay protests in Paris, part of global disruptions in anticipation of the Beijing Olympics in China, April 7, 2008, Hoche-Friedland, Paris, Île-de-France. Designer unknown. Photograph Peter Krefting. Flickr, Creative Commons License.

City Olympics, students protested against the repressive regime of president Gustavo Díaz Ordaz, leading to the Tlatelolco Massacre during which 260 protesters were killed by army forces only ten days before the games.[5] Student protests also took place in the context of the Seoul Olympics of 1988, and various dissenting voices disrupted Olympic events in Atlanta in 1996,[6] Sydney in 2000,[7] and Athens in 2004.[8]

In 2008, forty years after Mexico City, anti-Olympic protests led once again to violent confrontations with authorities. This time the protests were global, given a context of intense censorship within China that silenced local voices of dissent. Activists who wished to bring international scrutiny to China's politics systematically disrupted the torch relay ceremonies of the 2008 Beijing Olympics in various locations across the globe. During protests in London, Paris, and San Francisco, activists came into conflict with the police and representatives of the Beijing organizing committee. Most importantly, anti-Beijing activism operated as a synergy between pro-Tibetan protesters and various human rights organizations, such as those concerned about China's role in Darfur. The confluence is characteristic of the transnational coalition activism that has developed in recent times (Fig. 1).

Within the broad spectrum of counter-Olympics activism, we will discuss two types of dissenting acts that are also "designerly" acts. The first is based primarily on communication design and uses symbolic appropriation as a method of undermining the authority of official Olympic design. The second mobilizes the agency of space by disrupting or trespassing on public sites that have symbolic significance for the Olympic narrative.

Symbolic Appropriation

The appropriation of Olympic symbols is a recurring tactic used by various counter-Olympic movements, from 1968 to the present. In the context of the 1968 Mexico City Olympics, the student movement appropriated sanctioned Olympic icons (logo, pictograms, and the dove, which was the symbol of the Cultural Olympiad) designed by Lance Wyman, Pedro Ramírez Vázquez, and Eduardo Terrazas (Fig. 2). Nevertheless, it is largely accepted today that the graphic design program of the Mexico 1968 Olympic was not simply the target of protest. As a new visual language of communication, it had a powerful effect on the protesters when they crafted their responses.[9] The (now seen as canonical) Mexico City 1968 Olympic logo, with its radiating pattern that expands from the letters "Mexico 68" and entangle the Olympic rings, defied Olympic rules—at least by the standards of corporate identity conventions today that demand the clear separation of the rings from all surrounding symbols.

Fig. 2 Lance Wyman's process drawing for the design of the Mexico 1968 poster, based on the Mexico 1968 emblem. Courtesy Lance Wyman.

Fig. 3 Pictograms for the Mexico 1968 Olympic Games designed by Lance Wyman and Eduardo Terrazas and their appropriation by student protesters. Courtesy Lance Wyman.

Fig. 4 Appropriation of Wolff Olins's design for the London 2012 emblem, August 1, 2007, Brick Lane, London. Anonymous designers. Photograph Iain Tait. Flickr, Creative Commons License.

While the Mexico City Olympic logo appropriated and localized the rings into a new (pre-Columbian and op-art inflected) composition, the protesters appropriated the logo into new entanglements that criticized the militarization of the regime and lack of civil liberties. The Mexico 1968 sport pictograms also provided student protesters with an icon-based language for communication that defied modernist abstraction. This visual language allowed students to express their sentiments of discontent, rage, and determination against the regime. By "paraphrasing" the Olympic pictograms' depictions of sports tools, students drew attention to the tools of urban warfare and suppression. The students' icons expressed their dissent through the exchange of a cleat for a military boot, a ball for a hand grenade, a boxing glove for a gas mask (Figs. 3, 4).

The visual language of the Mexico 1968 Olympic Games design, paradoxical as this might sound, had a major impact on the future careers of protesters who followed design-related professions. Some of them were students of design who later became influential design professionals and educators. Such was the case of Juan Antonio Madrid, later the director of the Escuela Nacional de Artes Plásticas. In 1985 at the University of Mexico in Mexico City, after a lecture by Lance Wyman, Madrid expressed his gratitude to Wyman for "giving him a language,"[10] and presented him the book Gráfica del 68, which includes a collection of the various graphics produced by the student movement in 1968.[11] This indicates not only a moment of reconciliation, but the blurring of the official and the unofficial, the authoritative and the subversive, in the long trajectories of design history.

Today, the boundaries between professional and non-expert designers are increasingly obscured. The Wolff Olins consultancy, designers of the official London 2012 emblem, was inspired by visual languages used in nonprofessional design. Their logo was meant to encourage further designerly expressions and participation by the public. For Wolff Olins,

> The emblem is unconventionally bold, deliberately spirited, and unexpectedly dissonant, echoing London's qualities of a modern, edgy city. Containing neither sporting images nor pictures of London landmarks, the emblem shows that the Games are . . . for everyone, regardless of age, culture, and language. The emblem is designed to be populated, to contain in-fills and images, so it is recognizable enough for everyone to feel and be part of London 2012.[12]

Wolff Olins recognized the changing role of contemporary audiences, from passive consumers to active participants in the design process, and aspired to provide opportunities for nonconventional means of engagement with their design. Their intention was to "hand over some tools that would allow people to make everything they wanted,"—a design that would be "off the podium, onto the streets."[13] Their emblem design was meant to be used by wider populations as a language rather than as a fixed form. They also invited the public to populate the large letterforms of the logo with in-fills of images and patterns of their choice. With this, they are the first official Olympic designers who wanted to see their design become appropriated by the general public rather than be used strictly by the corporate Olympic Partners (TOP), a goal that they only partially achieved (Fig. 4).

Fans of the Olympics, designers and citizens alike, found the design to have no obvious relation to accepted notions of Britishness or London. Soon after its release, negative descriptions of the logo went viral, and an unprecedented volume of new designs—from parodies to sincere alternatives—were produced by expert and non-expert designers and circulated online.[14] This was a paradoxical development. While the emblem was rejected and disparaged by the public, it actually inspired a level of engagement with design that its designers had hoped for. But Wolff Olins's aspiration to see the design appropriated by the public for the generation of new meanings was almost impossible to realize, given the strong corporate control of the IOC. Only TOP and those authorized entities that participated in the Festival of London and the "Inspired by London 2012" program were allowed to use the logo.[15] Any form of appropriation was strictly prohibited and prosecuted. Nevertheless, despite its lack of popularity, Wolff Olins's work constituted a major paradigm shift that endeavored to defy the limitations incorporated in the Olympic charter.[16]

Spatial Agency

Objects are not the only materialized forms of dissent. It is also carried out by the actions of individuals or collective bodies. Bodies in action operate within specific spaces but also use space as a medium of resistance. Urban disruption and trespassing are two established tactics that utilize the potential of space to be transformed into agency.

Urban Disruption

Counter-Olympics activists often use methods of urban disruption to express their dissent. The main design tool in such operations is the deployment of critical mass. The mass of bodies in action aims to disrupt day-to-day and ceremonial functions of the Olympics by temporarily occupying strategic public spaces or Olympic sites. Accompanied by rhythmic sounds and distinctive appearances, using masks or other forms of identity concealment as in the black bloc anarchist operations, the assemblage of bodies, objects, and spaces acts as a mobile disruptor of public life and evokes a range of reactions in passersby— from astonishment to distress, from euphoria to claustrophobia, from compliance to rage. Bodies in action are occasionally augmented by various forms of equipment, from bicycles to tents, that provide different possibilities for agency. Urban disruption in the form of street protest has been used by counter-Olympics activists from the Mexico City 1968 Olympics to more recent demonstrations against the Beijing 2008, Vancouver 2010, and London 2012 Olympics, often leading to confrontation with local authorities.

Continuing the anarchist tradition of the Northwest Pacific region, Vancouver activists did not hesitate to use uncompromising direct action from the beginning of their anti-Olympic action. The dialogue between protesters and the state disintegrated early on, and positions were entrenched. Protests focused on various intertwined fronts: environmental destruction, the wastefulness of taxpayer money on the games at the expense of indispensable social services, the threat to civil liberties by massively militarized police forces, and the encroachment upon indigenous peoples' rights through the use of aboriginal Coast Salish land as one of the Vancouver Olympic sites.[17] Anti-Olympics activists, including existing and newly established groups such as No One Is Illegal, Pivot Legal Society, and No Games 2010 Coalition, employed strategies from earlier anti-World Trade Organization protests, using local spatial occupation and coordinated operations of public disruption. The spatial tactic of the encampment is an example of disruption used by activists. It took the form of the Tent Village and Red Tent campaign that took place in February 2010 in two different Vancouver sites as a means to turn the city's attention to the issue of homelessness, a persistent problem neglected by Olympic organizers despite their $1.84 billion budget (Fig. 5).

Urban disruption was also used during the 2012 London Olympics. On July 27, 2012, as part of their monthly bicycle ride through the city, participants in London's Critical Mass made the Olympic stadium their biking destination and planned their arrival to coincide with the beginning of the Olympic Opening Ceremony.[18] Throughout their trajectory from South London to the Olympic site, participants were met by resistance from the London police. The demonstrators succeeded in transgressing the defined boundaries by gaining access through the Rotherhithe tunnel that connects London north and south of the Thames. Although several bikers were arrested, the event went mostly unnoticed by the local and international media, as was the broader anti-Olympic opposition in London, in contrast to the anti-Beijing campaign, which had attracted wide visibility in the western world.[19]

Trespassing

The act of trespassing the barriers to Olympics sites is a common form of dissent used by activists. After 2001, Olympics security increased by an unprecedented amount, both in expenditure and its representational presence. Trespassing can be seen as an act that functions between spatial appropriation and disruption, which utilizes both spatial and performative means. The question of what lies behind the fence, literally and metaphorically, during the development process of new Olympic territory intrigues the imagination and ignites the rage of citizens who demand transparency and inclusion. Trespassing is also a means employed by investigative journalists to obtain first-hand accounts of the conditions behind the closed spaces or as a test of Olympics security measures. But it is also used by designers, artists, and photographers interested in scrutinizing the urban and environmental transformation triggered by the Olympics.

The fence around the London 2012 site came to vividly symbolize the "defensiveness and paranoia of the Olympic Delivery Authority."[20] During preparations for the Games, activist-artists literally transgressed the fence, while others did so in subtler, indirect ways. "Point of View," a project by the Office of Subversive Architecture, was placed just outside the Olympic border. Though its users did not physically trespass the Olympic site, the structure provided the

Fig. 5 Red Tent Campaign, part of a housing protest, February 27, 2010. Vancouver, British Columbia, Canada. Designer unknown. Photograph Stephen Hui. Courtesy of the photographer.

possibility of trespassing through vision. It comprised a viewing platform with a few steps erected in front of the fence for solitary observation. Only one's head and eyes were allowed to trespass the restricted zone[21] (Fig. 6).

"Trespassing the Olympic Site," by Stephen Cornford, was a performance-based project that took place from 2006 to 2008, prior to the installation of the 5,000-volt electrified fence surrounding the London 2012 site. Appointing himself "artist in residence," Cornford witnessed the "process of clearing the site, the gradual erasure of its history," before the construction process began. The findings of his exploration were reported online through photography and journal writing.[22]

From our point of view, works like these juxtapose the intense surveillance of the Olympic operation with intentionally low-tech means of action or observation that rely on resources that are easily available. Involving discrete objects and bodies in action, they are meant to act as prosaic security valves to assess or warn about the impact of the Olympic design from a human-scale perspective. As embodied, yet designerly, actions, they are not meant to restrain the large design operations of the Olympics, but rather to allow their participants to obtain a first-hand, unmediated experience of a given condition, that has been otherwise restricted by the authorities. Works of this type avoid direct confrontation and suggest acts of disobedience rather than disruption.

Potential of Counter-Olympic Dissent

It is true that, in comparison with some well-known cases of successful urban resistance, the numerous counter-Olympics movements have no success stories or triumphal results to demonstrate, such as those that came out of the protests against the urban renewal order of the 1960s.[23] Instead, some of the most important contributions of counter-Olympics acts of our recent times, besides the strengthening of local movements' capacities for self-organizing, are the synergies established with areas of expertise that have to do with material figuration. These are mobilized through both professional and non-professional forms of engagement, for the development of programs of socio-technical action, such as those described in this essay. The capacity for change through these vigorous, though sometimes inconspicuous and always unfinished, counter-Olympics products and acts should not be underestimated. Political theorist Victoria Hattam, in her essay on the use of color in revolutionary politics, suggests that "visuality more generally opens the door to the affective and in so doing expands our conception of the political." [24] Seen this way, images and all other forms of sensorial affectivity "provide an important link to the projectivity of politics through which we expand, reimagine, and enact new possibilities."[25]

Fig. 6 Point of View by Office for Subversive Architecture (OSA), London, 2012. Photograph by Karsten Huneck. Courtesy of OSA (London office).

Counter-Olympics activists' appropriation of official symbols into new networks of associations, and their adoption of tactics of embodied action that directly or indirectly confronts authorities in the urban realm are both dissenting and designerly. Embracing tactics that expose what has been suppressed by Olympics rhetoric, they bring into light the coercive nature of the Olympics and deconstruct their rhetoric of renewal and progress. These counter-Olympics acts are as transnational and multimodal today as the Olympic design operations themselves; their geographies bridge the local and the global, while their strategies range from the "pragmatic to the poetic." Similarly, with propositional design, they aim to "promote individual agency, engage communities and propose systemic changes within a global framework of mutual obligations."[26] Though they may not resolve all disagreements or advance design alternatives, they do offer effective, non-scripted encounters that "expand the conception of the political into vital non-verbal domains."[27] From our perspective, these actions, "never finished, always in progress," participate in the debate of design as "the art of the possible."[28]

GARMENTS AS AGENTS
OF CHANGE: LUCIA CUBA

Hazel Clark

Changing Fashion Geographies

The relationships between fashion and geography are many and complex, and they date back centuries, encompassing the complex trade routes between East and West. From the late 1850s, Paris became the center of haute couture, the pinnacle of fashion design, following the establishment of the House of Charles Frederick Worth. A century later couture lost its supremacy to prêt à porter, comprising off-the-peg garments that made fashion more available to more people in more places. By the twenty-first century fashion's reach has become unprecedented; the geography of the production, consumption, and mediation of fashionable clothing is now global in its economy, origination, and impact. So great is fashion's role that it has become a tool in nation branding.

For countries rising or aspiring to world prominence, hosting biannual fashion weeks has served to promote indigenous design talent and attract buyers and the all-important international fashion media. The term "fashion city," which was once only applied to Paris, New York, London, Milan, and, arguably, Tokyo, has become aspirational and has expanded to include cities such as Jakarta, Santiago, Zagreb, and Montreal. In 2000, the mayor of Shanghai declared that his city would become the "world's sixth fashion centre" by the end of the first decade of the new century.[1] Even when these ambitions have not been met, their very utterance provides evidence of the shift of the global fashion map away from the big four fashion cities. In parallel, the dark side of fashion's geography has also been revealed. The collapse of the Rana Plaza garment factory in Bangladesh, in April 2013, killing over a thousand people working to produce clothing for large western "fast fashion" brands, highlighted the scale and nature of the human rights abuses quietly condoned in the name of cheap clothes. Where fashion originates, how it looks, the role it plays, and the responsibilities it might have are no longer obvious or fixed.

Fashion theorist Barbara Vinken has referred to the period after the 1970s as one of post-fashion. Whether or not we agree with her moniker, we cannot argue with her highlighting the differences before and after that time. She observes how fashion has become a coproduction between the *créateur* and those who wear the clothes, with "people in the street" being as equally responsible for what they wear as professional designers.[2] Something else has also altered; more designers are seeking to "create a counter-rhythm" to the seasonal frenzy of fashion collections, that is, to define fashion as being based on duration rather than change.[3] Vinken cites 1981 as another key date, the year when Japanese designer Rei Kawakubo first showed her Comme des Garçons collection. But Kawakubo and her compatriots Issey Miyake and Yohji Yamamoto and the Belgian designer Martin Margiela initiated not only a new sense of fashion time but also new fashion design geographies. Originating from a country then considered outside fashion's creative ambit, except as a source of exotic motifs for western designers, the Japanese Big Three opened the way for the development of more conceptual approaches to fashion and were followed by Margiela and the Antwerp Six, fashion graduates from the Antwerp Academy of Fine Arts.[4]

Fast forward to May 2012, when the first eighteen graduates from the MFA in Fashion Design and Society at Parsons The New School for Design, in New York, showed their final collections. With its international cohort of students, the program facilitates understanding of the global fashion industry, including design, production, and distribution cycles, and aims to develop social and critical perspectives. Students not only come from different parts of the world but from a variety of personal backgrounds, which are not only contributing to the expansion of fashion's geographies of origination but are also setting new agendas for fashion and the work it might do. In the remainder of this essay, I will discuss *ARTICULO 6: Narratives of Gender, Strength, and Politics*, the MFA collection of Lucia Cuba, as a recent example of fashion's changing geographies and its new agendas.

New Fashion Agendas: Lucia Cuba

The form and content of Lucia Cuba's *ARTICULO 6*[5] collection directly reflect her own culture and geography as a citizen and a resident of Peru before coming to New York on a Fulbright in 2010. While the collection draws upon some traditional forms of dress, it does a great deal more by engaging with significant issues of gender and human rights that plagued that country's recent troubled history. In creating *ARTICULO 6*, Lucia Cuba contributes not only to the continuing shift in fashion's geographies, but she also demonstrates how fashion can respond to new agendas, which in the process take the role and potentialities of fashion beyond the commodity sphere.

To describe *ARTICULO 6* as a fashion collection is simplistic. It is best characterized as an activist design project that aims to raise awareness about a little known incident in Peru's recent history. From 1996 through 2000, the government of president Alberto Fujimori forced sterilization on more than an estimated 3,000 people, mainly Andean women living in rural areas.[6] In speaking out against this action, the project is named after Article 6 of the second chapter of the General Health Law of Peru, which provides individuals with the right to choose the contraceptive method they prefer and to have access to appropriate information prior to making that decision.[7] By law, the application of any permanent contraceptive method requires the prior written consent of the recipient.

Lucia Cuba became familiar with the case in March 2008 as part of her research for a PhD at the public health faculty of the Universidad Peruana Cayetano Heredia (UPCH) in her native Lima. Already a consultant in public health specializing in youth sexual and reproductive well-being, Cuba had undergraduate and graduate degrees in social psychology and educational psychology and had practiced as a fashion designer. Her activities included coordinating sustainability and development programs, teaching psychology and fashion design courses, and participating in projects for the development of arts and culture in Peru and Latin America and other initiatives aimed at advancing the development of local emerging fashion systems. These included creating and coordinating the LUCCO independent design lab in 2004, a collection of urban casual wear for men and women,[8] and PROJECT GAMARRA, an activist design initiative.[9] The latter is ongoing and aims to raise awareness among designers, researchers, business owners, workers, neighbors, and consumers about the importance of understanding the Gamarra Commercial Emporium in Lima, not only as an industrial cluster but as an urban ecology—a site of creativity and a space of confluence of diverse peoples and cultural identities—in an attempt to promote self-reflection, social development, and the strengthening of social cohesion and sustainable practices in this urban context.

In common with many contemporary practitioners, such as designer Hussein Chalayan or Parsons' MFA Design and Society Director Shelley Fox,[10] Cuba moves fluidly between media and venues, selecting the most important vehicle for her work, which results in or comments on the production of fashionable clothes as will be discussed in more detail. As a result, after graduating from Parsons, she was awarded a residency at the Textile Arts Center in New York City.

Cuba has been described as an activist designer who, when asked by a journalist what she ultimately hoped to accomplish through her approach to fashion, responded, "To allow people to consider the agency of clothes and to connect in a stronger way with one of the most known elements in every society: garments. Also to allow this familiarity with garments to become an opportunity to inform, be analytic, and raise awareness about how our society develops, and what we can all, as citizens, do about it."[11]

She describes her work as a critical approach to fashion design through the construction and exploration of garments as performative and political. Her aim is to create a broader understanding of the role of fashion design objects, including their social, ethical, and political perspectives, in addition to their functional and aesthetic roles. The work reflects her desire to question the established language of fashion based upon its commodity status or condition by acknowledging the agency of clothes. In their different forms, her garments and installations often employ photography and video in an attempt to broaden the potential grammars of critical action through clothes as wearable devices and as affective and embodied conveyors of cultural meaning. Cuba uniquely combines fashion, art, and activism with her background in public health and psychology. It is her commitment to addressing issues of body, gender, and bio-politics that informs the *ARTICULO 6* project.

Garments as Agents of Change

ARTICULO 6 consists of a collection of thirty-four pieces of clothing and 12 Actions. The clothes are made from mixed media, using embroidery and prints on cotton twill and canvas. The formal aesthetic is inspired by native Andean *polleras*, or skirts, which have been subject to deconstruction and reinterpretation (**Fig. 1**). The blouses that accompany the skirts are intended to reference the uniformity and militarization enforced by public policy and to evoke the strength and capacity of victims to defend themselves and overcome the physical and psychological irreversibility of the forced sterilization. The images and symbols printed and embroidered on the fabrics comment on the range of institutions, activists, press, and individuals related to the case.

The 12 Actions occupy a variety of forms and venues. The first was a photographic interaction taken in the countryside in Azpitia, Peru, in April 2012. The individual garments were presented on models whose plaited hair falls over their faces, symbolizing the way in which the individual identities of

Fig. 1 Lucia Cuba, *ARTICULO 6*, Action 1: Photographic Interaction. Model Carla Rincón. Photograph Erasmo Wong Seoane. Courtesy Erasmo Wong Seoane.

Fig. 2 Lucia Cuba, *ARTICULO 6*, Action 1: Photographic Interaction (detail). Model Carla Rincón. Photograph Erasmo Wong Seoane. Courtesy Erasmo Wong Seoane.

the victims of atrocity were disregarded. These images are visually striking, as are the designs themselves, at first masking the disturbing nature of their content. Reviewing Action 2, the installation of the collection as part of the MFA graduate collection in May 2012, *The New York Times* fashion journalist Eric Wilson commented on, "[A] simple design on canvas, it was printed with repeating black-and-white photographs of a small boy standing at attention. You might have thought the jacket verged on adorable,"[12] until it was pointed out that this was a childhood image of Fujimori, the perpetrator of these human rights violations (**Fig. 2**).

At the time of this writing, a total of eight of the 12 Actions have been completed. Action 3 was a conversation, staged in Lima, where the designer discussed the creative stages and processes leading up to the collection. The next, Action 4, entitled Meta Devices, presented objects designed to be worn with and complement the clothes, including footwear and facemasks. For Action 5, NYFW/Runway Performance fashion models wore the garments and objects as part of the MFA runway show held at Milk Studios during New York Fashion Week in September 2012 (**Fig. 3**). Action 6, Interactions, was presented in an exhibition as part of the II Iberoamerican Design Biennale (BID-DIMAD), in Madrid from November 2012 to February 2013. *ARTICULO 6* received the BID 2012 fashion design award and a special design for development award mention, and one of the garments was selected for inclusion in the biennial's itinerant exhibition over the next two years.

Action 7 took a somewhat different form, being presented as three independent manifestations called Exposed. The first resulted from the runway collection, after which stylists for the performer Lady Gaga requested access to some of the garments.[13] They chose to dress the celebrity for an MTV interview, shown on September 14, 2012, to launch her perfume, Fame. Lady Gaga wore two pieces printed with the text of Article 6 of Peru's general health law that states: "all persons have the right to choose freely the contraceptive method they prefer, and to receive information on the methods available and on the risks." Although the celebrity was not making a statement about the project herself, wearing the pieces generated an immediate and positive reaction locally, triggering a massive media response about the designs and the significance of the text. This Action spurred conversations about the case as well as new ways of informing and touching upon different social issues in Peru using garments as agents.

Fig. 3 Lucia Cuba, *ARTICULO 6*, Action 5: NYFW/Runway Performance. Photograph Pablo Moura. Courtesy Pablo Moura.

Fig. 4 Lucia Cuba, *ARTICULO 6*, Action 7: Exposed 2, street posters in Lima, Peru, 2012.

The second exposure of Action 7 was to produce posters printed with Article 6, which were placed in different streets in Lima and other cities in Peru (**Fig. 4**). The third exposure of Action 7 featured the garments being worn on the streets of New York during Fashion Week, in February 2013, and reported on by stylist and fashion blogger Lily Gatins for *Le Report*. Action 8, Forzadas.pe, took a different form, comprising a digital record of the many articles, videos, and reports that had documented and resulted from the project. Forzadas.pe also articulates the efforts of different people and organizations working toward the resolution of the case. The final four Actions comprise "Video/Performance"

136

Photograph Luis Ángel Gonzáles Taipe. Courtesy Luis Ángel Gonzáles Taipe.

(Action 9) and an exhibition (10) "Estados Unidos de . . ." that took place at the Invisible Dog Gallery, New York, in September 2013. "2,075—A Silent Action" (11) will be staged in Lima by a group of 2,075 volunteers, the number of the sterilization victims, wearing *polleras*. Finally, a travelling exhibition, *ARTICULO 6*—Exhibition (12), is currently planned for 2014.

From these different platforms, Lucia Cuba's work has shared the knowledge about the unresolved case of forced sterilizations in Peru. Cuba's overall objective is to provoke conversations about sexual and reproductive rights in Peru, contribute to collective memory, and have an impact directly on individual cases against the government that were reopened for the third time in March 2011, after having been the subject of considerable discussion in the 2011 presidential campaign, during which Fujimori's daughter, Keiko, was one of the strongest candidates. The case is currently under the jurisdiction of the district attorney. However, though there was an explicit electoral promise by Peru's current president, Ollanta Humala, to seek justice for the victims, the public is largely unaware that the case has been reopened. As Cuba speculates, this may be a consequence of the prevailing power of Fujimori's party in different governmental institutions throughout the country.

Yet forced sterilization is not just a regional issue pertaining only to Peru. Action 10, titled "Estados Unidos de . . ." (United States of . . .) drew attention to the global nature and the currency of the condition. In particular, it referenced the forced sterilizations that were carried out in the United States as part of the Eugenics Program in North Carolina in the early part of the twentieth century and continued until as late as 1974.[14] The exhibition also called attention to the current, and controversial, one-child policy in China.

ARTICULO 6, while enormously ambitious in scale, demonstrates the work that fashion might do. Lucia Cuba describes her garments as "agents of change."[15] Their agency bestows on the clothes a longevity that transcends the short-lived conventions of the fashion cycle. The garments also demonstrate, quite powerfully, that fashion's changing geographies need not be absorbed only by commodity fetishism and that they also have the opportunity to set new agendas, rather than being bound by past practices and definitions. The project expands our awareness of fashion and the role of the fashion designer. In the twenty-first century, the global reach of fashion's production, consumption, visualization, use, and the simple fact the virtually all human beings wear clothes, provide huge latent political potential.

Acknowledgment

Sincere thanks to Lucia Cuba for providing information and images and for agreeing to allow ARTICULO 6 to be the subject of this essay.

RETURNING DUCHAMP'S URINAL TO THE BATHROOM? ON THE RECONNECTION OF ARTISTIC EXPERIMENTATION, SOCIAL RESPONSIBILITY, AND INSTITUTIONAL TRANSFORMATION

Teddy Cruz

It is obvious by now that the celebrated metropolitan explosion in the years of the last economic boom also produced in tandem a dramatic project of marginalization, resulting in the unprecedented growth of slums surrounding major urban centers, exacerbating the socioeconomic and demographic conflicts of uneven urbanization and putting urban asymmetry at the center of today's crises. In the context of this shift, the design professions are paralyzed, silently witnessing the consolidation of the most blatant politics of unaccountability, the shrinkage of social and public institutions, and the absence of a single proposal or action that might suggest a different approach or different arrangements. Rather than an economic and environmental crisis, ours is primarily a cultural crisis resulting in the inability of institutions to question their ways of thinking, their exclusionary policies, the rigidity of their protocols, and silos. Within this radical context we must question the role of architectural research and design today.

The primary site of artistic intervention for research and design today is the gap between cultural institutions and the public—a space now instigating a new civic imagination and collective political will. It is not enough to give art the task of only revealing metaphorically the socioeconomic histories and injustices that produced these crises, but it is essential that art becomes an instrument to construct specific procedures to transcend them and develop a more functional set of operations that can reconnect art and architecture to the urgency of the everyday and to a rethinking of its institutions. The formation of new platforms of engagement in the creative fields can only be made possible with a sense of urgency, pushing us to rethink our very procedures. The need for expanded modes of artistic practice, alternative sites of research and pedagogy, new conceptions of cultural and economic production, and the reorganization of social relations seem more urgent than ever.

Expanding Artistic Practices: From Critical Distance to Critical Proximity

A revision of our artistic procedures is essential today because the ideological divide permeating politics today is also implicit in art and architecture's current debates. On one hand we find those who continue to defend art and architecture as a self-referential project of apolitical formalism, made of hyper-aesthetics for the sake of aesthetics. These voices continue to press the notion of the avant-garde as an autonomous project requiring a critical distance from institutions so as to operate critically in the research of experimental form. On the other, are those who feel the need to step out of this autonomy in order to engage the sociopolitical and economic domains that have remained peripheral to the specializations of art and architecture. This contingency questions our professions' powerlessness in the context of the world's most pressing crises.

The latter—a growing body of emerging practices—seeks instead a project of "radical proximity" to institutions, encroaching on them to transform them from the inside out in order to produce new aesthetic categories that can problematize the relationship of the social, the political, and the formal, questioning the creative fields' unconditional love affair, in recent years, with a system of economic excess that was necessary to legitimize artistic autonomy. How to reconnect artistic experimentation and social responsibility, a major aspiration of the historic avant-garde, must be the central question of today's debate.

What is sought, then, is an expanded mode of practice, where architects are responsible for imagining counter-spatial procedures, political and economic structures that can produce new modes of sociability and encounter. Without altering the exclusionary policies that produced the crises in the first place, our professions will continue to be subordinated to the visionless and homogeneous environments defined by the bottom-line urbanism of developers' spreadsheets and the neoconservative politics and economics of a hyper-individualistic ownership society. In essence, then, the autonomous role of the artist needs to be coupled with the role of the activist. I don't see one as more important than the other because both are necessary today.

Rethinking the Sites of Experimentation: New Paradigms in Research and Design Will Emerge from the Margins

The world's architecture intelligentsia, supported by the glamorous economy of recent years, flocked en masse to the United Arab Emirates and China to help build the dream castles that would catapult these enclaves of wealth into global epicenters of urban development. Other than a few isolated protagonist architectural interventions, whose images have been disseminated widely, most of the high profile projects produced in such regions of growth have, in fact, only perpetuated the exhausted recipes of an oil-hungry globalization. In other words, no major ideas were advanced there to transform existing paradigms of housing, infrastructure, and density or to resolve the major problems of urbanization today—problems that are grounded in the inability of the institutions of urban development to engage with informality, confront socioeconomic inequity, and address the lack of affordable housing and infrastructure.

While the attention of the world has been focused on these enclaves of economic power in recent years, the most radical ideas advancing new models of urban development were being produced on the margins, across Latin American cities. Challenging the entrenched neoliberal urban logic of development founded on top-down privatization, homogeneity, and exclusion, visionary mayors in cities such as Porto Alegre and Curitiba, in Brazil, and Bogotá and Medellín, in Colombia, began to initiate new institutional protocols by enabling public participation, civic culture, and unorthodox cross-institutional collaborations, rethinking the very meaning of infrastructure, housing, and density and mediating top-down development and bottom-up social organization. I cannot think of any other continental region in the world where we can find this type of collective effort, led by municipal and federal governments seeking a new brand of progressive politics to produce an urbanism of inclusion.

We urgently need to reorient our focus to other sites of research and design intervention. The examples of Porto Alegre, Curitiba, Bogotá, and Medellín argue that some of the most relevant experimental practices and projects moving socioeconomic sustainability forward will not emerge from sites of economic abundance but from sites of scarcity and zones of conflict. On the periphery, conditions of social emergency are transforming our ways of thinking about urban matters and matters of concern to the city.

Radicalizing the Particular: Moving from the Ambiguity of the Public to the Specificity of Rights

We must move beyond the abstractions of the global in order to hit the ground running and engage the particularities of politics inscribed in local geographies of conflict. Within the specificity of conflict, contemporary artistic practice has to reposition itself so that it can expose the particularities of hidden institutional histories and reveal the missing information that will allow us to piece together more accurate, anticipatory urban research and design interventions. To be political in our field requires a commitment to exposing the particular conditions of conflict in the territories and institutional mechanisms that have perpetuated such conflicts. What produced these crises in the first place? Only the knowledge of the specific conditions that produced them can enable us to think politically. And the only way to produce a truly experimental architecture in our time involves the specific reconfiguration of the political and economic ground. The very conditions that produce conflict between top-down forces of urbanization and bottom-up social and ecological networks, between enclaves of megawealth and sectors of marginalization, can provide the material for and of design.

What is needed is a more critical role for design as a set of actions that encroach upon the fragmented and discriminatory policies and economics that produced these collisions in the first place. It is not buildings but the fundamental reorganization of socioeconomic relations that is necessary for producing new paradigms of democratization and urbanization. Artists and architects have a role in the conceptualization of such new protocols. The construction of the political is at stake here, not just political art or architecture.

It has been said that the civil rights movement in the United States began on a bus. At least that is the image that consolidated an argument that detonated a constitutional transformation, a small act that trickled up into collective awareness. While public transport at that time was labeled "public," it was not accessible to all. It is necessary to move from the neutrality of the term "public," as it is used in current political debate, in order to arrive at the specificity of rights, the rights to the city and to the neighborhood. We have to open up the idea that architects and artists—besides being researchers and designers of form, buildings, and objects—can be designers of political processes, alternative economic models, and collaborations across institutions and jurisdictions.

With this approach, design can take the form of small, incremental retrofits of existing urban fabric and regulation, encroaching on the privatized public domain and infrastructure, as well as on the rigidity of institutional thinking. The most radical interventions of our time may emerge from specific, bottom-up urban and regulatory alterations, modest in nature but with enough resolution and assurance to trickle up and transform top-down institutional structures.

Communities of Cultural Production: The Informal as Praxis

While in recent years the global city has become the privileged site of an urbanization of *consumption* and display, local, informal neighborhoods on the margins of such centers of economic power remain sites of cultural *production*. These are peripheral communities where emergent economic configurations continue to take place through the tactical adaptation and retrofit of discriminatory zoning and exclusionary economic development. Such improvisations and reconfigurations have the effect of producing a different notion of the political at the intersection of formal and informal urbanization and in the spaces of conflict between top-down policy and bottom-up social contingency. From these informal, worldwide settlements, a new politics of urban growth for the contemporary city may be shaped, taking into account bottom-up sociocultural productivity in the restructuring of unsustainable top-down urban policies.

But as we return to these informal settlements for clues, their stealth urban praxis also calls for artistic interpretation and political representation. This should be the space of intervention for contemporary architectural practice, engaging the specificity of the political within the performativity of the informal as the main creative tool to expand notions of design (**Fig. 1**). As architects, we continue to be seduced by the image of the informal, seeing it as only an aesthetic category, and we do not translate its operative dimensions, its socioeconomic and political procedures. The informal is not just an image of precariousness. It is a compendium of practices, a set of functional urban operations that counter and transgress imposed political boundaries and top-down economic models.

The hidden urban operations of the most compelling cases of informal urbanization across Latin America and the world need to be translated into a new political language, with particular spatial consequences from which new interpretations of housing, infrastructure, property, and citizenship may be produced and other modes of intervention in the contemporary city inspired. Generating these alternatives is incumbent on five imperatives.

1. Challenge the normative notions of architecture that conceives of itself as an autonomous, self-referential system that freezes and spatializes time. How to engage, instead, the temporalization of space found in informal urbanization's management of time, people, spaces, and resources? Within this new paradigm, conventional zoning ceases to be a punitive tool that prevents socialization

143

Fig. 1 ETC Manufactured Sites 2: Housing Urbanism Made of Waste, Teddy Cruz, 2000–ongoing. Courtesy Estudio Teddy Cruz.

but instead becomes a generative tool that organizes and anticipates social and economic activity. Density is no longer measured as an abstract quantity of objects per acre but as the quantity of socioeconomic exchanges per acre. This assertion suggests that the future of the city will be small. In conditions of socioeconomic and environmental crisis, urban growth will depend on the pixelation of the large by the small. In other words, an urbanization of retrofit. The micro-socioeconomic contingencies of the informal will transform homogeneous, large-scale official sites of urbanization into more sustainable, plural, and complex environments.

2. Question the identity of the global city based on the dominance of private development and economic value alone, which sponsors a fixed image of progress driven by budgets and profits. Engage social value as the catalyst for the incremental, low-cost layering of urban development found in informal urbanization by rethinking existing property models. Redefine affordability and the value of social participation, enhancing the role of communities in coproducing housing, and enabling a more inclusive idea of ownership.

3. Reimagine the logic of jurisdictions, where conventional government protocols give primacy to the abstraction of administrative boundaries over the social and environmental boundaries negotiated by informality as devices to construct community. How to enable more meaningful systems of political and jurisdictional representation at neighborhood scale that can tactically calibrate individual and collective interests? This shift in perception from the abstract to the particular requires mediating agencies that can produce new forms of local governance and social contracts that can enable guarantees of protection for these communities to share the profits of urbanization and prevent gentrification.

4. Critically intervene in the gap between institutions and communities. How to produce more meaningful roles for local nonprofit, community-based organizations, empowering them to co-own and co-manage, with communities, the resources of development and become the long-term choreographers of social and cultural programming for housing? These agencies can be urban curators, enabling the reorganization of social systems and economic resources at local scale. They can amplify and enforce the critical interface between top-down government infrastructural support and the creative bottom-up intelligence and sweat equity of communities and activists.

5. Denounce the consolidation of economic and political power that has installed an anti-tax, anti-immigration, and anti-public-spending culture today—a power that is cementing the final erosion of civic participation from the political process and a culture of impunity in the upper echelons of institutional structures everywhere. At a time when the welfare state seems no longer

145

possible, we must remember that social and environmental justice is not only about the redistribution of resources but the redistribution of knowledge, the right of marginal communities to access to education.

The common conceptual threads and lessons that run along the many exemplary projects in Latin America mentioned at the beginning of these reflections elevate the need for an urgent collective imagination, an investment in an urban pedagogy—the transfer of knowledge across governments and communities—and the pursuit of a civic culture as the basis for an inclusive urbanization. Within the informal, other conceptions of the public and of citizenship will be found.

Toward an Urban Pedagogy: The Visualization of a New Civic Imagination

Fundamental to a rethinking of the exclusionary political and economic frameworks that define the logic of uneven urban development in recent years is the translation and visualization of the sociocultural and economic entrepreneurial intelligence embedded in many marginal immigrant neighborhoods. But the hidden cultural, social, and economic value of these communities' informal transactions across bottom-up cultural activism, economies, and densities remains off the radar of conventional top-down planning institutions. If we consider citizenship as primarily a creative act, enabling the transformation of institutional protocols and the spaces of the city, a new conception of civic culture can emerge within these marginal communities of practice. In this context, I see informal urbanization as the site of a new interpretation of community, citizenship, and praxis in which emergent urban configurations produced out of social emergency honor the performative role of individuals constructing their own spaces.

These invisible urban praxes call for interpretation and representation in order to form the spaces of intervention, institutions of art, culture, and governance that are vital to engagement. How to design the conditions that can mobilize this activism into new spatial and economic infrastructures that benefit these communities of practice in the long term, beyond the short-term problem solving of private developers or institutions of charity?

Often, these communities lack the conceptual devices to understand their everyday procedures or how their neighborhood agency can trickle up to produce new institutional transformations and shape alternative politics and economies at the scale of everyday needs. In the context of these conditions, a different role for artistic, architectural, environmental, and community activist practices can emerge, one that goes beyond the metaphorical representation

Tactics of encroachment: as the Latin American Diaspora travels Northbound, it inevitably alters and transforms the fabric of San Diego's older subdivisions, generating non-conforming mixed uses and high densities that retrofit Levittown with difference.

Non-Conforming Buddha: a tiny post-war bungalow in a San Diego mid-city nieghborhood has been transformed from a single-family residence into a Buddhist temple.

An urbanism 70' deep: thirty some tunnels have been dug beneath Homeland Security in the last eight years. One of the largest ones was discovered last year. It had retaining walls, water and air extraction systems and electricity. It connected a house in Tijuana and a factory in San Diego.

South to North: Neighborhoods made of non-conformity. Tijuana's informal land use patterns encroach into San Diego's sprawl.

North to South: Neighborhoods made of waste. San Diego's Housing waste is recycled into Tijuana's slums.

Migrant housing: Mexican builders recuperate post-war bungalows that are slated for demolition in San Diego, and bring them across the border. Once imported into Tijuana they are assembled above one story steel frames. These floating houses define a space of opportunity beneath them, that will be filled with other uses.

Housing urbanism made of waste: one city recycles the leftover of the other into a second hand urbanism. Used garage doors and wooden crates make wall systems.

Recycled rubber tires are cut and dismantled into folded loops, creating a system that threads a stable retaining wall.

Fig. 2 Transborder Neighborhood Flows, Teddy Cruz, 2008. Courtesy Estudio Teddy Cruz.

of people, where a community's symbolic image is amplified instead of its operative dimension.

The development of a new form of urban pedagogy built on questions is one of the most critical sites of artistic investigation and practice today. This work is rethinking the gap between cultural institutions and the public. How to produce new interfaces with the public to raise awareness of the conditions that have produced environmental, economic, and social crises? The conventional structures and protocols of academic institutions may be at odds with activist practices, which are by their very nature organic and extra-academic. Should activist practices challenge the nature and structure of pedagogy within the institution? Are new modes of teaching and learning called for?

It is essential to reorient our gaze toward the drama embedded in the reality of the everyday and in so doing engage the shifting sociopolitical and economic domains that have not previously been grasped by art and design. Or, as artist Tania Bruguera said to me recently, "It is time to restore Duchamp's urinal back to the bathroom." We need to stress the urgency of a more functional relationship between research, design, and the production of the city and restore the ethical imperative between individuals, collectives, and institutions.

In my own research-based practice and teaching over the last ten years, the Tijuana–San Diego border has served as a laboratory for research of the politics of surveillance, immigration, and labor, the polarization of informal and formal systems of urbanization, and the expanding gap between wealth and poverty. This has led me to understand that we need to rethink our practices, seeing them as sites of intervention, not only to enable bottom-up creative intelligence to scale up but also to participate more meaningfully in the retrofitting of political and economic systems.

Ultimately, it is irrelevant whether architecture and urban development is wrapped in the latest morphogenetic skin, neoclassical prop, or LEED-certified photovoltaic panels if such approaches continue to camouflage the most pressing problems of urbanization today. I have been thinking lately about what Bernard Tschumi wrote many years ago when he reminded us that, as architects, we continue to be obsessed with the conditions of design. Instead, he suggested, we must engage the design of conditions. This is the task of research today, designing the conditions for socioeconomic and environmental justice from which a more experimental architecture can emerge (**Fig. 2**).

PICTURING CITIES

Sze Tsung Leong
interviewed by Susan Yelavich

On June 17, 2013, Mexican-born, British-American artist Sze Tsung Leong sat down with Susan Yelavich to discuss his photographic series Cities, *shown in these pages, and its resonance with issues raised by globalization. Their conversation considers how his work reflects the role of history in the present and the values represented in urban configurations around the globe.*

SY: If there is a unifying theme among the essays in this book, it is the exploration of the capacity of people to materially change the world. Designers do it intentionally and increasingly collaboratively. You look at the world differently. Can you describe your views on human capacities to shape and reshape the world?

STL: The way we shape the world around us is a large part of this work, and what draws me to cities is that they record human activity on a very long scale of time. I hope that my images give a sense of the way that we impact the world on a very large scale, beyond the individual and more on the level of civilization and society. These activities are translated into form, and it's this visual manifestation of human activity that I want to depict in my images.

SY: You photograph both ancient and modern cities. Given your interest in the scale of information they offer, do you see newer cities as a different phenomenon than older cities or as a part of a continuum?

STL: I think it's a combination of both, because there are aspects of city making that are specific to particular histories and locations and others that persist through the ages and in different places. For example, the basic form of the grid has persisted from ancient Roman ruins to brand-new cities in China, in these and many other cases because centralized power made possible the rapid layout of large-scale city grids. Organic forms—patterned on the gradual transformation and formalization of the movement of people, the paths of livestock, or natural features—also persist throughout time, from medieval cities to today's informal cities, such as Cairo or La Paz. At the same time there are patterns that are the very specific results of contemporary social conditions and technology. We can see this also in Cairo and La Paz, where a similar palette of red brick and a similar state of unfinishedness is the result of a tax structure that increases once a building is completed.

SY: By nature, all cities are unfinished. But you just provoked an interesting thought: you talked about the grid and then you talked about organic cities, and you made a distinction. For example, you tend to call the organic city, the informal city. Do you sense an ideology in the gridded city that is different from the organic city?

STL: The form of the grid, when seen on an urban scale, automatically implies some degree of planning, and planning automatically implies the workings of authority or government power. The grids of ancient Rome, the boulevards of nineteenth-century Paris, and the new cities of contemporary China are all the result of strong, centralized authorities that shaped the cities we now see. An important aspect of this work is the way that power affects form, and cities are probably the clearest and largest examples of this relationship.

SY: Speaking of power, the architectural historian Christian Norberg-Schulz described the baroque as a nonlinear style marked by systems that radiated outward to infinity, a style that was part of the Church's visual spectacle of persuasion. Are there cities that are visually organic but actually reflect a tentacle-like power?

STL: By saying that the grid is a manifestation of power is not to say that the organic is absent of power. One of the main distinctions is that the grid can be laid out at one time, while organic form grows in a slower, more cumulative way. The cobweb patterns of medieval cities are a good example of organic forms that radiated out from the central authority of the church and town hall.

SY: I'd like to shift now from the nature of the city to the nature of your work. Let's talk about how you think people might perceive it. Barbara Adams, my co-editor, noted that your work reminded her of maps and mapping. Have you thought of your work that way?

STL: I have, and I am very interested in the relationship between photographs and maps. We usually think of photographs depicting a point of view, especially an individual point of view. A good example is the genre of street photography that reflects the experience we have of walking through cities. On the other hand, we think of maps, not from the individual point of view, but from above, a kind of total, all-over view. I am trying to shift the viewpoint away from the view of the individual to something approaching the all-over view from above, so that you can see the city as a pattern, as an accretion of different shapes and forms that come together on a very large scale.

SY: You chose not to be an aerial photographer. Instead, you go to the tallest place in the city to take your pictures. Why did you choose to do this when you could shoot from a plane?

STL: In my photographs, I am trying to simultaneously depict a wide range of scales, from individuals walking on the street to large urban patterns, and to create an awareness of how we exist in relationship to the larger scales of our environments. In other words, I want to create a view that simultaneously includes the individual as well as the built structure of society. High vantage points, such as rooftops or cliffs, are close enough to capture details such as people, signage, and surface textures, while being far away enough to capture the larger picture. They are also unfamiliar views that we don't normally see when experiencing cities.

SY: Exactly. There is one image of Chicago in the suite you've contributed to *Design as Future-Making*. It breaks the frame of the city and at the same time documents it. I find it particularly disorienting.

STL: The disorientation is an important part of the experience of looking at these images, because there's a very interesting process when looking at an image of a place of trying to place ourselves. We search through our repository of knowledge to make the unfamiliar familiar, but often we experience the opposite, when the familiar becomes unfamiliar. This happens especially from the high vantage point, because it's not a common way to experience the city and makes us look at something that may be familiar in a completely new way.

SY: I never ride the bus in Manhattan, but I was forced to do it one day, and suddenly I realized I was seeing the second story of every building and thought, "Here is another city." That is what you are giving us from a particular vantage point, an interesting distortion that does not play on the notion of distortion. What about the commonalities between cities? After doing all of this work you must occasionally think: "Here it is again." What are the common tropes you have noticed?

STL: The things that are familiar to us travel with us wherever we go, so being in an unfamiliar place will always be seen through the lens of what we know. Today the commonalities are becoming more of the driving force behind the development of cities as our economies are more intertwined.

SY: Traveling so much, there can't be too many places that make you feel alien. I am wondering if there is a place that you find unknowable.

STL: Because I grew up in many places across the world and have been fortunate to experience many cultures, there is always some aspect of being in a new place that is knowable or familiar. One place, though, where I felt a particularly intense concentration of new, unfamiliar experiences was India, especially the way in which the continuum between life and death permeated daily life. There was an upswell of life that I had never experienced before, of crowds of people, animals, and activity, juxtaposed against events such as cremations in the heart of the city and in one case a wrapped body floating down the Ganges.

SY: We have managed in Eastern and Western cultures to dispel death and pretend it doesn't exist. So that is a fairly profound distinction. I am always curious about distinctions because in our particular moment of globalization, identity and location are all up for grabs. I am wondering if it is important to you that your viewer knows if your photograph is a view of Cairo, Bangalore, or Mexico City?

STL: I don't think it's so important, as it's more meaningful what each individual viewer experiences in their immediate encounter with the image.

There's a process of placing ourselves, of questioning what is familiar and foreign to us, that can be independent of knowing where the photograph was taken. The process may recall memories, initiate trains of thought, provoke questions, and it's this process that is the most interesting. I think that we often read the world through what we know by putting labels on what we look at, but by taking the labels away, we have a more direct and inquisitive experience to what we are presented with.

SY: **My experience of your work is that it blocks a common tendency, one that can be detrimental, namely a tendency to claim territory—the feeling that "I own this" because I know it or because I live there. Your response the to the last question reminds me of a painter I know who does portraits, but whose first priority is to make the portrait a painting, not a likeness. Similarly, you're making the city a photograph—photographs that seem very resonant with our culture of dislocation and our uncertainty about where we are in the world. To what extent are you conscious of that?**

STL: Yes, I try to create images that exist on their own and have an openness that can be looked at and interpreted in many ways. I also think that an openness of interpretation can be a way to positively confront uncertainty and dislocation in that it makes us form a relationship with our surroundings that is our own.

SY: **Speaking of relationships with our surroundings and our claims on them, do you think cities have greater identities than nations?**

STL: I think you could say that, but the idea of nations or the boundaries we draw to separate things can be arbitrary. Although cities have very particular identities, which are in turn shaped by the nations they are in, there are also so many overlapping circles of influence that form identities that do not conform to national boundaries.

SY: **Speaking of scale and what can and cannot be captured in a photograph, it seems you are trying to let us take in as much as possible.**

STL: Yes, I want to produce a feeling of being overwhelmed by visual information and a sense of the vast ranges of coexisting scales. On a technical level, the lens I'm using takes in more information than what we can see with our own eyes. The angle of vision of our eyes is about 60 degrees, while this lens takes in closer to a 100 degrees.

SY: So there is more artifice than I realized. How did you come to decide that you wanted to use this type of lens and not, for example, a panoramic lens?

STL: I think this point of view produces a very interesting kind of "in-between" image that looks almost normal to us. I didn't want something that looked too distorted. If you get wider, you start to get fish-eye effects. Instead, this is an unsettling area that feels slightly unfamiliar.

SY: This is something that often gets short shrift these days, the formal decisions, technical decisions that inform the process of making what we see. I think the tendency to separate form from content and affect is misguided. But you also see with prior knowledge, which isn't directly apparent to the viewer. For example, you've lived in Mexico City; you know things about its geography, its substrata of water, which affected your choice of vantage point. How much research do you do for each city you photograph? What gives a city an identity?

STL: The identities of cities work on many different levels. On the most obvious and most familiar level are a city's monuments, the Eiffel Towers and Empire State Buildings. On another level there is the city fabric and the textures of buildings—the gray tile roofs of old Beijing or the pale stone of Jerusalem. There's also a more experiential level. When I was growing up in Mexico City, things such as the color of the curbs, the types of foliage, the texture of concrete walls formed a significant part of my experience of the city. These are the kind of things that one absorbs, that become a part of the identity of a city that we can look at and feel we know where we are. Another way is through signage. Some may have some trouble locating the city in the photograph until they start looking at details and locating signage in a particular language or the way that things are worded.

SY: It's interesting that the city for you is an amalgam of things like signage, curbs, and buildings, as well as the spaces between them, and that you also see the agriculture patterns and the market pathways preserved in today's roads that carry the memory of the old traffic. Do you think of your work as a temporal historical record—as an archive—or solely as photographs?

STL: I think there are aspects of all of those. I try not to ascribe one particular label, but I want my work to be open so that it can be seen as all of these things. Besides being visual compositions, they are also temporal and historical records in that they record and describe particular moments in time.

SY: I would say that the work you did in China offers a historical record of the rampant urbanism that destroyed the *hutong* [alleys lined by vernacular courtyard houses]. Would you go back and revisit it? An ethnographer or anthropologist goes back. I don't know if an artist needs, or wants, to do that.

STL: I am interested in historical change, but in a different way. With photography a common way to show change is to revisit a specific site and see how it has changed over a period of time. But I want to show historical change over a very large arc, to show how cities reflect the changing of eras, from ancient to medieval to Renaissance and so on. That is, to show on a global scale how cities have changed throughout history.

SY: In some of your images—I'm thinking of the one of Amman—you can see the present as well as the past, but in other images, you can't see that palimpsest. Does that matter to you?

STL: The way environments can be built completely from scratch, without a trace of the past, is incredibly interesting. My previous series, *History Images,* which you alluded to before, looked at how history can be almost completely erased on an urban scale.

SY: I think of your work as bearing witness. In some cases there is a poignancy to the work, in other cases there seems to be a neutrality. To what extent are you aware of arousing emotions?

STL: The viewer's emotional response to an image is very important to me. I try to strike a balance between making an image that shows things in a straightforward way but also has a poignant gravity.

SY: That said, I don't think your images are overtly manipulative. They are more political. But you have to come to them with a certain familiarity with the place and its circumstances to read them that way.

STL: Politics is a very emotional subject because we all exist within a political context that affects our lives profoundly. We may not necessarily need to know the details of these circumstances, but politics, government, and power shape our societies and built environments in ways that affect us as individuals both consciously and unconsciously.

SY: There is an essay by Jamer Hunt in this book about scale, how fungible it has become and what a challenge that is to designers. Your work also raises issues of scale. But there must be something else, besides the 100-degree angle, which gives the viewer such access to detail in your work. The tension between enormous high-rises and fine-grain details of curbs and signage is uncanny. How do you get that range?

STL: I present these photographs through large-scale prints, whose viewing experience of course can't be shown in the context of a book. I print large, up to about 50 x 60 inches, so you can have several readings from a distance, where you see the totality of the image, and then you go up close, and you can see details. This is the product of using an 8 x 10 camera, which records an incredible amount of information.

SY: Your 8 x 10 negatives are another bit of scalar information that I hadn't considered before. Near and familiar, far and near, far and familiar are phrases that have come up in our conversation, in other writings and interviews. Do you want to comment on that or speak to the idea of being far and familiar yourself?

STL: This subject has permeated much of my work, including another series of photographs of mine called *Horizons*. We normally look at the world by drawing distinctions, whether something is close or distant, familiar or foreign. My interest is to complicate that relationship by saying that these opposites can be simultaneous. One might encounter an image without knowing exactly where it is, or without a label, and go through a process of trying to decipher it, a process of oscillation from what is known to what is unknown.

SY: Why don't we talk about each image keeping that thought in mind? With the first image in this series, we are looking at China (Fig. 1).

STL: This is Shenzhen, showing how the modern city has grown around and overtaken rural villages. In the foreground, the dense cluster of buildings used to be a village, while the modern high-rises used to be farmland. As the farmland filled in, the villages became more urban while retaining an independent form of government. Their economy was transformed from growing produce to developing real estate, with factories and apartment buildings for workers. That's why you get this very, very dense, hyper-urban condition.

SY: It looks as if there was an effort to keep the older city intact, but I imagine it is fairly fragile. You have this ring around smaller buildings of the agrarian city. We usually we think of older buildings being on the periphery, and that's what is really stunning about this. Are they endangered now? Why have they been left untouched?

STL: I think it's because of the way that village and city governments are separate entities and operate according to different rules. The village government has a certain border, an authority over their land, and the city government grew around it. The shape is a result of a border. At the same time, the structures of government in China can change very suddenly, so whether this is endangered or not, you just never know.

SY: The next image is of Amman, Jordan (Fig. 2). Tell us about this image and why you chose this perspective?

STL: You see a very interesting juxtaposition between the ancient Roman city, one of the first instances of globalization, juxtaposed with the contemporary Jordanian city built over the last fifty years or so.

SY: We tend to think of the Roman as only in Italy, forgetting the vastness of the ancient Empire. This amphitheater is a great reminder of its reach. What else about this city drew you?

STL: There is something very appealing about this uniform urban fabric because it has been built in such a short amount of time, and the types of buildings are relatively anonymous. There are not many indicators of where this is, until you look at the details and you see the minarets. There is also a billboard of King Abdullah II.

SY: Here is a pair of images with buildings that appear similar (Figs. 3, 4). They seem to have the same ceramic tile roofing, and they seem to share a quasi-grid, or a few grids colliding.

STL: I paired these two images because they are examples of globalization from the sixteenth and seventeenth centuries. On the left is Madrid, on the right Quito. Here is an urban form that was translated from Spain to many areas of the world.

SY: Madrid is on a flat plane. It is interesting to see how urban form meets topography.

STL: Quito is nestled in the Andes, where the colonial city has been translated into a very specific geography of hillsides and mountains.

SY: So, a colonial version of Madrid on a different topography. Now with Mexico City we are in familiar territory for you (Fig. 5). What part of the city are we in?

STL: This is the historic center, which is composed of many layers. It was originally a few islands surrounded by a lake, upon which was built the capital of the Aztec Empire, Tenochtitlán. This city was razed after the Spanish conquest, and a new city was built on top of it. The Spanish used the grid, one of the fastest ways to organize new territories, to lay out their city. More recently, one of the major events that affected the city was the devastating 1985 earthquake. In the foreground you can see much of the new reconstruction. You can see also some buildings that are leaning as a result of the seismic activity but are also reminders of the original lakebed the city is built upon, because the leaning is a result of sinking into the ground. The city records this long history in various ways, which is then recorded in this image.

SY: We seem to have a propensity to ignore geography, topography, stratification. I think our cities are also testimony to our blindness, including our blindness to our own mortality. We build on landslides and flood zones. The challenge now is how to build and not be blind, because we can no longer claim we don't know the consequences, because we do know.

STL: On the left of the next pair of images is Nairobi, a city about a century old, which was originally a stop on the rail line that then grew into a city. In the image you can see different histories embodied in architecture that ranges from British colonial buildings to Muslim religious buildings to modern commercial buildings. On the right is Ghent, a medieval city centered on the cathedral and the cathedral square (Figs. 6, 7).

SY: This next image is not the Hong Kong most of us know (Fig. 8). It's not the forest of white sticks, white skyscrapers, we usually see.

STL: This shows a combination of generic skyscrapers that we see all over the world and buildings that are very particular to Hong Kong from the 60s and 70s that have a kind of patina from age and the harsh weather. You can also identify this as Hong Kong through the signage, the traditional characters.

SY: Are we seeing informal, ad hoc architecture here in the additions on the roofs?

STL: Yes, some of these buildings have accumulated informal additions on the roofs. It's almost like a small village. The next two images are of La Paz and Chicago, two cities spreading out as far as the eye can see over the landscape (**Figs. 9, 10**). Most of La Paz was actually built very recently, in the last fifty years or so, so most of it is an informal city, not built according to government laws or guidelines. Chicago has a very structured grid that relates to the first laying out of the land as the West was being settled. You also see the contrast of economies—Bolivia being the poorest country in the Americas versus Chicago being in the wealthiest—and how that impacts urban growth.

SY: As a formal conceit, you show a looping road cutting through the terrain of La Paz and in Chicago, a looping highway, creating an odd correspondence between them. I can't say Chicago looks particularly compelling. The outskirts of cities in the States are functional to the point of hideous, and we know that in order to cover this terrain we are going by car. In La Paz we don't know how we are going to do it.

STL: Postwar development in the United States was shaped by the car and the highly regulated plans and layouts of highways. The curves are functions of cars, while the curves in the path in La Paz are functions of navigating a hill on foot in the most direct way possible.

SY: La Paz is so densely settled, it looks like a carpet. Wasn't it one of the richest cities in the Americas?

STL: During the colonial era, La Paz was part of the silver mining trade route from Potosí, which had the largest mine, and the coast, making it part of the wealthiest region in the Americas. A few signs of this wealth remain in historic structures such as the city's lavish cathedral, but they are surrounded by signs that indicate the fact that Bolivia is now one of the poorest countries in the continent.

SY: Now we're in Antwerp, but an unfamiliar modern Antwerp (Fig. 11). What are we looking at?

STL: These are housing projects built in the 70s, just across the river from the medieval center of Antwerp.

SY: What attracted you to this social housing complex? Is this a particular interest of yours? Is it a city within a city?

STL: One of the reasons I was drawn to this area of the city is that these forms represented a particular view of how society could be organized at a particular moment in history.

SY: The last image shows a part of Cairo that known as the City of the Dead (Fig. 12). These are graveyards, but they've been built as a city, a dense urban condition. Which reminds me, we haven't talked about the fact that we rarely see human beings in these photos.

STL: The last image is naturally absent of people since it's a graveyard, but in the majority of my images there are people in the photographs. Because of the scale of the images, people appear very small. Unfortunately the size and resolution of reproduction in books makes many of the details that you would see in the actual prints more difficult to see, but the combination of sweeping viewpoint and fine detail of the images allows the viewer to have an overall view at an enormous scale and then look close to find individuals in the city. Ultimately, I hope that this range of viewing experiences heightens our awareness of our relationships to the scales and contexts that we live in.

The photographs on the following pages are from the series Cities. All are chromogenic color prints © Sze Tsung Leong. Courtesy Yossi Milo Gallery, New York.

CITIES: A PORTFOLIO

Sze Tsung Leong

1

3

4

6

7

9

10

12

UP-ENDING

SYSTEMS

UP-ENDING SYSTEMS

Barbara Adams

This section of *Design as Future-Making* in many ways mirrors the first. The activities of making and acting that are central to crafting capacities are equally important in upending systems. But making and acting are complicated by contemporary confusion about and within systems themselves. As the authors in this section contend, our current conditions are not adequately served by the systems in place. This concern has been broadly theorized across a wide range of disciplines. For example, sociologist Zygmunt Bauman tells us the inherited frameworks that organize our ways of relating in and to the world are disintegrating in the face of "the new lightness and fluidity of the increasingly mobile, slippery, shifty evasive, and fugitive [strongholds of] power."[1] Anthropologist Michael Taussig argues that we now experience a doubleness of social being, in which we oscillate between normalcy and panic as part of "a nervous system" that changes shape just as we think we have gotten hold of it.[2] And literary critic Fredric Jameson points out how difficult it is in the context of global capitalism "to think a system so vast that it cannot be encompassed by the natural and historically developed categories of perception with which humans normally orient themselves."[3] But we needn't only turn to theory to see that existing systems are becoming more and more difficult to sustain and navigate—we can simply open the newspaper or reflect on our own experiences and participation in the world.

Mishka Henner, Ammunition Depot in Staphorst, Overijssel, 2011. From the series *Dutch Landscapes*.
Courtesy Mishka Henner.

With a palpable sense of our situation as precarious and our condition as one in which risk is omnipresent, we respond in a variety of ways including denial, apathy, and transformation.[4] Tremors of transformation can be felt when we push at, and sometimes through, the limits of existing systems. From Wikileaks to the recent protests in Turkey and throughout the Middle East to the creative tactics we deploy to negotiate the everyday forces of order that confront us—tactics like sharing and bartering not just goods but also intellectual and social capital—we reveal systems as partial and always incomplete. These transformative efforts show how the various elements of a system exist as uncoordinated potentialities until they are organized and mobilized via some form of action so that they might function in a particular relational scheme. Systems, understood in this way, are prone to change. They are more than the codes and rules and inputs that constitute the infrastructure—they are rich with unanticipated associations, confluences, and circuitry. This opens the possibility for upending systems where seemingly ossified schemas might be delinked through heretical propositions that depart from standardized and ritualized ways of doing.

Yet the rigidity of systems stands in tense relation to this more pliant stance. Accordingly, designers are discovering that the secret to negotiating this tension might be less about confronting the rigidity of rules and more about changing tack. Consider Do Tank, a laboratory initiated by New York Law School, where digital interfaces are designed to help examine "the role of legal and political institutions, social and business practices . . . not only to foster community, but to take action."[5] In other words, to develop a culture of civic participation. This approach is also evident in the work of DESIS (Design for Social Innovation toward Sustainability), an international network of design labs, which emphasizes scenario building to promote social and environmental sustainability. Their focus on the design of public policy asks people to engage in social learning projects that generate new relationships and practices.

Design strategist and coordinator of DESIS Ezio Manzini sees design as a catalyst that can activate the cooperative invention of alternative scenarios—from cohousing to urban farming—that are small, local, open, connected, and rich with the capacity to skirt normative systems and their failures.[6] On a quite different scale, the European Commission has turned to design to rethink the public sector with Sharing Experience Europe (SEE), a platform that touts design thinking and practice as "the way to overcome common structural flaws in service provision and policymaking."[7] The design consultancy IDEO, through both its for-profit and nonprofit divisions, has also worked closely with the public sector to rethink entrenched bureaucratic practices from the work visa process in Singapore to voting participation in Peru to filing for social security benefits in the United States.[8]

Practices such as these tend to de-emphasize finite solutions in the interest of generating questions. What is design's role in our ability to inaugurate new forms of dwelling in the world? How can design assist in the navigation of current systems and the initiation of new imaginaries? How can design participate in disaggregating the systems in place and challenging what computer scientist and critic Jaron Lanier calls their "locked-in" nature?[9] How is it possible for design to create passage where there has been none, to open and extend action into time? The gestures and negotiations advanced in Up-Ending Systems address these dilemmas; they creatively corrupt fixed forms of production and unmoor the normative practices and philosophies that underwrite design. These authors interrogate the assumptions embedded in such fundamental concepts as scale, speed, nature, and artifice. In the process, they reveal how design is implicated in changing our inner clocks, in affecting consumption and waste, in allowing access to information, and in creating or inhibiting equitable access to resources for survival. They mark points of change, indicate crises, and engage convertible, incomplete landscapes that present uncertainty, risk, and error. In doing so, these authors resignify politics, place, practice, and person through the lens of design. Stressing potential over possibility,[10] the essays in this section of Design as Future-Making relinquish rote models and modules in favor of openness to unlikely alliances, unexpected connections, and always the possibility of transformation.

Attunement to futurity is requisite for upending systems. When framed as attunement, design rejects the impotence experienced by the angel of history who was unable to look away from the wreckage and catastrophes of the past to see where he is headed.[11] Beyond attunement, our condition requires that a commitment to futurity be demonstrated in meaningful action. Once in motion, action has no end and, as a result, poses risk and uncertainty that recall the fragility of the human condition. This activity is heavy with consequences and responsibilities. In spite of the uncontrollability of provoking action, designers are increasingly being called upon to contribute their particular knowledge and experience to the hornet's nest of contemporary crises exacerbated by the habitual default to obsolete systems. They are also being asked to anticipate the consequences of their work in admittedly unstable conditions. For example, in the face of wasteful systems of production, distribution, consumption, and elimination, philosopher Peter-Paul Verbeek asks designers to consider the sensorial aspects of using products (not just their emissions or material mass) as a way of changing the temporal dynamics of product cycles and as one way of addressing the environmental crisis.[12]

The authors in this section of the book do not say we should, or could, launch a wholesale overhaul of existing systems. Rather, they present lateral moves. Acting on systems, as understood in the essays that follow, involves critical gestures that conjure new stories. These stories reimagine how a narrative might move from point to point and recast who might act as a protagonist. As Otto von Busch points out, "world-building is also about producing infrastructure, rules, and culture for a fictional world; the ludic parameters for shared imagination, the world in which explorative *paideia* is let loose."[13] Because systems regulate the vantage points from which we view the world, it can be easy to forget that there are alternate ways of world-building in this sense.

Elucidating the inequities suffered when such alternatives are muted, unexplored, or unrecognized, philosopher Jacques Rancière explores the limitations of the audible and visible within political and aesthetic regimes. He is concerned with what can be apprehended by the senses, how that which is sensible is distributed, and how this defines the extent of what we can know, how we think, and what we can experience.[14] According to Rancière, social and political order is founded on the distribution of the sensible. Some groups and ideas can be sensed (heard, seen, etc.), while others remain outside sensibility. By "undoing and rearticulating the connections between signs and images, images and times, or signs and space that frame the existing sense of reality,"[15] we can remap our cartographies of perception and see systems differently. Reshaping systems of visibility, according to Rancière, involves inventing fictions that have the capacity to create new alliances and forms of action. "Fiction invents new communities of sense: that is to say, new trajectories between what can be seen, what can be said, and what can be done."[16] The essays that follow seek to redistribute frames of visibility and patterns of intelligibility that can generate new communities of sense.

We seem to be at an impasse. We understand that the classic coordinates of our most familiar systems—our understanding of time, space, identity—were staked out in another context, yet we continue to orient ourselves using these conceptual points (which can only take us off course). If it is true, as Hannah Arendt argues, that the modern age shifted our perception of the human condition from wonder to doubt, from frailty to uncertainty,[17] then how might design reckon with this state of affairs? Arendt offers a tentative response: "The life span of man running toward death would inevitably carry everything human to ruin and destruction if it were not for the faculty of interrupting it and beginning something new, a faculty which is inherent in action."[18] The essays that follow advance action that interrupts and upends fraught systems.

REASONS TO BE CHEERFUL, 1, 2, 3 . . .*
(OR WHY THE ARTIFICIAL
MAY YET SAVE US)
Clive Dilnot

I.

All societies have a sense of the future. Ours, largely, does not. This immediately
suggests, rightly, the peculiarity of our situation. The break with the previous
century in this respect is decisive. Modernity is defined by the creation of the
future as compensation for the loss of the organic continuity of the past. "Is
not to be modern to know clearly what cannot be started over again?"[1] After
1900, to design is to design for the future, it is to bring the future into being as a
contemporary possibility. Politics worthy of the name is little different. The vision
there is on behalf of a future that can be made better than the past. The slogan
"from the existing to the preferred situation" becomes a generalized credo.

 Yet the most memorable cultural statement of the last forty years—
The Sex Pistols' "No Future!"—has none of these connotations, except in their
absence. Since then, notwithstanding paid enthusiasms for the virtues of the
market or for the everlasting development of new technologies (both really
repetitions of the same), we have existed in a kind of stasis. Francis Fukayama
was roundly condemned for his thesis about the end of history, yet this was only,
perhaps, because he hit a nerve by saying something no one wanted to hear.[2]

* With apologies to Ian Dury and the Blockheads ("Reasons to be Cheerful, Part 3," 1979).

The truth is that the future has, for us, disappeared—at least as an affirmative possibility.[3] Despite the almost magical hopes that some vest in Silicon Valley (or in endless economic growth if one is Asian), the future is, for most, that which conjures up an underlying fearfulness about what may be to come. Yet so distant are we from this, so wrapped in the short-term, that not even fearfulness is allowed to reach the condition of impelling action.[4]

That we feel our future is no longer assured is not surprising. The exponential increase in destructive capacity (represented not only by the two world wars but the apparatuses of human desolation perfected in the concentration camps and the gulag) developed across the seventy or so years up until 1945 issued in the postwar nuclear standoff. This intensification of destructive capacity threatened the possible annihilation on a daily basis for almost forty-five years.[5] Though the fall of the Berlin Wall in 1989 did not quite usher in Francis Fukayama's end of history, and the quick (atomic) end to history seemed to recede a little with the end of the Cold War, the sense of impending fatality was replaced soon after. Any sense of furturority was assailed not only by a succession of economic crises, culminating in the bank failures of 2007–8, but also by increasing evidence of man-made climate change, and at scales that threaten a severe break with patterns of climate, ecology, and settlement that we have known as a species since the end of the last ice age. Today, no serious person denies the strong likelihood, close to certainty, of global warming and climate change. Yet the very lack of action with respect to this threat means that, on the contrary, as the headlines of a despairing pair of articles recently had it, on current evidence, "We will watch the rise in greenhouse gases until it is too late to do anything about it."[6]

It is not just the scale of what we are now engaged with that warrants pessimism.[7] The real problem lies elsewhere, in the gap between our compulsive inability not to act disastrously in pursuit of accumulation, and our equal but perhaps even more abject inability to act collectively to deal with these threats.[8]

II.

Yet this reading of our situation is still too immediate. If we are going to attempt to move from nihilistic despair (however disguised this might be by technological enthusiasm), we need a more structural look at our position. In particular, we need to understand that the totality of what we are experiencing today is not just more of the same, or a continuity with what was only with newer technology, but represents a qualitatively new historical condition. As well as containing an acute potential for disaster, this new condition contains other possibilities for acting and becoming. It is on this basis that we can hazard the possibility, though as yet remote, that we can avoid catastrophe and conceive of the chance of a humane future.

The easiest way to grasp what is involved here—not just as continuation of what is, but as the emergence of a new historical condition, one in which the artificial constitutes world and forms the horizon and medium and the prime determining condition of how we are—is to consider these three diagrams (Figs. 1, 2, 3). Crude to the point of absurdity, their value is not for all that negligible.

In the first, artifice is central but limited. We can agree that there is no human becoming without artifice and the artificial, but under the conditions of hand labor artifice is always difficult, always limited. Things are crucial but rare. The ability to have an effect on nature is limited except in defined locations, such as by stripping forests. In this era, attention is bound to be on the vagaries of chance. Here is the invention of the gods, or God, and the attempt to access fate by determining and obeying law.

In the second, artifice is shown as a logarithmic spiral. The industrial revolution's vast increase in productive capacity was enabled through the combination of the exploitation of fossil fuels as power and technology-as-method, both propelled by the sense of the possibility in the drive for accumulation. By 1917, Fordism has set up developments that after 1945 make industrialization a global phenomenon. But if nature remains still the ultimate horizon, then, in Nietzsche's terms the "gods have fled." The fiction that what is made is not made becomes seen for what it is, first in relation to kings, second to the gods. The latter now command only religion. Scientific law and its research models command mentality.

In the third diagram, artifice encompasses: it constitutes world. Today, it is gradually becoming apparent to us that, from around 1945, the world entered into a sixty- or seventy-year transition in which industrialization became global, and what we can call the incomplete artificial world of the early twentieth century was transmuted into the condition we are now beginning to experience, in which the artificial, and not nature, is the horizon, medium, and determining condition of the world: its totality. The historical markers of the transition are destructive: the A-bomb, the acceptance of global warming, and the definition of our age as "anthropocene." But the new conditions opened by the artificial are by no means the only ones.

Two overarching qualifications apply.

The first is obvious but requires reiteration. The artificial is by no means confined to technology.[9] Today, it means the combination of technical systems, the symbolic realm, including mind and the realm of our transformations and transmutations of nature.[10]

The Place of Artifice and the Artificial in Human History

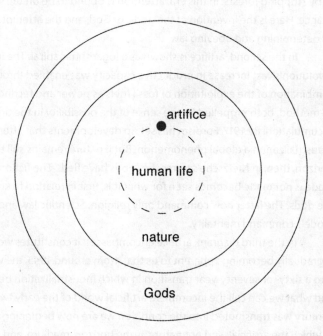

Fig. 1 Artifice and the
artificial in the epoch of
craft-making up to c. 1800.

1800 - 2000

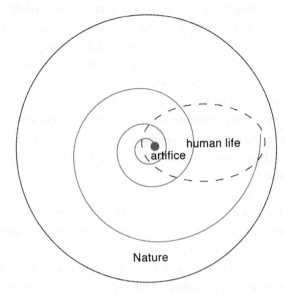

human life

artifice

Nature

Fig. 2 The explosion of
artifice in Industrialization
c. 1800-2000.

2000 ⟶

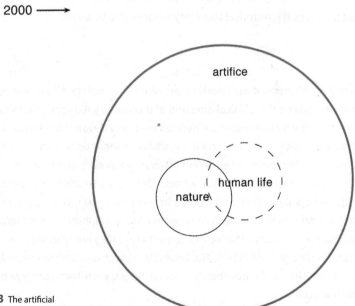

artifice

human life

nature

Fig. 3 The artificial
as world 2000–.

The second is that the artificial does not oppose nature in a simple binary opposition. It, or rather we, affect a synthesis. A genetically modified tomato is neither purely natural nor purely artificial. It belongs rather to the extended realms of living things that are, as we ourselves are, a hybrid between these conditions. Neither nature nor the artificial nor the human are today pure.[11] No longer, as we still wish to think, merely a quasi-autonomous (and inferior) realm within the world (the "standing reserve" of made things that we can do with as we wish), the universal infiltration, reach, and ubiquity of the artificial constitutes a historical transition in the conditions of our becoming. The revolution portended by this development should not be underestimated. It opens an epoch for humans that is essentially unsurpassable. In an essential sense, we are now condemned to the artificial as the essential horizon and medium of our becoming.

It is perhaps not surprising that in any explicit manner we cannot yet think this. But this is also a source of our unhappiness. Not to be able to think the conditions of our time means not to be able to think what determines us. To be blind to what is emerging is not just to be blind to what conditions our acts, it is also to fail to see the possibilities that the artificial opens. In terms of escaping our destiny toward catastrophe, it renders impossible any affirmative apprehension of the artificial. Because we cannot think the artificial, because we cannot see it, because we fail to understand it, we cannot think what resources it might offer us. Because we cannot think about these resources, so we cannot think past the present.[12] Abject capitulation to the norm is maintained by our inability to grasp what is opened by the historical trajectory we are living through.

III.

The form that the artificial will take is by definition incomplete. This is precisely the issue. This will be the political question of this century, along with how we overcome the destructiveness of an inverted economy devoted to individuated private accumulation and greed. Yet if the artificial cannot be known as such, its outlines, or at least some of its salient aspects, are already visible. In terms of redeeming the title of this essay, I will consider seven aspects of the artificial as worlds that open possibilities for praxis beyond those we historically inherit. By no means definitive, they are in some ways more metaphorical than literal, more indicative than recipes for action. Nonetheless, they are relevant in noting directions for thought and action. The issues I will touch on concern law and its absence, propositions, the possible, mediation, negotiation, technology and its overcoming, ethics.

1. No Law/Configuration

Given the manifest indifference of nature to our fate, it was natural, or so we say, that in earlier human epochs we would seek to personify fate and attempt to formulate laws that explained and accounted for fate. As this gradually transformed into seeking to grasp the nature of what is, it became equally natural to seek not only God's law but the laws of nature. It is equally natural, or so we say, that the realm of laws that effectively connect finite, brief, and tenuous life to what is enduring should be valued over mere realms of appearance. Even as the more theological aspects of this projection lose force under the pressure of the rise of science, science provides compensatory logic for the relevance of law in that, as Francis Bacon intimated, it is precisely access to natural law that gives us the knowledge to create instruments of power beyond those gained by empirical experience alone. Heidegger too has maintained that law is the very subject of experimental science; that one experiments, in the modern sense, in order to prove or disprove law, to prove or disprove that which is the case. Law, then, is central to the modern project, for on it depends the certainty of things in their condition of objective measurability.

But when we turn to the artificial we find a peculiarity, or rather two. The prime condition of the artificial is not that things are, but that things could be other. In the artificial there is no absolute "what-is," which means that there is no law. Since this statement seems at first sight absurd, let me explain. Previously, it seemed possible that law could wholly determine artifice, thus giving the artificial something of the authority of the given, making artifice an objective fact. This is the point that Herbert Simon makes when he says at one point in *The Sciences of the Artificial*, "I have shown that a science of artificial phenomena is always in imminent danger of dissolving and vanishing. The peculiar properties of the artifact lie on the thin interface between the natural laws within it and the natural laws without. What can we say about it? What is there to study besides the boundary sciences—those that govern the means and the task environment?"[13]

But in fact, as we pursue this notion or pursue the character of the artifact, we see that in artifice no law is ultimately possible. To be sure, as Simon pointed out, "those things we call artifacts are not apart from nature. They have no dispensation to ignore or violate natural law."[14] But this is to state the matter very incompletely. That which cannot ignore or violate natural law nonetheless cannot, in its configuration, be subject to law. A simple example will suffice. Consider a half-dozen chairs of different configurations. While each may obey, in detail, the natural laws appertaining to the forming of timber or the bending of metal, in their configuration they obey no law. Plato was thus wrong in this instance. No ideal chair exists. In artifice there are only chairs. This reflects the general truth that the artificial does not know law but only instances and possibility. What matters in the artificial is the configuration that things take.

2. Proposition

Configuration in the artificial is always the negotiation of complex incommensurable requirements; requirements that meet and are, to some degree, resolved in the artifact. But since the artifact is always in the end the contingent and unpredictable outcome of an essentially unstable relation of forces, no final resolution of a configuration can ever be achieved. All artifice has, therefore, the character of a proposition. It is an exploration of the possibility of what an X might be. What replaces law (rule) and the certainty of method is the radical uncertainty of the proposition, in which the artifact—any artifact— inhabits a double condition, one that can scarcely be expressed verbally but can be expressed typographically in the form "This!?" The artifact is "This!": existent, possessed of reality, possessing these attributes, and showing them forth, that is, exemplifying them. And also "This?": the artifact as quasi-fact, as like nature in its quasi-objectivity as a proposition, constituted as a form, which implicitly, if not explicitly, offers a question to the world.

3. The Possible

That the artificial is therefore, in strict terms, a world beyond law and beyond certainty means that the propositional is structurally inherent to the artificial; that in the artificial there are no absolute facts means that the artificial is a world of the possible, not as extrapolation or as subjective will ("I demand!") but as its deepest condition. The artificial, we might say, brings possibility into objective being or, rather, it reveals, according to the principle that the higher reveals the lower, that possibility is now not only the future and everlasting condition of the human—the human as becoming not being—but is perhaps the very condition of the universe.[15] In short, in the artificial we grasp a universe of possibility, of becoming, not of being. In that sense, we break with what Adorno called the "pure self-presentation" of being, imagined as a fixed and determinant point. Instead, we now objectively occupy the realm of culture as possibility. To put this in reverse, as the artificial constitutes the realm of our possibility, so possibility now becomes the very realm of our being.

One might well argue that this is the definition of the human, that the possible is what human culture has always stood for. Yet this is not how we have historically seen it. All too often culture, particularly in its classical anthropological uses, has been seen as an instrument of continuity, a reproduction of sameness and resistance to change. Culture in that context stood for inertia, not movement and change.[16] By contrast, the onset of the artificial as objectively the realm of the possible means that notions of the artificial and of culture as possibility resonate sharply: "Culture ... is about making things different from what they are; the future different from the present. It ... is that which accepts that ... 'things are not necessarily what they seem to be' ... that 'the world may be different from what it is'."[17] It stands not for continuity but for the

> concern with keeping the forever inexhausted and unfulfilled human potential open, fighting back all attempts to foreclose and preempt the further unraveling of human possibilities, prodding human society to go on questioning itself and preventing that questioning from ever stalling or being declared finished. ... To say "culture" is to make another attempt to account for the fact that the human world (the world molded by the humans and the world which molds the humans) is perpetually, unavoidably and unremediably *noch nicht geworden* [not yet accomplished],

as Ernst Bloch beautifully put it.[18]

4. Mediation

If the artificial performs transmutations on the status of law and the possible, it is also necessarily concerned with the centrality and position of mediation. All artifice is essentially mediation. Seen through the artifact, this is Herbert Simon's basic proposition:

> We can view the matter quite symmetrically. An artifact can be thought of as a meeting point—an interface in today's terms—between an inner environment, the substance and organization of the artifact itself, and an outer environment, the surroundings in which it operates. If the inner environment is appropriate to the outer environment, or vice versa, the artifact will serve its intended purpose.[19]

Rather than "meeting point" or "interface," the more accurate term here would be mediation. Relations go at least two ways, not, as Simon suggests, merely one.[20] All artifice is made on behalf of human subjects.[21] Any artifact is, therefore, the meeting point of at least two external relations or outer environments; that of human subjects and their relations, to whom it is irreducibly addressed, and that of existing artifacts and the wider physical environments in relation to which, or in the context of which, it acts. The inner configured environment of the artifact itself, referring here simultaneously to its mode of internal organization and its modes of operation, is therefore a negotiated mediation between the realm of the subject and the objective conditions of the complex contexts in which it operates.

Put differently, if the artificial is mediation (if that is its essential, radically contingent status), then transformational acts within the frame of artifice as world, be they design or politics, are by definition acts of complex mediation that take place between irreducible demands and conditions that cannot be bracketed or wished way, nor merely dominated, but must be taken up in their weight and negotiated in terms of a propositional configuration ("This!?"). In this situation, the situation of the artificial as world, the speculative, propositional, and negotiative conditions of configuration and mediation (critical affirmation) become the prime, and necessary, characteristics of practice (praxis) as a whole.

5. Negotiation of Incommensurability

Much of technology, in the tight sense of the term, has been devoted to the attempt to deny its condition of mediation, first, through the lessening of the status of the configuration of the artifact in favor of laws determining it; second, as a disavowal of complex negotiation.[22] Thus, for example, in scientific technology, relations are twofold: obedience to understood rules as the determination of the configuration (certainty); minimal second-order adaptation of the technology to the demands of the environments—economic, technical, human, social, ecological—within which the artifact will operate.[23] By contrast, the moment we move to accepting complex relations, we are confronted with incommensurable moments and demands. These moments are incommensurable because in belonging to qualitatively different realms (i.e., speed *and* safety in travel, dependence *and* independence in aging), they can neither be subsumed within a null environment nor adequately represented a priori before their always incomplete resolution in a configuration that is necessarily the relational outcome of complex negotiation between incommensurable moments and demands.

6. Surpassing "technology"

Forty-five years after Simon first drafted *The Sciences of the Artificial*, what he perceived as emergently in process, has intensified, expanded massively in scale and impact, and today constitutes an effective, though by no means seamless, totality. We have seen that by the late 1930s, Heidegger was already disinclined to see technology purely as such. Today we can go much further. The realms of technical systems, symbol systems, and the artificial adaptation of nature, which in 1968 were still relatively distinct (at least in our minds, though less so then in praxis), have today become almost co-terminus, or at least it is now impossible, in practice, to make a clear distinction between the one and the other.[24] The

194

most obvious and far-reaching linkage is between technologies and language, where the old distinctions between work and interaction, upon which an entire sociology was built, have given way to a much more uncanny condition.[25]

Of significance here, both intellectually and practically, is this merging of symbolic and technological capacities that renders the idea of a pure technology redundant. To put it another way, technology as a concept can now be seen to belong only to the short industrial era. Born out of a division of labor useful in utilitarian terms to differentiate what could be objectified and treated as if it lacked relation to the subject, objective movements within technology itself are pushing beyond the limits technology gives itself. A small case in point is Kevin Kelly's book, *What Technology Wants*. At one point Kelly lists thirteen aspects or virtues that his technology seeks to realize. It will strike anyone reading this list that technology seeks increasing "efficiency, opportunity, emergence, complexity, diversity, specialization, ubiquity, freedom, mutualism, beauty, sentience, structure, evolvability,"[26] and that comparatively few of these terms apply or are consonant with technology as we know it. Most go beyond. A few are all but incompatible when thought within traditional limits. Technology arrives, then, for humans at the point at which even internally it reveals itself in excess of itself as concept and finds itself dissimulated in a world of the artificial that cannot be other than our world.

That technology is overcome by being surpassed, that it is incorporated into the wider notion of the artificial, makes us more aware of the degree to which our mental capacities, including of course language but all symbol-making capabilities, are not simply natural but are themselves artifacts.[27] If, on one side, this calls forth the hubristic projects of Artificial Intelligence, with their declared ambitions of creating an artificial brain, this also causes us perhaps to be more aware that human mental sensibility was formed, came into being as such, through artifice; that the artificial is therefore both the condition of human becoming, that without which the human could not be, and through which we may become, in Vattimo's telling phrase, "(finally) human."[28] The condition of the latter is seeing our own conceptions of what constitutes artifice transformed under the workings of the artificial itself. The end of technology, which is also the end of representation—we are living through the high wave of the latter now at the point where representation, so constitutive of the modern, begins to be eclipsed—is the beginning of the artificial proper, where what becomes central, as already suggested, is the resonance and attuning of artifice to subjects, worlds, and nature. Thinking the artificial in this sense is, therefore, that transitive appropriation of what-is as that-which-we-have-made, which overcomes the older splitting and brings us back to technology, not as a pseudo-mastery, which actually masters us, but as a dialogical and dialectical relationship of mediation.

On that basis destructiveness can be accepted and incorporated without illusion and without mastery.

7. Ethics

What obtains with respect to praxis is paralleled in terms of ethics. The replacement of law by the possible, and the primacy given to mediation and negotiation, transforms the ethical situation that obtains between possibility or the proposition and mediation. Simon's famous definition of design as the "devising of courses of acting to move from existing to preferred situations"[29] reminds us that the artifact is not the end of poietic activity, that its end lies in the situation and, even more precisely and essentially, in the humans who are the actors or subjects in that situation. Since situations are irredeemably bound to the human, then activities that engage actively with them—as design and politics do as essential moments of their acting, the situation as the very nexus of their work—are necessarily ethical and in two senses. First, because the situation is the very locus of ethics:

> There is no need for an "ethics" [in general] but only for a clear vision of the situation . . . to be faithful to the situation means: to deal with the situation according to the rule of maximum possibility; to treat it right to the limit of the possible. Or, if you prefer, to draw from the situation, to the greatest possible extent, the affirmative humanity that it contains.[30]

Second, because the situation that necessarily has the human as its center calls for a concomitant responsibility by the subject. If the subject is always immediately or ultimately the subject of artifice—that to whom it is without exception addressed—then subjects must acknowledge, vis-à-vis the world, vis-à-vis others, vis-à-vis generations to come, this radical anthropomorphism; they must take on board the responsibility (costs, consequences) for being the necessary center of all situated activity.

The first of these two ethical transformations gives content, demand, to Simon's "preferred situations" and, thus, to mediation in general. The second delineates the radical responsibilities that the inescapably anthropomorphic subject must take on board as the price paid for centrality. The onset of the artificial as world is the condition where this responsibility can no longer be so easily sloughed off. A politics adequate to the condition of the artificial as world begins here.

IV.

Nothing that is said here exhausts the artificial. On the other side, if it scarcely justifies the title (we have no warrant to be cheerful in the face of disaster, but there is placed on us a requirement to act to the best of our ability to avert disaster) the orientation toward intervention is affirmative in the sense that Alain Badiou beautifully caught when, in a sharp critique of the modern, purely critical (passive) stance of philosophy, which he aligns at one point to distance from the real, he argued that thought today—and that means also practice today—must intervene into the paradoxical real. But if you intervene, says Badiou, this act necessarily shifts you from criticality to affirmation:

> Why is it affirmation? Because if you intervene with respect to a paradoxical situation, or if you intervene with regard to a relation that is not a relation, you will have to propose a new framework of thought, and you will have to affirm that it is possible to think this paradoxical situation, on condition, of course, that a certain number of parameters be abandoned, and a certain number of novelties introduced. And when all is said and done, the only proof for this is that you will propose a new way of thinking the paradox.[31]

The paradox of our time is that we have made that which we cannot yet think. The artificial, understood aright, is our possibility as well as the source of the dangers that beset us, though these lie, as we have seen, as much if not more in the attitudes we bring to the artificial rather than to any essence of the artificial. Thinking the paradox of the artificial—in action, through the manner in which we remake the world—is turning the prosaic nihilism of our age towards a resonant affirmation of what is possible for our history beyond accumulation and catastrophe. Reasons to be cheerful? Not quite. Reasons for possibility? Certainly.

DESIGN AWAY

Cameron Tonkinwise

"My field? Um, Design Studies, with a sustainability bent, you could say."

"Well, what I mean is, I don't teach students how to design; my job is to get them to think about what they are going to design—and why."

"Yes, I suppose that's right. My colleagues teach the students to design stuff, and I teach them not to."

Having had this conversation more times than I care to, I might now have something to add. The way this exchange runs, it looks like we in Design Studies are doing the opposite of teaching students to design, as if questioning and rethinking were not ever part of the practice of designing. But I want to suggest that not-designing is also a kind of designing; it can be proactive, a deliberate strategy to undesign, to make existing designs disappear. The opposite of the *vita activa* of making, of designing things into existence, is not merely the privatively passive *vita contemplativa*, but rather the very active act of unmaking aspects of our locked-in world—designing things out of existence.

In a seminal article, "Prometheus of the Everyday: The Ecology of the Artificial and The Designer's Responsibility,"[1] Ezio Manzini asks: if a primary driver of human being is "doing," as in, accomplishing, affecting, achieving, what does this driver look like in an era of material limits? Prior to any widespread

Fig. 1 Shiba Sheikh, *Ingredients: things destroyed to bring you value*. Courtesy Shiba Sheikh.

ENJOY BY NOV 13 03
A3WN 0910

100% juice

shake well!

the
fruit
inside*

1 ¾ oranges
½ mango
1 ¾ apples
& a hint of banana†

*per bottle
†sustainably grown & harvested

ecological awareness of finite resources and the vulnerability of ecosystems, "to do" meant "to make," to make things better by making many more better things. Environmental constraints necessitate a shift in objective, from the quantitative to the qualitative, from a culture of producing to a culture of reproducing. Designers need to become caretakers of "a garden of objects."

To strain the metaphor, gardening also requires weeding, pruning, composting. To do more with less also means getting to less, getting rid of more. Can there be a practice of undesigning, what Tony Fry has called "elimination design"?[2] Should there not be such a practice, given the imperatives for enhancing the sustainability of our societies? And could such a practice qualify as a satisfier for a new generation of designers? Would not designers—as hunters, cullers, eradicators or, less violently, waste managers, cleaners, problem dissolvers—make an importantly "productive" contribution to transitioning our societies to less stuffed futures?

Usually, the act of design seems a beautifully creative and intelligent craft. By contrast, destruction seems stupidly simple, a brutish, quick act. I will point out that, in fact, eliminating some aspect of our everyday material existence from our society is a complex and difficult task requiring very skillful strategies. Before doing so, I want to make clear that undesigning is already an act practiced by every designer when designing.

Creation = Destruction

Tony Fry has pointed out that the essence of design ethics lies in the fact that no act of creation can avoid also being an act of destruction. The most straightforward version of this equation is the fact that to manufacture any thing, some "natural" resources must be destroyed. A tree must die for it to be the material cause of a wooden table.[3] For all the warmth that timber appears to exude in our built environment, each plank is an autopsical slice, as dead as it is unnatural.

This is obviously never a one-to-one relation. The timber is never derived from the roots or leaves or branches or bark, only ever from the straighter sections of the trunk not so close to the heart of the log or its edge. The majority of the tree is simply wasted.[4] Other, ancient trees, now concentrated into oil, have been combusted to run the saw or transport the timber or form glues and lacquer. Frederick Schmidt-Bleek's notion of an "ecological rucksack" captures this well, for any weight of a final useful product, a gold ring for example, there is a vast array of materials that have been combusted or contaminated or dispersed—in the case of gold, 250,000 times the weight of the ring.[5]

At this point, we are still only approaching matters materialistically. It is not just a solitary tree that gets destroyed to become a table, but a home to birds and mammals, to insects and fungi and other plant species for sure. If these are not killed in the tree's felling and processing, they are stressed by being displaced. The tree is also part of a wider home, an ecology, such that its removal (it is rarely just one solitary tree that is cut down) will impact all that is interdependent within that ecology with neighboring species thriving in certain light and soil conditions, all species functioning within current climatic conditions, and so on. Life Cycle Assessment of ecological impacts has taught us that designers can be the source of widespread destruction in the name of creating better communications, products, and environments.

What is destroyed even extends to humans. Invariably, the process of reordering materials into higher performance qualities involves the creation of concentrations, in products and byproducts, that are dangerous to those who produce those materials or live near the environmental release of those byproducts, and sometimes to those who use the final products (e.g., lead paints on metal toys or synthetic estrogens in plastic containers) (**Fig. 1**). Indirectly, wider ecosystem damage can also result in epidemiological-scale human health problems.

We know all this, don't we? Again and again, we see lists of planetary systems in distress as a result of all that designers do to make and sustain our built environments. But do we know it in any forceful way? Do designers graduate from design schools fully aware that a successful career will involve vast amounts of natural material and ecosystem destruction and even health risks to fellow humans? Do they think of themselves as one of the most dangerous modern professions, as Victor Papanek pointedly made clear?[6] Or do they instead just internalize being celebrated as newly minted members of the creative class?

Creative Destruction

To some extent, what I have talked about so far are the inevitable, yet mostly unwitting acts of destruction involved in designing. But it is worth underscoring that innovation is itself a deliberate act of destroying aspects of existence. To make a better product is to have the intention of rendering the existing version of the product redundant. As Karrie Jacobs pointed out, when you hire a communication designer to do a corporate rebrand, get your waste receptacles ready: all existing articulations of the brand will have to be dumped—a phenomenon that, ironically, is even more extensive if that client is a good corporate citizen engaged in logo-bearing sponsorship of community and arts initiatives.[7]

In this way, we start to see that designing something into existence, something that people think is valuable enough to adopt and adjust their (time) budgets to incorporate into their habit(at)s, is a way of designing something in the world out of existence. This is not what Schumpeter famously called "creative destruction." That notion refers more to innovation opportunities that come from moments of widespread destruction. In the original Marxist formulation, the economic system appears to inevitably go through moments of destructive crisis from which capitalists always stand to benefit, despite initial appearances of wealth devaluation. In the neoliberal reformulation, managers are encouraged to welcome, and even initiate, occasional destruction of components of their businesses to stimulate innovation. I am talking about the reverse: where the destruction results from the innovation.

It must be remembered that no product is an island. Every product exists within artificial ecosystems.[8] There are the infrastructures with which any product must connect (e.g., electricity outlets, water faucets and drains, etc.); there are contiguous products required for most products to function (e.g., a toaster needs bread, butter and jam, knives and plates; a printer needs paper and toner and a computer, etc.); then there are the other products that make up the environment in which that product makes sense (e.g., a refrigerator, filled with food, exists in kitchen, a place with the kinds of products and décor that orient us toward it as appropriate for meal preparation).

A new product must negotiate that ecosystem. It could just become one more thing in its designated ecosystem or something that can seamlessly replace just one of the things in that ecosystem. But if it is of significant value, it will alter that ecosystem and the practices involved in that ecosystem. Work on "value constellations," from handles-and-razorblade systems to digital-mobile product-service-systems, indicates that design innovation can involve interventions into whole networks of products. These often appear to be merely attempted monopolistic extensions, but from the designer's perspective, they are justified ways of ensuring the interaction experiences the designer intends, a total design of the product-in-its-ecosystem, which includes streamlined habits-of-its-user. The point is that designers engage in creation by destroying whole systems of existing products when they can, to limit the possibility for unanticipated product contexts and uses.

Enabling Value

So designers do a lot of material destroying on their way to being creative. But there is obviously another side to this equation, the value of what is created out of this sacrificial destruction. Fry's design ethic becomes: Is what you make worth what you have destroyed to make it and have it taken up in the world?

Designers, as opposed to artists, aim not to create artifacts as ends unto themselves, but artifacts-as-means. Judging the value of a design means judging the value of what it enables more than the artifact itself, what is done with the thing rather than the thing itself.

This asymmetry between destroyed materials and created activities makes the equation very difficult to apply. Is a 100-year-old tree—and the associated flora and fauna impacted by the creation of a table from said tree—worth all the family meals that are less easy to have without that table? Should that table enable at least 100 years' worth of meals, making it an heirloom to pass between generations?

Before getting to these calculations, it must be acknowledged that there is further destruction on the creative value side of the equation. Artifacts are given designs, designed forms and functions, to make the use of those seemingly neutral instruments (or communications or built environments) easier, more productive, or enjoyable. The resulting affordances make their use more likely.[9] As mentioned, this "orienting-toward" that effective design achieves will always be at the price of whatever else is no longer so easy or productive or enjoyable.

Design not only gets users to "attend-away-from" (in Michael Polanyi's sense[10]) the "present-at-hand" (in Martin Heidegger's sense[11]) features of the thing that has been created, but also focuses the attention of the user toward certain kinds of experiences or activities, before which the design withdraws into "ready-to-handedness." Don Ihde's formulation is most appropriate in relation to our dialectic of creation and destruction: designs mediate our engagements with the world by channeling our perceptions toward only certain components of the world. Ihde's example of this "amplification-through-reduction" is quite pointed: the periodontal probe, which channels all the dentist's perceptual world into the tip of the hooked needle with which to feel for cavities in teeth.[12] In this sense, designs create the possibility of certain ways of being in the world, but only by destroying or, less dramatically, back-grounding other experiences of the world. Designs free us to do things by freeing us from other worldly noise or burdens.

In this way, the value of designs lies in the new habits they create. Having been habituated to the freed-up, or well-disposed, world that a design in one domain enables, invariably those now ratcheted-up expectations get transferred to other domains. Norms of convenience made possible by destructive creation are transposed to other contexts as a driver of more destructively creative designing, prompting questions such as: Why is this phone slower than my laptop? My clothes washing is a one-button-press system, so shouldn't my car have one too? I can multitask at the café, so why is there no Wi-Fi in this theater?

This orienting power, this capacity of designs to dispose us toward certain activities and qualities of experience, and thereby dispose of (i.e. get rid of, at least temporarily) other activities and experiences is the source of long-standing fights about design and the politics of artifacts. Plato will worry that writing disables our memory, puritans will insist that labor-saving devices do away with the suffering that a god intended for us, educators claim television deforms the brains of the young, designers lose their capacity to craft when using only digital tools, and so on.

Obviously, one can and should argue about the extent to which actual destruction is occurring. Designs can be persuasive, but as we hopefully learned from the failure of modernism, they are not determining. Even for the most closed use-scripts, there are still work-arounds and hacks. And if skills or activities or approaches to the world are designed away from, that does not mean that they are unrecoverable. People can, for socio-political reasons, voluntarily de-ratchet expectations and re-skill—consider the Transition Town movement, for instance.[13] The point is that, at the very heart of the value that designers create by enabling people to accomplish any number of things, there is a destructiveness, a decision to promote through materialized supports certain kinds of being-in-the-world. As Fry has again usefully identified, design futures; it makes certain futures materially possible and likely. But in so doing, it can defuture, limiting the number of futures we have now, and limiting the quality and quantity of the futures of those futures.[14]

I hope it is clear the extent to which all design involves destruction, material, and cultural. Designers seem insufficiently aware of this aspect of their practice. It is shocking the extent to which they have not seen this as the very source of their power as value creators. It is, therefore, no wonder that the value of using this aspect of their practice more directly—to deliberately eliminate some products, and so the practices they sustain, enable, promote—is not widely sensed.

What to Destroy

But if not done as part of a larger project of creating, why seek to just destroy? I indicated at the outset that a general reason concerns the fact that, at the moment, design has habituated us to living with too much stuff. Most of that stuff continues to destroy other stuff by being energy consuming, if not literally requiring other resources: toner and paper for a printer, fertilizer and pesticide for lawns, deodorizer and stain remover for carpets. Often, previous products are considerably less efficient than current models. In these cases a straightforward calculation can be made as to when there are net reductions in resource destruction when replacing in-use models with newly created more-efficient ones: always-on household items, like refrigerators, should, on current efficiency improvement trends, be replaced at least every eight years, well before their functional use-life ends.[15] Hence, government schemes that offer encouraging rebates, "cash for clunkers." "As soon as possible" is the prevailing attitude toward getting rid of incandescent light bulbs in place of compact fluorescents or LEDs.

In some cases, products have been made parts of artificial ecosystems without sufficient analysis of their ongoing ecological impacts: carpets, for instance, are not only in most cases toxic to produce and dispose of, but are also the source of off-gas chemicals that cause sick-building syndrome at room temperature (especially in buildings sealed to create more efficient HVAC systems) and, further, become traps for walked-in toxins, such as pesticides on the lawns we just mentioned. Carpets make floors soft and warm to walk on,[16] but there is a much under-acknowledged cost to this relatively small gain. Carpets, then, as opposed to area rugs, could be targets for elimination design.

Just because something exists does not mean that there has been a well-thought-through evaluation of whether the value it creates is worth what it destroys. Leaf blowers are a good instance of what Umair Haque calls an "unnovation."[17] Of course, one would have to argue each case.

If blanket annihilation is too much, James Pierce points out that decisions could be made about restricted use, deploying the design of affordances in reverse to make use more effortful (what Pierce calls "displacement") or to restrict that use to certain times and places (via "inhibition").[18] Promoting these conversations about what deserves to exist, or not, in our societies and, if so, when and where and for whom, and how easily—as opposed to just accepting what the market system makes available—is exactly the point of contemplating elimination design.

Ways to Kill a Design in Use

So, let us say that a consensus has been reached to remove a particular design from being used. If a designer decides to deliberately and explicitly use the destructive side of the creative process to that end, how easy is it to accomplish? I will run through four design discipline-specific strategies for undertaking elimination design.

Vilify (Communication Design)

Communication Design ordinarily tries to promote ideas by making
- what is invisible about that idea more visible (e.g., illustration),
- those ideas more readily understandable (e.g., information design), or
- by associating them with other ideas that a target group values (e.g., branding).

Each of these strategies can be used negatively: to expose the hidden ecological destruction involved, to make the value creation deficit behind that destruction immediately apparent, and to associate the design and its ecosystem or use with things that a target group disapproves. The overall intention is to encourage a target group to want to dissociate itself from a product. In this case, designing is not directly doing the eliminating, but instead creating the conditions in which elimination would be tolerated or even assisted.

What I am suggesting goes to the heart of the matter with which I began: that design presents itself as a creative practice. Though the process of design is essentially structured around criticism—the constant micro-critique of "reflection-in-action"—designers are not satisfied with being merely critical. This perhaps explains why, ironically, design criticism remains, relative to academic and popular criticism of other creative industries, immature and marginal.

Consequently, eliminative communication design is not merely a formal activity. It is inseparable from content generation, namely, being critical of existing designs. To put it the other way around, eliminative communication design is a form of activist design criticism. Not content with merely verbally pointing out the flaws of a design, eliminative design criticism takes up the tools of communication design to give its criticism force, visualizing in affective ways why the product is not only deserving of strong critique, but deserving of elimination.

An intriguing version of this is what Tony Fry and Anne-Marie Willis once called "Prefigurative Criticism."[19] In this practice, the intention is not to eliminate an existing product but to eliminate a coming product. If successful, this intervention would eliminate future destruction caused by the arrival of that product. Because it is "futural," it can only be a communication design project. Prefigurative Criticism happens by taking sketches and prototypes of what the product would be and situating them in an undesirable context. Done well, the product becomes associated with those negative values before those producing the product have had the chance to positively brand it. As I write this, Apple is promoting its new MacPro desktop computer. It will not be available until later this year, so only images of its black cylindrical form exist at the moment. This affords a prefigurative design opportunity to associate this new form with the ecological destructiveness of its manufacture, and so eliminate some of the scale of subsequent runs of this product.

Replace (Product Design)

It may seem nonsensical to contemplate eliminating products by designing products, but I argued earlier that the introduction of new products leads to the destruction of existing products. Sustainable design has, to date, been a strategy of replacing existing toxic or inefficient products with "greener" alternatives. Of course, much of the problem was that, apart from being greener, the products rarely showed more significant, "comparative advantages," as Rogers specified, is required for "The Diffusion of Innovations,"[20] and consequently failed to displace existing products.

Ideally, elimination by design involves a net reduction in materials intensity by virtue of one new product eliminating two or more existing products. This requires "convergent design," a notoriously difficult thing to accomplish. Donald Norman illustrates unusable design with a concept for a multimedia unit,[21] which, in interaction design at the time, held that every new function a device could accomplish required either yet another unique button or another click in a complex menu tree.

Since Norman gave that example, there have been a series of quantum shifts in digital design. Processing speeds and memory sizes, as well as the associated quality of hardware, such as screens and speakers, have increased exponentially, allowing the nature of interaction with digital devices to draw on a more diverse palette than dedicated buttons, multiple clicks, or keyboards. Tangible interactions, plus the capacity of devices to be more situationally aware, as well as just the maturation of the practice of interaction design, have made negotiating function convergence much easier. Digital devices can now accomplish a wide variety of activities, each with levels of quality that were previously only possible through dedicated devices. There is, therefore, in most cases, no loss of "comparative advantage" in listening to music and reading e-books on the same device on which I do my emailing and phoning. Finally, as was noted above with respect to the ratchet effect, being able to do many things on one device becomes a normative expectation, not least so that less needs to be carried when living a harried mobile life.

There is an interesting limit to convergence though. Recent work on "social practice theory" suggests that we tend to chunk activities into discrete practices, which comprise constellations of devices, skills, and meanings.[22] Laundering, commuting, preparing a meal, and exercising can be only done in ever more semiconscious ways because of the distributed intelligence possible when they are handled through distinct work environments with a distinctly regulatable rhythms, in what Theodore Schatzki calls the "timespace" of a practice.[23] This suggests that humans still cope with everyday life by having one set of things per each major activity. Convergent digital design recognizes this when devices allow apps for particular actions to take over the whole interface, orienting the use to that appropriately focused virtual environment.

Fig. 2 Shiba Sheikh, *"Accidentally" in a position to upgrade*. Courtesy Shiba Sheikh.

Another aspect of digital devices that facilitates elimination is the "decouplability" of the service the device provides from any particular device. The immaterial quality of information and communication and the pervasiveness of cloud-based data mean that what is "me" about a device does not reside in the physical qualities of a device. I can drop my iPhone in the toilet and get a replacement one with a seamless transition because "I" can be quickly reinstalled (Fig. 2). This allows a certain class of physical products to be eliminated via convergence, again without comparative advantage loss; but this also clearly allows the proliferation of things, whether diversifying "me" onto a range of screen-sized devices or cycling rapidly through one season's devices to the next.

Nevertheless, this substitutability as affording elimination goes in the opposite direction to the other dominant form of sustainable design: product use-life extension. Designing products so that they last longer is another indirect form of elimination design, in this case eliminating the need for subsequent replacements. "Heirlooming" is also difficult because it combines an engineering expertise (in terms of design for reliability, maintainability, repairability, upgradability) and a socio-psychological expertise (understanding "product attachment," how and why people value a product enough to sustain its use).[24] There are also economic issues: understanding the upfront capital costs compared with whole-of-life operating costs.

Finally, and picking up on this economic issue, a product can be eliminated by another product within that product, as when the components and materials in a product become more valuable than the original product. People will eliminate a ring from their life for the cash value of the gold that can then be resold to become someone else's more valuable ring. This becomes a product design strategy when products are designed in ways that facilitate post-use-life component and materials recovery.

Restructure (Built Environment Design)

Ursula Tischner, a sustainable design researcher and practitioner, once collaborated with Friedrich Schmidt-Bleek, founder of the Factor 10 Club (which advocates for a 90-percent reduction in the developed nation materials intensity) to develop a concept for a refrigerator with one-tenth the lifetime material usage of a conventional refrigerator.[25] To accomplish what is essentially an elimination design challenge, Tischner proposed, in essence, a return of the cool room. This space, built into a building's internal structure, would be already cool as a result of the building's thermal mass and, therefore, do away with a refrigerator's need for insulated sides and doors. An occupant would need only have some lightweight, removable shelving, and a small portable refrigerant-

Fig. 3 Sankalp Bhantnagar, *Buildings that make umbrellas redundant*. Courtesy Sankalp Bhantnagar.

compressor to lower the temperature of some shelf units more than others. With this example, it becomes possible to see that products can be eliminated by "built-ins." A city can eliminate the need for umbrellas with covered sidewalks or winter coats with underground passageways between buildings (**Fig. 3**). Public transport systems eliminate cars, and vice versa.

A rich example is Dolores Hayden's history of what she calls "material feminists" at the end of the nineteenth century in North America.[26] These activists envisioned emerging urban density coupled with steam-powered industrialization affording the socialization of women's domestic labor. As Hayden documents, these women recognized that capitalizing on these opportunities required architectural innovations: new kinds of kitchen-less apartments with access to shared dining, laundering, and childcare services. Women could be liberated from atomized domesticity, and all the products associated with that oppression eliminated, by structuring into our urban landscapes' collective domestic economies. Apart from some socialist, and sometimes religious, experiments, these designs were not realized, though a legacy of these times persists in the form of serviced apartments.

Cities that developed before more suburban single-family forms were instituted into the design of high-rises continue to do a kind of elimination designing. A majority of apartments in New York City to this day do not have the room or infrastructure for in-apartment laundering, effectively eliminating domestic washing machines from many areas of the metropolis. But as this example indicates, eliminating one kind of product institutes another, in this case, commercial laundry facilities (though this equipment tends to be more efficient and longer lasting). As Jan Gehl quipped, small refrigerators in apartments that eliminate the possibility of large refrigerators make for walkable cities, because people must shop more often, driving the demand for closer fresh food provisioning. But the latter will require more pop-up stall facilities for farmers markets and an increased number of trucks rattling into the city each day.

Architectural scale design might have significant elimination potential, but it has limited practicability. Buildings are expensive to build, especially in cramped cities, and the people who live in existing buildings must be displaced while rebuilding occurs. Consider trying to eliminate the inefficient window air conditioners that are pervasive in New York City. The architectural strategy would be HVAC systems with opportunities for significantly increased efficiencies. However, retrofitting the buildings without building-scale cooling services would involve effectively depopulating whole boroughs for a significant period. As Hommels has noted, cities are obdurate when it comes to "unbuilding," not just in terms of their materiality, but also socially.[27]

Disown (Service Design)

Elimination design can aim to be absolute: a whole category of thing eradicated from our societies. Or it can be relative, reducing the overall number of those things in our societies significantly. The most straightforward example is sharing: in theory there should be as many less of a product that is shared as the number of people making shared use of it.

When the European Union pursued dematerialization as a sustainable research topic, case studies were done of "functional sales," where businesses sell the use of a product (leasing, rented washing machines, or pooled resources like a Laundromat) or, better, the results of expert use of a product (laundry services).[28] One of the findings of this kind of work was that it is comparatively rare that products have been designed for use by multiple users; the standard use case is the single owner-operator, when instead the focus should be on the relatively new practice of "service design."

Being prepared to eliminate (the need for) ownership of a product, at least with respect to the "no comparative disadvantage" innovation diffusion measure I have been using, means that access to the appropriate product, when needed, must be the focused-on outcome of the system. Often in the promotion of "collaborative consumption" or "product-service systems," there is talk of functional equivalency: "you don't need a car, you need mobility; 95 percent of the time your car is idle." While it may be idle, it is not doing nothing; it is being-available-for-you. Consequently, the functional equivalent of owning a car is not mobility, but "wheels when you want them" (the registered tagline of Zipcar), regularly but also occasionally at short notice. The latter requires a sophisticated infrastructure and a flexible system, things that are most effectively (if not cost-efficiently) provided by people, service workers in a well service-designed system, for example.

Importantly, this observation draws attention to the historical fact that the rise of consumer capitalism in the twentieth century was driven by households switching their modes of resourcing from people to things. Appliances eliminated servants, video recorders eliminated theater ticket collectors and popcorn vendors, microwave ovens eliminated late-night seatings at restaurants, and so on. To engage in elimination-oriented service design is to try to reverse this trend, returning customers to people-based systems of need provision.

Again, the challenge, in terms of ecological and economic sustainability, is to deliver a system of access to a product that does not drive up the need for other kinds of products to sustain that access—smart phones, databases on servers, a well-distributed and maintained fleet. Obviously, as with Borges's one-to-one map, the most convenient service system for a product would have the same distribution scale as owned products. So product elimination by service design always requires a modification of expectations or, rather, new kinds of benefits that cannot be disadvantageously compared to the benefits provided by an owned product. It's not just that car share mobility is cheaper than the operating costs associated with an owned vehicle, but that the service design of car share allows you to go places, meet people, and have experiences you just couldn't or wouldn't otherwise.

I began with what I hoped was a shocking proposition: that designers (under instruction from their Design Studies mentors) can and should engage in destruction rather than creation. As we have proceeded however, I suspect that this has been transformed into a very mundane proposition. Far from an act of terrorism, eliminative destruction lies at the very heart of the design process, though under-acknowledged. When it is foregrounded and undertaken as the prime objective of designing, it looks like only a minor variation on communication, product, built environment, and service design.

There is much more to say about what designs the elimination of designs—policies and demographics for example. But for all the prosaicness of elimination, it should not be forgotten what is stake. Not just at the global level of unsustainable materials intensity, but just at the personal level. It is one thing to know or feel the need to throw something away. It is another to do it, as all the devices and trinkets sitting in unopened draws in every household attest.

PACE LAYERS

Bruce Sterling

Design struggles with a world of broken, ugly objects and services, while we science fiction writers are painfully bored by a world that's duller than we can bear. Why is the world like that? Why hasn't the whole system been swiftly upended by one designer judo-throw? Why haven't a flock of chrome-plated black swans arrived from outside the box?

Why can't design and science fiction seize the world with a rush and a push, junk all the broken rubbish, and dwell henceforth in a *Gesamtkunstwerk* Norman Bel Geddes Futurama, where design and science fiction would likely be both equally contented and have plenty of work on their hands?

In order to explain this state of affairs, I have to resort to a futurist schematic on the brink of literary metaphor. I learned this from Stewart Brand, who learned it from Gregory Bateson. It's called "pace layering."

Pace layering is not scientific. It's not falsifiable, it can't be quantified, and it's basically a form of Californian mysticism (**Fig. 1**). However, whenever I'm asked to speculate about what's likely to happen, I commonly have recourse to pace layering. I use it because it works so well; the results are plausible and sound commonsensical.

Many better-known methods of futurist speculation commonly boil down to pace layering. An awareness of pace layering can save a lot of heartbreak for a would-be system revolutionary.

Fig. 1 Bruce Sterling with stereoscope, Turin. Courtesy Bruce Sterling.

The core idea of pace layering is that there is not just one system in the world. The world is multisystemic; it's onion-like. The upper layers are light, airy, and swift-moving, while the deeper layers beneath them are dense, seismic, and slow.

Everything changes, just as Heraclitus said, but never at the uniform speed of his rushing stream. Changes arrive at different speeds, wheel within wheel. Some things go, while others hang around quite a while, which is why science fiction writers still quote the quips of Heraclitus.

The surface, in which designers and science fiction writers both frolic in the happy daylight, is the fastest pace layer. This layer is called "fashion." Fashion is hyperactive, but its churning transformations rarely have lasting consequence.

Mind you, fashion is not new, it's ancient (**Fig. 2**). Tattoos, cosmetics, and hairstyles are all prehistoric. So fashion is no younger than the other layers; it just generates artifacts that come and go with the shelf life of a Pantone color choice.

Below the pace layer of fashion is "commerce." If fashion is the street, then commerce is the marketplace. Commerce is also very old, although its pace is rapid. Chanel jackets change every fashion season, but the Chanel business enterprise has well outlived its founder's mortal lifespan.

There is no way to make fashion slower than commerce, or to make commerce faster than fashion. I can't explain why this is so, but it is. Pace layers rotate like nested spheres in a Ptolemaic universe. If commerce becomes somehow hot and frantic, then fashion will become feverish and hysterical.

Below business and commerce is the pace layer of "governance." Here science fiction and design are strangers to the scene, aliens from a distant pace layer. No designer ever designs her way into the U.S. Senate (though one would think that proper interaction design would make that task pretty easy). America's most politically accomplished science fiction novelist, Newt Gingrich, is a daffy, ranting visionary with no staying power.

Fast-moving creatives from the fashion layer lack the time for grave political commitments. They shy away from politics because they know that "nothing is going to happen." If you testify to Congress, arranging this act of political theater takes weeks. You will spend ten minutes speaking at grandees who are visibly ignoring you. People become upset if you disrupt that process with novel or surprising information. Creatives will vote and also complain a lot, but they lack the *Sitzfleisch* of career power-politicians, who can sit through anything.

This is the native pace of life at the governance pace layer. If government works any faster, then the layers above them, commerce and fashion, are placed in immediate peril. So it won't be business-as-usual any more, and fashion will

Fig. 2 The Muse of History, Milan. Photograph Bruce Sterling. Courtesy Bruce Sterling.

likely be rationed. In the jolting, crisis-laden era of King Stork, everyone prays for King Log.

Mind you, all the pace layers are entirely capable of rapid, sudden change—revolutions, epiphanies, catastrophes even. But they'll be fewer and farther between as the depth increases. Since the faster layers are piled atop the slower ones, the effects of change will mostly propagate upward. A fire on the ground floor leaps to ignite the roof.

Below the pace layer of politics is "infrastructure." In theory, infrastructure is under political control, but in practice it isn't. Infrastructure is slower in pace than electoral cycles. This is why bureaucracies commonly outlast and out-wait any whims of elected officials. It's also why the three vast titans of the military-industrial complex, the medical system, and the fossil-fuel business basically own the American government.

It's easy to see that all three of these vast, sluggish systems are badly designed and broken. The military has endless wars, the health system kills off the population, while oil and coal have wrecked New York, New Orleans, and the drought-stricken flyover states. They're broken, but not from entropy, thoughtlessness, or neglect. They're broken because the breakages serve the interests of the owners of the infrastructure. The installed base is too big to fail. It outlasts the cricket-chirping of its critics.

The power of infrastructure is easy to see when one removes oneself from the shibboleths of a particular government. Russia, for instance, is a gas-pipeline infrastructure with a state perched on top. The Soviet Union sold oil, and collapsed. The Communist apparatchiks were replaced by Yeltsin's privatization moguls, who also sold oil and also collapsed. They were replaced by the Putin elite of FSB spies, who still sell oil. Putin can die, and his clique can be purged by whatever comes next, but the oil infrastructure will still far outweigh the public interests of the Russian populace. They will watch their tundra catch fire from climate crisis and wonder how such things could be in the world.

To understand that infrastructure goes deeper than politics was the great insight of Silicon Valley. It's why they always build without asking permission first. Infrastructure also explains the success of the current Chinese government, which consists of Red engineers rather than Red ideologues. It's the source of the unity of the European Union, which always avoids voters and promulgates infrastructure standards instead. Even designers dabble in infrastructure, when they make new materials and new processes fashionable.

Infrastructure is not the deepest pace layer. Below it is "culture," the layer of values, beliefs, and metaphysics. The current American political polarization—the "broken politics"—are broken on purpose. The purpose is deeper than mere political struggle: it's a fifty-year-old civil cold war about culture.

Tremendous shear forces exist between the layers of culture, infrastructure, governance, business, and fashion. A lot can be accomplished in the weak and slippery seismic zones between the layers; consider a trend that becomes a new business, an ambitious business that buys itself a senator, and so on.

It follows that the best timing for a change in the situation in your own layer is a time of spasm in the layer below you. To out-guess events in your locale, you need to see what's happening on this deeper level. Try to understand why it happened, then translate that change into the attitudes and practices of your own situation.

That can be done. Other things can't be done. For instance, there is no way to freeze all the layers in place and rationalize them from top to bottom. Though they all coexist; you can't synchronize your eager heartbeats to the changes of the seasons and the grinding of tectonic plates. Revolutionary "Year Zero" efforts will be subverted and overthrown. It's why totalitarian government resorts to book burnings and mass murder; to start over fresh means to liquidate everybody and demolish everything.

Reason and persuasion find their limits in culture. You can't argue people out of their culture any more than you can argue your French girlfriend out of being French. She is French, she will stay French, so you either have to love her for that, or else give her up.

Mind you, a cultural pace layer is in motion like all the others; it's just slower paced **(Fig. 3)**. The American children of your French wife will become Americans, because they've been subjected for a lifetime to American culture along with American infrastructure, governance, business, and fashion. They'll become obese kids with handguns who vote Republican and shop at The Gap. However, when someone sings "Frère Jacques" in dear old Maman's nostalgic tone, they will weep uncontrollably.

Below the pace layer of culture is the primeval layer, that of "nature." People sometimes imagine that nature is a static realm of eternal verity. It isn't. Nature can change just as suddenly and drastically as any other pace layer. There have already been five massive extinctions of life on Earth during Earth's natural history, and we're in the midst of a sixth one.

Changes in nature are the grand stuff of legend and prophesy. They're earthquake, typhoon, famine, and pestilence; they're Nuclear Winter and a new Dark Age. They're Green Revolution and personal immortality; they're Singularities and terraforming of other worlds; they're Artificial Intelligence and the Big Rock Candy Mountain, where the hoboes eat roast chickens that grow on trees. They're legends that are mostly romantic and imaginary, except when they're real.

When nature changes, the long-established moral values of the culture layer are tossed in the air like so much New Year's confetti. Even history goes up

for grabs, because the stories we tell ourselves about the past are reassessed in the light of the contemporary. In the cold light of a transformed world, even History will change her mind.

Consider the curious fate of the great designer Raymond Loewy, whose atelier created the iconic Coke bottle and the Lucky Strike package. In the fashion and business pace layers, those were two terrific successes; in the nature pace layer, they killed off millions of the consumers that Loewy struggled to serve. The market valorized them, while human anatomy disagreed.

It's not that Loewy made the wrong moral decision; that moral decision never came up for him at all. If Loewy had declared, "I refuse to work for Coca-Cola, for they make people fat; while Lucky Strike are merchants of cancer and asthma," Loewy would have been universally condemned as a kook. Coca-Cola was the very symbol of American industrial predominance. Tobacco was the oldest and most honored American narcotic. Morally rejecting tobacco was like kicking Sir Walter Raleigh in the shins. So Loewy did the proper thing at the time, as, all too commonly, we all do.

We've never had a moral value system that can out-think pace layers. Morality is deep and slow, but it's not the slowest and deepest; nature predates humanity, and it will post-date humanity, too. The best that morality can offer us in that very, very long run is the sour guide that "All is Vanity." Sure, it is, but in the long run we're all dead.

To say, "In the long run we're all dead" is a very science fiction statement. It's the Huxleyan natural history lesson of H. G. Wells in *The Time Machine* and the Alpine gray abstractions of Olaf Stapledon in *Last and First Men*. It's a contribution of science fiction that isn't pop rubbish; it's classic. We human beings are the mayflies of the deepest pace layers.

If we embrace that Lovecraftian point of view, though, it's obliterating; it taints the brief experiences that make life so worthwhile, such as a decent lunch. It happens to be a cold and stellar arena where science fiction triumphs over design, but, frankly, who cares? A tiny fraction of the population knows who Olaf Stapledon was, while everyone and his sister has a designed cellphone now. For a while, that is.

Most schemes used today to out-guess futurity are subsets of pace-layer thinking. For instance, most efforts within the design world will fit well within a simple cycle of four basic phases. "Question Mark, Rising Star, Cash Cow, Dead Dog." These four states of products and services are entirely typical of a world dominated by capitalism.

Fig. 3 Retroscope, a dead media device, Turin. Photograph Bruce Sterling. Courtesy Bruce Sterling.

Question Mark is the phase of basic research and development. It's a tight, cultish world of self-appointed tech elites who literally don't know what they are talking about. Some newfangled phenomenon has arisen, and there's a paradigmatic struggle to name it and to fund it.

Nobody makes much money in the Question Mark quadrant. On the contrary, they consume money: from academia, government, venture capital, crowd-sourced Kickstarter funds, anyone who'll fill the innovator's begging bowl. The most common answer to this Question Mark is simple: it's mere fashionable rubbish. It's a red herring; there is no there there. It's intellectually sexy, yet it lacks substance.

The next quadrant is the Rising Star. A consensus emerges that this phenomenon is more than a vaporous techie conceit; it's commerce. The Question Mark receives some exciting, specific answers: someone needs it, it has real uses and applications, it has taken material form. Designers flock to this boundary between the concept and mass acceptance. The Rising Star shines on design, because designers have more power and influence in this quadrant than they do anywhere else.

The third quadrant is the Cash Cow. A major corporation acquires a design atelier's product. A Cash Cow sells out. A Cash Cow is a slow, cud-chewing beast, but it supplies beef, leather, and milk. Government will number it and inspect it. Some infrastructure of stalls and troughs will be built around it. It'll become a cultural reality, an institution, taken for granted. It will bore science fiction writers, who will never write novels about it.

The fourth stage is the Dead Dog. It is obsolescence, the fate of the defunct and the useless. The Dead Dog is the haunting specter of the unsustainable. It is the vastest quadrant, huge, ever-growing. All is vanity, and every assembly line leads to the junkyard.

Designers are aware of this situation, but there are no specialized Dead Dog designers. Design as a discipline provides shiny new objects and services to the world; it never deliberately removes the rusty, dreadful, existing ones. Design has never created a functional hook with which to drag designed objects off the world stage.

Design has created some cleaner, more sustainable methods of production, such as cradle-to-cradle design and its many green cousins, but there are no design undertakers directly specializing in dead things. However, as the deepest pace layer grinds on, the dead things will be most things, and eventually all things.

We humans never clean up a mess; we just idly hope that, somehow, the outworn will sink down into the nature pace layer and vanish. The hope is that the toxic debris will rot faster than it can accumulate around us and within us. Unfortunately, that hope is mere wishful thinking.

A cousin of the Question Mark, Star, Cow, Dog quadrant is the useful "Gartner Hype Cycle." Beloved by modern technologists of a digital slant, the Gartner Hype Cycle is all about language, or, rather, about how techies talk about technology under capitalism. The Hype Cycle has its distinct stages, which are analogous to the quadrants and also to pace layers. In order of occurrence, these phases are the Technology Trigger, the Peak of Inflated Expectations, the Trough of Disillusionment, the Slope of Enlightenment, and the Plateau of Productivity.

In the jargon of the Hype Cycle, a Technology Trigger is a fashionable novelty. Tripping this trigger attracts some attention. The Peak of Inflated Expectations is the loudest moment of chatter among the speculatives and the speculators. Sci-fi writers thrive here. They're so eager for novelty that they'll do technology's public relations work for free. The Trough of Disillusionment occurs when the overblown hype is discounted. In pace layer thinking, this disillusionment is the shear force separating the fashion layer from the commerce layer. Cool ideas don't necessarily sell. Successful design is harder to achieve than pundits like to admit. The Gartner Slope of Enlightenment is the investor-pleasing change from an awkward calf to a mature Cash Cow. The Plateau of Productivity is the Cow mooing her way into the lasting good graces of government, infrastructure, and culture.

The Gartner Hype Cycle is pretty good, as far as it goes, which is not very far. Because the Hype Cycle is all about talk, it fails in confronting the aspects of reality that people don't talk much about: abject failure and inevitable obsolescence. The world doesn't work on hype, because it's real. In the real world, most tech startups fail. Many digital technologies are obsolete before they plateau, meaning that, in pace layer language, they are just fashionable gadgets; they are too frail to ever become governmental, infrastructural, or cultural; they're mere passing fads.

Pace layer thinking is quite philosophical about that prospect; it accepts that most fashion is mere churn and always has been. In the business world, that attitude is dreadfully unbusinesslike, for it condones unconscionable wastes of the time and energy of the wealthy. It's a comedy to those who think, a tragedy to those who feel.

One thinks more soundly when freed from the hype of any single pace layer. New things in the world have complex fates. They're not the exclusive properties of any single sponsor; the street finds its own uses for things, and things also find their uses for the street. If you want to judge whether an innovation will thrive, it's good sense to run a reality check on every layer.

In the nature pace layer: Is the idea even feasible? Does it defy the laws of nature, like a time machine or a warp-drive both do? Then that's not a product at all; it's sci-fi. Do not be deluded by its dramatic appeal, its cool metaphysical implications, or how great it looks as a prop in some comic book blockbuster movie. It's otherworldly. It's not going to happen.

Culturally speaking: Does the pope hate it? Then expect some long-lasting trouble. The pope may not have battalions, but he's got his methods. The pope's business is two thousand years old.

Infrastructurally: Does it scale? Is it too big to build and maintain? Is there no feasible way to physically remove a rival structure that is already sitting there, fully installed? Are entire thriving cities, maybe whole nations, specialized in making it and maintaining it? You're charging the windmill, Quixote. Better not try that alone.

Governmentally: Is it illegal? Everywhere? How easy is it to regulate? Is the fix already in at City Hall? Are you designing beautiful cardboard pro-bono shacks for the homeless while the cops are already deputized to move your clients right along? Your tears and good intentions won't help that situation. The clients aren't homeless because they lack designer cardboard; they're homeless because of legally established urban property relations.

Commercially: Are you going to manufacture it, sell it, distribute it, store it, and employ people? If so, then you're actually a product manager and an entrepreneur, not a designer. If you attempt to work in both layers at once, you'll be torn. Next time you get some brilliant, groundbreaking design notion, you will have to neglect that. The longer-term consequences of your first stroke of genius will consume all your time and attention.

The wheels are always turning. As the clock ticks, the contents of the layers tend to sink downward. Those that don't sink to the relative safety of a slower pace will tend to simply vanish from the earth.

A fashion that persists has business implications. A business that survives has legal and political implications. A nation-building government conveys a heritage of infrastructure. Infrastructure is not mere concrete and iron; it persists as a settled way of life, as a mode of cultural being.

In the metaphysics of pace layering, everything that beats the clock is dragged toward the core; when it's said and done, then it's culture, it's part of who we are. When it's no longer said or done by anybody, it's the mute Gothic silences of nature. Ashes to fertile ashes, the dust that is tomorrow's soil.

FORMS OF SPACE AND TIME

Anna Barbara

If twentieth-century architecture was dedicated to planning the forms of space, we may suppose that, in the current century, architecture is already focused on forms of time. These temporal architectures exist inside spatial architectures that, thanks to time-based architectural planning, are re-invented, re-shaped, re-built, and given new functions to include all *tempi dell'abitare* (times of dwelling).

The future is already present in the ways we inhabit spaces using new media—simultaneity, ubiquity, and super-fast transport—which can warp space coordinates. Time-based architecture creates hierarchies that are different from traditional spatial logics. This is because the possibility of subverting the *consecutio* of spaces allows us to work on the folds of time and in the future.

The modern city challenged gravity to conceive skyscrapers, launching the twentieth-century megalopolis. Today's city challenges the dimensions of time to envisage new urban morphologies and architectural typologies. The contemporary city aims at blending *chronos* and *kairos*—linear, objective time and the subjective perception of time—continually changing its configurations, functions, and habitats. Buildings become organisms absorbing the temporal excursions of the different activities they host. The activities that represented the functionalist matrix of nearly everything modern are not only units of surface but temporal algorithms that synchronize different times, compressing and expanding space according to necessities and desires.

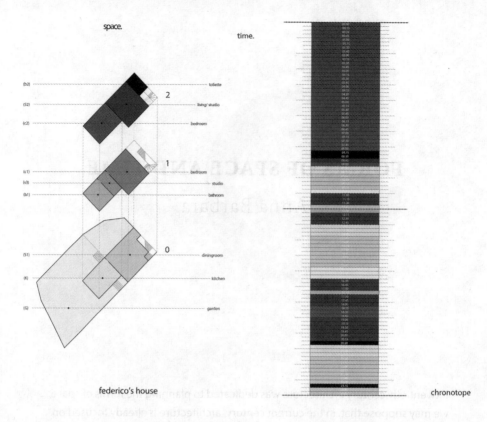

space.

time.

(b2)   2   toilette

(S2)   living/ studio

(c2)   bedroom

(c1)   1   bedroom

(x3)   studio

(b1)   bathroom

(S1)   0   diningroom

(K)   kitchen

(G)   garden

federico's house   chronotope

The architectural issues touching time and its variables are extremely contemporary:

- consumption/occupation of new territories and the reuse of empty spaces
- synchrony of different times
- new relationships between inhabiting, working, and producing
- so-called smartness
- inter-scalar mobility
- relationships with new communication media
- global interior/local exterior
- many facets of proximity

The idea that many existing buildings cannot be reused because their functional mandate has expired is a defeat not only for the environment and the economy but also for planning and architecture. Buildings conceived to last a few centuries, dedicated to commercial programs following the short

226

time.

Figs. 1a, b, c *Time-space 01-02-03.* Studies for chronotopes of house in Piacenza indicating time spent in each room, 2013. Anna Barbara and Federico Zucchi. Courtesy Anna Barbara.

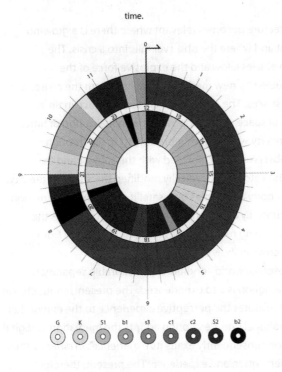

daily chronotope

life-span of a brand, should be planned with the possibility of transformation, so that a shopping mall can turn into a school or a museum into a temporary residence whenever it has to change its end use or needs more than one purpose simultaneously.

In the general analysis of what happens to time in spaces, we cannot overlook the great revolution introduced by new media, concerning the perception, production, manipulation, and projection of places. The utilization (and even the sheer presence) of these media in spaces allows relevant changes, as for instance the relationship between inhabiting and working. This is no more a functional on-off relationship; it belongs to a whole seamless existence. Thanks to communications media, all sorts of spaces—private, public, social, political—are present simultaneously at the same level. New media can no more be considered basic services for dwelling. Instead, they enter, for all intents and purposes, the innovative planning of life spaces as generators of languages, priorities, actions, and imageries.

Time-based architecture becomes relevant where there is a growing contraction of the present and where the observer falls into a crisis. The speed that new mobility vehicles allow and the explosive force of the perceptive simultaneity fueled by new media eventually deform the *consecutio* relationship of times and spaces. The effect is the erasure of space in time leading to fragmentation of space, or the opposite, the spatialization of time, involving an imitation of reality with images reproducing space through time (**Figs. 1a, b, c**). The observer, who coincided with the subject and the protagonist, even when the automobile radically modified the shape of the city, ultimately steps out of her body and settles on a satellite for all her information about reality. This is undoubtedly a Copernican revolution, since it puts the observer outside the surrounding reality on a level that is abstracted from experience, allowing objective analysis of the world.

In the modified observer/world condition, an inexorable separation between perception and emotion is also experienced. The present, contracted in vertiginous derivatives, accelerates the perceptive experience to the extent that it detaches it from the emotional one. Perception adopts the mediation of digital technologies while emotion subsequently exalts its experiences *in differita*, thus creating a gap between perception and experience. The present, therefore, becomes a moment of reality scan and accumulation of information, which can be experienced later and somewhere else, perhaps assisted by accessories that can accompany and improve the metaphor.

Space is definitely dynamic and the dimension of depth is substituted by a mobile coordinate, which is a temporal sequence. Therefore, the structure of the city, which used to produce itineraries and narratives, dies out. The space of storytelling and deduction, which conveyed modernity, is replaced by the hypertextual space and intuition.

In this new appearance, crossing over places becomes a series of layers, of sliced up spaces, like sequences of thin architectures devoid of luminous and spatial shadows. "Layerable" is, therefore, a condition of certain places we inhabit, fragmentary and discontinuous, where the crossing has no meaning since the distance factor, the primary equation linking space and time, is lost.

The issue of time is, by its nature, linked to space through movement and its equations. The different temporalities simultaneously at work during mechanical, virtual, and physiological actions trigger a sort of schizophrenia similar to jetlag, typical of the world of mobility without movement. High speed makes important poles of the continent closer, notwithstanding their actual distance and their historical connections. This creates new affinities, new networks of appeal, new coalitions.

The time of new infrastructural network is no more proportional to distance itself but to the typology of transport and its speed. In these spaces, inhabitants are replaced by passengers, users, consumers, listeners, viewers identified by name, address, date of birth, passport, and PIN. Through a PIN, the relationship between community and city is radically modified, because the city is no more a unique entity, a territory, or a border. Its identity becomes a brand following marketing logics rather than territorial policies.

We are back into a time warp of space, like the one introduced by low-cost flights that trigger an unusual rethinking of matched cities and airports: Frankfurt/Hahn, London/Luton, Milan/Orio al Serio, Paris/Beauvais. The new airport realities are appealing because of their supposed proximity to certain big cities, activating services, and performances. These new twin cities, now dubbed "air cities," are terminals devoid of any real connections. One is simply the discount store of the other, a fictitious appendix.

Extreme conditions, safety stress, the need of shadowy places to allow work on digital screens, the desire of environments tuned on our desires and therefore governable make inhabited spaces more and more introjected and the city less open. In certain cities you rarely meet someone walking on the pavement; everyone moves from one indoor place to another without going outdoors.

The digesting city is a sequence of continuous spaces, without a horizon, with a claustrophobic architecture. It is swallowed by a series of connected spaces devoid of perspective, where space is enclosed and the sky nowhere to be seen. It is an apparatus of places connected and subsequent, one after the other, with no possibility of choice. In this multicellular and functional city, the main movement is peristaltic, pushing people and goods toward predefined directions and temporal mechanisms. The digesting city is disturbing but also comforting, because its organs see to the consumption and processing of goods to extract energy, to feed the city itself and its inhabitants, and to eliminate its wastes, just like the digestive system.

This city does not need eyesight, because the landscape cannot guide it anymore, being too close to be in focus. It's a chemical architecture of taste and smell, a city of interiors without outside/around, an enclosed space without limits that evokes the architectural utopias of Étienne-Louis Boullée and Claude-Nicolas Ledoux.

It was the era of Japanese commercial centers and theme parks, sensorial places where experience was accelerated and contracted according to the duration of the ticket. And then these Las Vegases of the everyday rapidly entered our ordinary ways of dwelling, as a solarium to enliven anemic happy hours, as artificial snow to sublimate ski runs in the mountains, as wavy beaches to get a homeopathic dosage of holidays during decidedly urban weekends.

To efficiently transfer environmental realities to other places, it is necessary to work on the physiology of the body, on the excitement or relaxation of certain glands to produce doping effects according to the characteristics of the building. Producing artificial snow to intensify the experience of mountain skiing is not enough. You need rarified, hypo-oxygenated air, alpine light that comes from below and decreases the production of melatonin, and maybe a fake chalet with an artificial fir tree on the entrance door. But the metaphor relies on something that is less visible and blatant: the manipulation of time.

The citadel of the present is besieged by actions that unsettle the project in space and time. Mobile phones and computers, along with GPS systems, ultimately do not replace reality but overlap it. Experiences of new media do not substitute for real life but impose space-time compressions and expansions that we are not used to yet. Sometimes we don't even give our bodies, in their very physiological acceptation, enough time to familiarize themselves with this novelty.

Planning time in its most efficient spatial mechanisms becomes extremely relevant to architecture, urban planning, and design, where plurifunctionality, the absence of context and new vocational status of commerce and leisure, become programmatic. The temporal scanning in these places has nothing to do with the chronological time marked on our watches with external time, but it follows an internal timer tracing the necessities of the metaphor. The time of sensorial places, being snowy mountains, tropical islands, or submarine rooms, is accelerated or contracted according to the experience that should be generated. Senses are the purpose, not the medium, of architecture.

At the basis of these experiences, there is a sort of emotional bulimia to placate, a contemporary anxiety to saturate the experience of time and place. It looks like a horrible present, with no escape, where time offers space the logistical, multifunctional, programmatic variables that relentlessly try to make our lives more efficient and stimulated. Yet there are clear signs of an impending reversal. Space will surrender to time in order to develop new planning actions, new forms of dwelling, and new architectural compositions without apocalyptic nuances.

This feeling seems to derive from the romantic *horror vacui*, an insane fear of emotional voids, of dull spaces, and of waiting. Possibly the most bulimic areas are the so-called non-places, which, given their inherent dullness, have to make up metaphors for the users in order to keep them active. The reaction of places is

Figs. 2a, b Day/night view from the same window. Gifu, Japan, 2006. Photograph Anna Barbara.
Courtesy Anna Barbara.

almost exclusively commercial: they translate experience in the most compulsive instinct to shop.

The constant, uninterrupted production has been for centuries seen by the Church as a usurpation of God's power. Believers were required to sanctify feast days and to rest on the seventh day. Even in the most secular European societies, this limit still represents an obstacle to the optimization of schedules, a theological vision of the use of time.

Buildings that remain open around the clock are temporally intermodal because they synchronize different times, compress and expand space according to needs and desires, and do not generate dense times. Intersecting a longer temporal chain, they can be paradoxically decongested, offering services at any time and letting people live in their favorite time spans (Figs. 2a, b). This mode of temporal use of space also affects the typologies of transport, developing public transportation to regulate collective fluxes while experimenting with other mobilities to guarantee an individual circulation over small distances.

The constantly open city will allow a free choice of the time frame in which to live, sleep, love, or work. This will mean being able to synchronize one's own schedule to the time zone of the community of choice, which may not necessarily be physically the closest.

"WHEN WE UNDERSTAND THAT SLIDE, WE'LL HAVE WON THE WAR." SYSTEMIC COMPLEXITY AND THE IRREGULARITIES OF SCALE

Jamer Hunt

If complexity is our condition and uncertainty is our code, then scale is our mission to the moon. We are living through a time when the subtle and unexpected effects of changes in scale are warping our perceptions of our world and our ability to effect change within it. This is happening at the same time that we are losing touch with scale, and in the process relegating it to an overlooked given. The three anecdotes that follow will help to illustrate just how far out of touch we are with scale. Hopefully, through these examples we can also begin to look at scale anew. Refamiliarizing ourselves with the unusual behaviors of scale will provide surprising insights into rethinking and redesigning systems in ways that mitigate our current tendency to endlessly proliferate dysfunctional systems.

In 2011 Sarah Lyall, writing for *The New York Times*, reported on an unsettling discovery: the kilogram no longer weighed a kilogram. The problem, as she reported, was that that physical artifact was no longer doing its job. Due to unexpected and unwanted weight loss, the reference standard for the kilogram—hewn of platinum, housed under three successive bell jars in Sèvres, France, and accessible by only three people in the world—had apparently lost 50 micrograms. While scientists had abandoned utilizing physical objects as standards for most quantities of measure decades ago—precisely because most physical properties are subject to miniscule but significant fluctuations—the international standard for the kilogram was still a physical object. To compound matters, according to Lyall, the dictionary definition of a kilogram tautologically referred to back to this very standard: "a unit of mass equal to the mass of the international prototype of the kilogram." As a result of this weight loss, the search is now on to replace that imperfect measure with a "physical constant." The meter, for instance, no longer refers to a metal bar the length of a meter, but to "the length of the path traveled by light in a vacuum during a time interval of 1/299,792,458 of a second."[1]

If I open up a document on my computer desktop in the word processing application Microsoft Word and I select the size of a letter-sized document, a familiar rectangular-shaped white space opens up on screen. By U.S. paper standards, a letter-size document is 8.5 inches wide by 11 inches tall. I can then choose, while still in Microsoft Word, to view that document at 100 percent on the screen before me. If I then take out a standard, physical ruler and measure the dimensions of that white rectangle on my screen, I get 5.5 inches by 8 inches. So, 100 percent of an 8.5 x 11 document is 5.5 x 8?

In 2010, General Stanley McChrystal, then leader of American and NATO forces, was being briefed on the strategic plan for the NATO invasion of Afghanistan. As is now the convention, his team was using Microsoft PowerPoint, a common slide presentation software, to deliver this particular briefing. Illuminating the screen was a densely tangled diagram consisting of more than ninety-five discrete nodes knotted together in what visual designers commonly refer to as a "spaghetti diagram." This infernally complex and thickly snarled mess included strategic factors such as "Coalition Execution Capacities and Priorities," "Western Affiliation Backlash," "Terrain Harshness and Breadth," "Ethnic/Tribal Rivalry," and "Counter-Narcotics/Crime Ops." It purported to render a comprehensive account of mission-critical forces and obstacles for the incursion into Afghanistan (**Fig. 1**). When he set eyes on the PowerPoint slide for the first time, General McChrystal famously quipped, "When we understand that slide, we'll have won the war."[2]

Each of the above anecdotes reveals, as in the parable of the blind men and the elephant, a different facet of the same phenomenon. That is, changes in the nature of our relationship to scale are destabilizing us in unexpected ways. Understanding these changes is critical today because massive changes in our natural, built, and immaterial environments are compromising our ability to manage their complexity. The rise of the Information Age (with its concomitant shift from atoms to bits), combined with the proliferation of networks (that the Internet birthed), has left us lost in a labyrinth that stretches too far, too wide, and too deep. But this explosive growth in size and complexity is not without its opportunities. For designers, whose own practices have drifted from producing artifacts toward designing and redesigning complex systems, shifts in scale may

Afghanistan Stability / COIN Dynamics

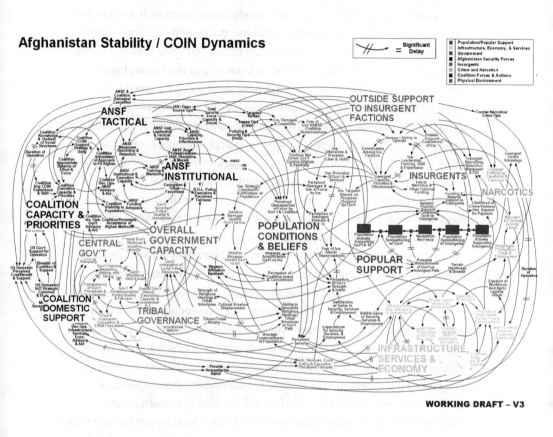

WORKING DRAFT – V3

Fig. 1 Afghanistan Stability/COIN Dynamics—Security, 2009. Public document from the Office of the United States Joint Chiefs of Staff.

235

also present possibilities for regaining some degree of agency in the face of metastatic system complexity.

Scale is a blindingly obvious phenomenon. We encounter it so commonly that we've lost our sensitivity to it and its behaviors. Anesthetized to its power and its effects, we are also slowly losing touch with it—literally. Our leap into more digitally mediated habits, spaces, and social relationships has altered our phenomenological relation to size and scale. Where we once defined most units of measure by their relationship to the human body, currently, we are in the process of a dramatic decoupling between scale and the human body. Thus, the earthly solidity of a platinum kilogram will undoubtedly soon give way to an immaterial constant, no more knowable than "the length of the path traveled by light in a vacuum during a time interval of 1/299,792,458 of a second." As Paul Virilio writes, "the basic concept of physical dimension . . . progressively [loses] its meaning and analytical power as a form of dissecting or dismounting perceptive reality. Instead we find other, electronic means of evaluating space and time, ones that share no common ground with the measuring systems of the past."[3]

This decoupling of scale and the human body does not just exist at the perceptual level and in relation to the human body. McChrystal's prescient comment demonstrates that we are also struggling to come to terms with conceptual complexity and scale. Stunning, but increasingly detailed, high-resolution graphics and diagrams—fueled by massive data sets and desktop supercomputers—bring to our fingertips quantities of information that often require even more processing just to make sense. Sophisticated software diagramming is revealing to us massive networks of interconnected data on fields that seem to stretch to the horizon. It is easy to empathize with McChrystal's bewilderment at the PowerPoint slide. There are just too many data points, too many variables, too many connections, and too many possibilities to consider. Short of handing over the decision making to algorithms, it is hard to foresee how we will put our human judgment and wisdom to use in the face of such convolution.

As with the ubiquitous image of the isolated polar bear on a cleaved ice flow that has become a synecdoche for an environmental catastrophe, the scope of which we cannot comprehend, we concoct overly simplistic and inapt depictions because the conceptual scale of these hydra-headed problems surpasses our ability to respond. They have taken on a scale that goes beyond the grasp of the human mind's finite ability to hold connections, relationships, and variables together in one frame. But rather than just freeze in the face of complexity, it is revealing to dig a bit deeper into scale and its behaviors so that we may begin to formulate an escape from its paralyzing effects.

In the 1960s, Frits Went, a Dutch scientist, posited a simple but illuminating two-part thought exercise: Would an ant be able to read if we shrunk the size of a book down to its scale? The key to the answer, Went revealed, had little to do with the remarkable little worker's ability to learn. Instead, he contended, the obstacle to an ant's ability to read an ant-sized book is that the forces of attraction between electrons at that scale would make it impossible for the ant to turn the pages. In other words, as scales shift, the nature of the problem changes. But could an ant take a shower, he next asked, if we could scale one down to its size? In this case the answer would appear be an obvious yes. Wrong. At the scale of the ant, the surface tension of a drop a water is simply too impenetrable, and the water would bounce off rather than sprinkle over the ant. Once again, as the scale changes, the problem changes.[4]

This phenomenon, known as scalar variance, occurs when changes in scale produce system effects that are disproportionate to regular changes in quantity. Increase the flame under a beaker of water, and the temperature of the water will continue to increase arithmetically until the fluid changes phase and becomes a vapor. Another way to describe this abrupt shift is that a quantitative increase leads to a qualitative transformation: a liquid becomes a gas. Change the scale, and the nature of the problem changes.

We can find this surprising scalar behavior across a range of different phenomena. In typography, for example, most typefaces maintain proportional relationships between the various components of the letterform as you change the letter in scale. For example, the letter "p" maintains its shape and proportion whether at 24 points or 8 points (**Fig. 2**). But a remarkable transformation occurs as letters shrink even further in scale. Thomas Huot-Marchand designed his typeface Minuscule to be legible even at sizes as tiny as 2 and 3 points. Certainly, the letterforms twist and distort themselves as they reach their minutest legible size. But what is even more interesting are the subtle manipulations that Huot-Marchand resorts to in order to keep the typeface legible. Close inspection of the letter "o" in the word "typographes," reveals that Huot-Marchand has radically altered the fundamental compositional rules. The letterforms, at incrementally larger point sizes, have rigorously followed a rule by which all of the strokes, or forms, are black and all counterforms, the empty spaces within letters, are white. In the letter "o" he reverses those relationships, making the counterform black and in effect making the body of the letter itself white, or absent (**Fig. 3**). Stroke becomes fill, figure becomes ground, and absence becomes presence. He inverts the foundational perceptual schema that grounds his system, and you may find that your brain actually fills in the circular stroke around the black counterform. It's not just that the letters change shape—this is not an instance of linear,

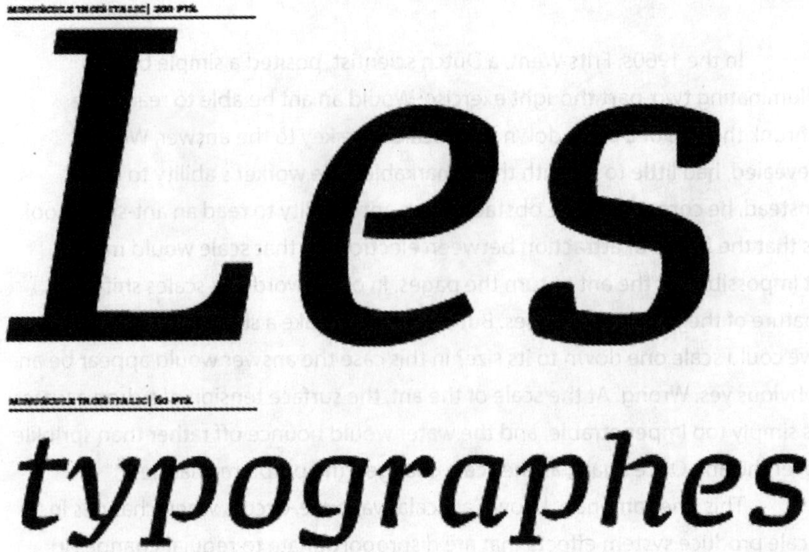

Les

MINUSCULE TROIS ITALIC | 200 PTS.

typographes

MINUSCULE TROIS ITALIC | 60 PTS.

Fig. 2 Minuscule Trois Italic. Thomas Huot-Marchand, 2007. Courtesy Thomas Huot-Marchand.

incremental changes in proportion—it's that the forms of the letters require a qualitative rewrite of the rules of the game. Change the scale, and the nature of the problem changes.

This phenomenon also manifests itself in another, very different domain: publishing. In 2009, Chris Anderson published his book *Free: The Future of a Radical Price*. The book purports to document an increasing and unpredicted trend in business: more and more companies are becoming successful by giving away their products. To back up this provocative claim, the book's publisher tried to walk the walk and give away the book for free . . . sort of. As the book critic Carolyn Kellogg struggled to explain, "the entirety of Chris Anderson's book *Free* is currently available free on the online service Scribd and at GoogleBooks. The not-quite-practicing-what-it-preaches rub: it's free to read online but not to print or to download. What you can get for free: a downloadable nine-page excerpt at Scribd and the complete audiobook.[5] The abridged audiobook is on sale for $7.49, and, no, I don't get the logic of that either."[6]

In this topsy-turvy economy, turned upside-down by Internet commerce, one can read the book for free but not print it, and the entire audiobook is free, but a smaller excerpt costs $7.49! That is to say, the impact of a chaotic new economy has unsettled the proportional relationship between quantity and value so that their proportionality no longer makes sense. Value has come unmoored from quantity, and, at least in this example, the rules of the system have broken down.

Les

typ■graphes

Fig. 3 Minuscule Deux Regular. Thomas Huot-Marchand, 2007. Courtesy Thomas Huot-Marchand.

This figure of speech—the broken system—has become the predominant way we now describe the ills that beset our cultural life, at least in the United States. Whether it is health care or politics, public education or finance, disaster resilience or food security—and the list could be much longer—politicians, pundits, and people of all walks of life are forever denouncing the failed state of our designed systems. No doubt this is due to many disparate factors, but there is also no doubt that the unexpected and unprecedented proliferation of interconnected networks has severely compromised our ability to manage these systems, if managing them is even a reasonable goal anymore. Their behaviors seem to be disconnected from rational control or even known causes. They have become "wicked problems," to borrow Horst Rittel and Melvin Webber's now inescapable turn of phrase. Or, to put it differently, the relationships between the parts of the system and its whole have become nonlinear.

Linear relationships within complex systems demonstrate regular, proportional, and predictable symmetries. So, for example, a small, failing bolt in a bridge can cause catastrophic damage, but its repair is straightforward: replace it with a similarly sized bolt. Engineers can accurately predict the forces and loads that bolt carries, and even if they cannot reproduce the bolt, they can find a substitute that will bear the necessary load. In nonlinear systems, however, we encounter behaviors that are neither predictable nor reproducible. The system scales up to a level of complexity where it no longer hews to models and predictions of its behavior. Cause and effect are scrambled. It would seem obvious, for instance, that widening roads would decrease traffic jams. To solve the problem of too many cars, make more lanes. If the problem gets bigger, use a bigger solution. However, evidence has shown that enlarging roadways inexplicably seem to generate traffic increases, perhaps because more people feel emboldened to drive on them.[7] In a nonlinear system, a small change can cause a massive headache: enough riders tapping on their brakes can cause a traffic jam, even when there is no actual obstruction in the traffic flow. In other words, as the scale changes, the nature of the problem changes as well.

Ecologists describe a similar, though more total, shift in system behavior from incremental, quantitative change to massive, qualitative change as cascading system change. The inadvertent introduction of an invasive species (algae, for example) into freshwater lakes can, for example, lead to a complete collapse of the lake's ecosystem. The system collapses, even though the invasive species would hardly seem a threat equivalent to the size of the macro-ecosystem. Cause, in these cases, becomes incommensurate with effect at the level of scale. Systems are particularly susceptible to these cross-scale transformations when they have reached the limits of their growth and become brittle: "the brittle state presents the opportunity for a change at a small scale to cascade rapidly through a system and bring about its rapid transformation. This is the 'revolt of the slave variable.'"[8] If small perturbations to a system can lead to outsize negative effects, should it not be possible to leverage small shifts in scale to create outsize positive benefits as well?

It would be a gross oversimplification to conclude that SMS messaging and Twitter led to the overthrow of brutal, autocratic political regimes during the Arab Spring of 2010, but it would be equally misguided to underestimate their power in catalyzing systemic change. Huge crowds of fearless citizens still had to stand up to bullets and bludgeons in public squares, from Tunisia to Egypt to Bahrain and beyond. But would these protest movements—and in particular their formulae for success—have cascaded so quickly across brutal and repressive regimes if not for the power of sharing tactics, clandestine video, and messages of support across diverse social media? Corrupt political systems finally gave way in part due to the surprising impact and mass mobilization of citizen tweets, texts, and tactics. By leveraging the power of small perturbations, protesters achieved massive system change in political environments that seemed otherwise intractable.

Confounded by a complex assemblage of traffic signals, road signage, driver behavior, pedestrian behavior, and urban planning that wasn't working, the city of Drachten in the Netherlands hired Dutch traffic engineer Hans Monderman to solve the challenge of increased traffic incidents at one central intersection. To most engineers the design problem would be simple: if too many cars, drivers, and pedestrians were leading to too many accidents and delays, then the straightforward solution would be to increase the carrying capacity of the roads while increasing signage and traffic signals to make drivers more aware of the rules. Monderman, however, had other ideas. He removed all signage, moved outdoor café seating perilously close to the intersections themselves, and increased the potential for confrontations between pedestrians and cars. The result: traffic flowed faster and the rate of accidents declined. Monderman sought out, in effect, a nonlinear answer to a linear problem. Rather than try to scale up the solution in response to the problem—the bigger the problem, the bigger the solution—he sidestepped the problem altogether. No longer did he rely upon passive drivers to interpret passive signals and signage, but he forced drivers and pedestrians alike to negotiate a signal-free traffic circle in which both groups had to actively communicate through gesture, eye contact, and social interaction.[9] To tame an increasingly complex problem, he had to change the nature of the problem itself.

Both the Arab Spring and the Dutch traffic examples demonstrate that unexpected and disproportionately small interventions into massive problems can transform otherwise intractable systems in surprising ways. Not coincidentally, both reconfigure the flows of information, leveraging the impact of social connection across communication channels to reboot the health of complex systems. Whether wittingly or not, they harness the peculiar powers of scale shifts to upend conventional wisdom, predictive modeling, and cause and effect. In neither instance did the protagonists simply escalate the scale of the problem with a typical arms-race solution: the Arab protestors did not, in most cases, use force to overthrow the national armies, and Monderman did not simply increase the carrying capacity of the roadway and reinforce it with even more signage. Solutions came from upending expectations of cause and effect, reframing the problem, and shifting the scale of response. Each, it seems, relies upon bottom-up processes that engage the power of many to unexpectedly effective ends. Top-down, centralized, master planning only seems to recapitulate the systems' already diseased ways. In these two examples, agency within the system is returned to or seized by the actors, not the regulators, of the system. This bottom-up approach is closer to evolutionary processes, wherein small mutations to a system's elements have the power to reverberate to powerful effect if given the space to proliferate. For designers, then, the approach must be to reframe the problem, identify the potentially catalytic agents, seed bottom-up effects, and let the system play. Flipping systems is not child's play, but it may be the only play left to us.

AFTERWORD: THE DESIGNER AND THE DESIGNED

Tim Marshall

Design is future-making. This collection of compelling and important essays attests to both the enduring and the changing nature of design. Design has always served as the midwife of technologies into our lives, creating collective practices and lifestyles. In so doing, design has been the medium of the material and technological transformations of our lives and, consequently, of our shared communities. If Churchill was right about the symbiotic effect that our built world has on us—how it designs us as we design it—then these forms of transformation are far more significant than is often acknowledged. This is why this volume of essays is so important.

In various ways and with reference to a variety of themes, the contributing authors all encourage us to confront this critical and profoundly important aspect of design's work in the world. We are asked implicitly and explicitly to think about the place and status of design. This is a notoriously difficult task: Who and what exactly are we referring to when we use the words design and designer? How do we deal with the ever-expanding implication of these words, which now travel across myriad boundaries, and thus with a diversity of meanings, understandings, actions, and critical implications? Is design becoming more powerful as a result of this movement? Or is it increasingly vacated and diluted, becoming a potentially meaningless catchall term? What are the implications of this expansion for those among us who declare themselves designers? If society is designing itself, if systems and institutions and technologies and politics and indeed life itself are all now so

Fig. 1 *Under Tomorrows Sky*. Fictional future city, developed by Liam Young and a think tank of scientists, technologists, illustrators, and special effects artists, for the 2013 Lisbon Architecture Triennale: *Close, Closer*. Photograph Catarina Botelho. Courtesy Catarina Botelho.

explicitly acknowledged to be designed systems, then surely the designer is now a title that is as freely associated as the application of the word design.

Design as Future-Making pries open and attends to these, and many other, questions, thus promoting debate and contemplation for the future of design itself. Indeed, a review of the authors' backgrounds underscores the very point that designers no longer have a guild-like ownership of design. Opportunities are presented, but great insecurity also follows from the displacement of privileged expertise. Many practitioners and observers now claim that the design process has been democratized through technology or via the access provided by technology. In my view, this claim of so-called democratization forces us to consider two important propositions: what design has done in the past and what the future promise of design might be. Serious reflection about these two matters would mean that we don't merely account for design's impact on the world simply in terms of form and instrumental function. Instead, designers must fully acknowledge various constitutive questions, such as: What was the project or what should have been the project? What were the unforeseen implications of any and all design acts? These questions serve to reinforce that most fragile dimension of the design practice—a critical perspective that is developed both within and outside of process. The critical perspective cannot be slighted since it enables the most essential feature of a design process that extends beyond the primary design act, if indeed there is one. That is, the critical process entails iteration, which itself necessitates a reflexive stance and the reflexive input of the designer. However, most importantly, it likewise involves the reflexive stance and critical capacities of the people for whom the design is intended. This collection of essays helps us to better understand various ways to approach or develop this critical perspective on the design process.

This is an important publication for that very reason: The editors put forth a convincing case for not reducing the design process to the purely technocratic practice of form-making, thus opening the workings and operations of design to social or critical debate. This move liberates the design process from designers in a way that should be taken not as a challenge to the hegemony of designers but rather as crucial to the transformation of design practice from a closed guild practice to a fully implicated social and material practice—a way of thinking and making in the world, and a way of thinking and making worlds. Design has no quality; it tells us nothing about how we will or can or want to live our lives. Design, in and of itself, and designers, by themselves, cannot possibly envisage all the horrors or pleasures that design can produce. Designers alone are incapable of determining the ethical and moral implications of the way designs act or proliferate in the world alone—how design designs. (This is far from the intention of having designers absolve themselves of responsibility for their acts of designing, hence the emphasis on "alone.") No group owns design. We cannot on the one hand celebrate the incredible power and reach of the processes and manifestations of design, while at the same time we attempt to dodge responsibility for the outcomes of our collective designed world.

So it follows that a sense of understanding about the processes and implications of design—an understanding of how design works in the world and structures our lives and interactions with things, institutions, systems, and each other—is now so important that it should be a subject of a broad liberal education. The design process is a question as much for citizenship as it is for experts or specialists. I suggest that this is the case because design cannot be the exclusive purview of the designer.

So what is the designer to do? The designer has a very particular role in the process of bringing together the conflicting and irresolute dimensions that proposing and imposing things in the world entail. The designer is both the specialist of a certain area (communication, architecture, clothing) and the facilitator of a community of actors working toward an incrementally improved situation or opportunity. The designer is a specialist in being a generalist, an expert in the configuration of specialist knowledge, the facilitator of the destruction of the division between the expert and the acted upon such that there is a reversal in the acknowledgment of expertise in the situation and in the outcome.

Ideally, then, design education should enable this double move for the future designer: To bring one's specific expertise to the table with the knowledge that any design expertise can potentially develop (it often does not) a very particular capacity to move across and between knowledge bases, skill sets, domains, systems, or institutions of authority and stakeholder interests such that the clumsy and necessarily compromised movement toward a sense of a better way to be in the world can be given the best chance to take hold or to stabilize as a given practice. A designer needs to know that people design in their acting with and on the object of design. And it is here that the veracity of design can be understood and assessed. Design education struggles, and needs to struggle more intentionally, with how to develop the most cogent design capacity of iteration, collaboration, and empathy.

The texts in this book clarify this point for us. None of the authors describes a design act in isolation of complex social, political, and environmental issues. None portrays the sole heroic designer fashioning outcomes according to a particular vision of the order of living. All explore the critical role of the designer in larger processes, urging us to see in the iterations of their work a cautious optimism that indicates that, indeed, design can be turned toward Herbert Simon's "preferred situation," but they add an essential missing ingredient in Simon's formulation: Whose terms do we take to be the determining standard that indicates an improvement?

ENDNOTES

Introduction

1. The author's translation of the affects of globalization on design is indebted to Arjun Appadurai's seminal work: *Modernity at Large: Cultural Dimensions of Globalization*, "Public Worlds," Vol. 1 (Minneapolis: University of Minneapolis Press, 1996).
2. For a thorough consideration of the nature of design as ethics: Clive Dilnot, *Ethics? Design?* (Chicago: The Archeworks Papers, Vol. 1, No. 2, 2005).
3. Michael Sorkin, "Eutopia Now!" *Harvard Design Magazine* 31, Fall/Winter 2009/10: 11.
4. Nelson Goodman, *Ways of World-Making* (Cambridge, Mass: Hackett Publishing Company, 1978), 22.

Crafting Capacities

1. C. Wright Mills, "The Man in the Middle," in *The Politics of Truth: The Writings of C. Wright Mills* (New York: Oxford University Press, [1958] 2008), 181.
2. Anne Balsamo, *Designing Culture: The Technological Imagination at Work* (Durham: Duke University Press, 2011), 6.
3. C. Wright Mills, *The Sociological Imagination* (New York: Oxford University Press, [1959] 2000). See in particular, chapter one, "The Promise," and the appendix, "On Intellectual Craftsmanship."
4. Mills, "The Man in the Middle," 183.
5. Louis I. Kahn's query of the brick has become a part of architectural folklore. It was his stock advice to students when they were stymied by a project. Allegedly, he first posed the thought problem to himself when he was working in Ahmedabad, India, in the early 1960s.
6. Gilles Deleuze, "Mediators" in Jonathan Crary and Sanford Kwinter (eds.), *Incorporations* (New York: Zone, 1992), 285.
7. Hannah Arendt calls assemblages of people acting and speaking together "spaces of appearance." See *The Human Condition* (Chicago: University of Chicago, [1958] 1998), 198–200.
8. Arendt, *The Human Condition*, 7.
9. Ibid., 52.
10. Ibid., 173. It's not only that *homo faber* has the capacity to create the conditions for speaking and acting, but also that *homo faber* redeems *animal laborans* from "its predicament of imprisonment in the ever-recurring cycle of the life process, of being forever subject to the necessity of labor and consumption (Arendt, 236). Moreover, it is through the faculty of action that *homo faber* recovers meaning. The human condition involves ongoing and complex interplay between the activities of labor, work, and action.

Thinking Differently about Life: Design, Biomedicine, and "Negative Capability"

1. http://en.wikipedia.org/wiki/BowLingual, n.d.
2. http://myfriendagain.com, n.d.

Fashion Hacking

1. Slavoj Žižek, "The Interpassive Subject," accessed February 15,

2013, http://www.lacan.com/zizek-pompidou.htm, 1998; and Robert Pfaller "Little Gestures of Disappearance: Interpassivity and the Theory of Ritual," in *Psychoanalysis: Humanities, Philosophy, Psychotherapies*, No. 16, Winter-Spring 2003.
2. Sherry Schofield-Tomschin, "Home Sewing: Motivational Changes in the Twentieth Century," in Barbara Burman (ed.), *The Culture of Sewing* (Oxford: Berg, 1999); and Paul Atkinson, "Do It Yourself: Democracy and Design," *Journal of Design History*, Vol. 19, No. 1, 2006: 1–10.
3. Eric Raymond, "How to Become a Hacker," accessed February 15, 2013, http://www.catb.org/esr/faqs/hacker-howto.html, 2001. Site updated Sept. 2013.
4. William J. Mitchell, *Placing Words* (Cambridge: MIT Press, 2005), 118.
5. Christopher Kelty, *Two Bits: The Cultural Significance of Free Software* (Durham: Duke University Press, 2008), 94.
6. Mister Jalopy, "Owner's Manifesto," in *Make* Vol. 4, 2005.
7. Carl DiSalvo, *Adversarial Design* (Cambridge: MIT Press, 2012), 2.
8. Ibid., 13.
9. Alexander Galloway, *Protocol* (Cambridge: MIT Press, 2004), 95.
10. Jargon File, n.d., accessed February 15, 2013, http://catb.org/jargon/html/.
11. Otto von Busch and Karl Palmas, *Abstract Hacktivism: The Making of a Hacker Culture* (London: OpenMute, 2006).
12. Galloway, *Protocol*, 165
13. Ibid., 166.
14. Stephanie Syjuco, "Anatomy of a Counterfeit," *Craft*, January 2007, Vol. 2: 60.
15. Ibid., 58.
16. Ibid.
17. Otto von Busch, *Fashion-able: Hacktivism and Engaged Fashion Design* (Göteborg: ArtMonitor, 2008).
18. Elizabeth Shove et al., *The Design of Everyday Life* (Oxford: Berg, 2007), 9.
19. Christopher Frayling, *On Craftsmanship* (London: Oberon, 2011).
20. Ibid., 76.
21. Ibid., 80.
22. Amartya Sen, *Commodities and Capabilities* (Amsterdam: Elsevier, 1985).
23. Ibid., 9.
24. Ibid., 10.
25. Martha Nussbaum, *Creating Capabilities* (Cambridge: Belknap Press, 2011), 20.
26. Frayling, *On Craftsmanship*, 80.
27. Nussbaum, *Creating Capabilities*,

Digital Crafting and the Challenge to Material Practices

1. Mette Ramsgard Thomsen, K. Bech, and M. Tamke, "Imagining a Soft Tectonics" in *Fabricate: Proceeding of International Conference* (London: Riverside Architectural Press, 2001).
2. George Beylerian and Andrew Dent, *UltraMaterials: How Material Innovation Is Changing the World* (London: Thames and Hudson, 2007).
3. Mette Ramsgard Thomsen, M. Tamke, M. Burry, and J. Burry,

"Design Environments for Material Performance," *Design Modeling Symposium Berlin*, October 2011, 321–29.
4. A. Menges, "Integral Computational Design: Synthesizing Computation and Materialization in Architecture," in *AMIT International Journal for Architecture and Modern Information Technologies*, Vol. 4, No. 3, 2010.
5. H. Alpermann, E. Lafuente Hernández, and C. Gengnagel, "Case Studies of Arched Structures Using Actively Bent Elements," Conference Proceedings IASS-APCS Symposium, Seoul, 2012.
6. Ruben Suare, "Innovation through Accountability in the Design and Manufacturing of Material Effects," in Branko Kolarevic and Kevin Klinger (eds.), *Manufacturing Material Effects: Rethinking Design and Making in Architecture* (New York: Routledge, 2008), 211–22.
7. A. M. Stoneham and J. H. Harding, "Not Too Big, Not Too Small: The Appropriate Scale" in *Nature Materials* 2, 2003: 77.
8. Greg Lynn, "From Tectonics to Cooking in a Bag," in Greg Lynn and M. Foster Gage (eds.), *Composites, Surfaces and Software: High Performance Architecture* (New Haven: Yale School of Architecture, 2011), 20.

Petrified Curtains, Animate Architextiles

1. Roberto Calasso, *The Marriage of Cadmus and Harmony* (New York: Alfred A. Knopf, 1988), 99.
2. Ibid., 101.
3. Ibid., 97.
4. Ibid., 100.
5. Nicolas Bourriaud, *The Radicant* (New York: Lukas & Sternberg, 2009), 51.
6. Richard Sennett, *The Craftsman* (New Haven: Yale University Press, 2009), 9.
7. Ibid., 8.
8. Corinna Rossi, *Architecture and Mathematics in Ancient Egypt* (Cambridge: Cambridge University Press, 2004), 148–61, cited in Victoria Mitchell, "Drawing Threads from Sight to Site," *Textile: The Journal of Cloth and Culture*, Vol. 4, Issue 3, 2006: 347.
9. Gottfried Semper, trans. Harry Francis Mallgrave and Wolfgang Herrmann, *The Four Elements of Architecture* (Cambridge: Cambridge University Press, 1989), 103.
10. Ibid., 104.
11. Ibid.
12. E-mail from Mary Taylor Simeti, April 29, 2010.
13. Maria Ann Conelli, "S. Maria Assunta dei Gesuiti and Sacred Theater," *Daidalos*, September 15, 1988: 72.
14. Alison Hilton, "The Peasant House and Its Furnishings: Decorative Principles in Russian Folk Art," *The Journal of Decorative and Propaganda Arts*, Vol. 11, Issue 2, Winter 1989: 14.
15. Mark Garcia, "Prologue for a History and Theory of Architextiles," *Architectural Design (AD): Architextiles*, November/December 2006: 14.
16. Joan R. Branham, "Penetrating the Sacred: Breaches and Barriers in the Jerusalem Temple," in Sharon E. J. Gerstel, *Thresholds of the Sacred:*

Architectural, Art Historical, Liturgical, and Theological Perspectives on Religious Screens (Washington, DC: Dunbarton Oaks, distributed by Harvard University Press, 2006), 15.
17. Nicholas Constas, "Symeon of Thessalonike and the Theology of the Icon Screen," in Sharon E. J. Gerstel, *Thresholds of the Sacred: Architectural, Art Historical, Liturgical, and Theological Perspectives on Religious Screens* (Washington, DC: Dunbarton Oaks, distributed by Harvard University Press, 2006), 164–65.
18. Nikos A. Salinganos and Kenneth G. Madson II, "Architecture: Biological Form and Artificial Intelligence," in The Structurist, No. 45/46, 2005-06: 59.
19. Interview with Philip Beesley in his studio in Toronto, January 10, 2012.
20. Calasso, *The Marriage of Cadmus and Harmony*, p. 383.
21. François Roche, "@morphous MUTATIONS," 2000, accessed September 9, 2013, http://www.new-territories.com/roche%20text.htm.
22. Ibid.
23. Alison Stone, *Luce Irigaray and the Philosophy of Sexual Difference* (New York: Cambridge University Press, 2006), 194.

Shifting Geographies

1. http://pl.wikipedia.org/wiki/Sepólno (Wrocław), last modified in 2012, accessed August 8, 2013.
2. Sarah Brooks, "Design for Social Innovation: An Interview With Ezio Manzini (Part I)," July 26, 2011, accessed August 12, 2013, http://www.shareable.net/blog/design-for-social-innovation-an-interview-with-ezio-manzini.
3. This call for entries evolved into the 2009 exhibition *Insiders: Experiences, Practice, Know-How*, at the Museum of Contemporary Art in Bordeaux, France.
4. Call for entries to "*Insiders, folklore coming*," Arc en Rêve, Centre d'architecture, Bordeaux, 2 and 4.
5. For a fuller discussion of cosmopolitan contamination, see Kwame Anthony Appiah *Cosmopolitanism* (New Jersey: Princeton University Press, 2006), Chap. 7, 87–113.
6. Appiah, *Cosmopolitanism*, 2.
7. *Existenzminimum* literally means subsistence dwelling. It became associated with the political beliefs embodied in social housing built in the interwar period. These (largely German) architects insisted that amenities such as electricity, indoor bathrooms, and access to sunlight, fresh air, and gardens—which necessitated smaller, sparser living spaces—were the true minimal conditions for living. Political forces on the right believed these efforts were too opulent for the masses; forces on the left believed they would ameliorate class differences by offering a new standard of dwelling and living.
8. Scott Lash and Antoine Picon, in conversation with Kenny Cupers and Isabelle Doucet, "Agency and Architecture: How To Be Critical?" *Footprint*, Spring 2009: 10.

Urban Ecologies: Quatre systèmes de conception pour la fabrication de "la Cité"

1. Lisa Graumlich Costanza, Will Steffen, Carole Crumley, John Dearing, Kathy Hibbard, Rik Leemans, Charles Redman, and David Schimel, "Sustainability or Collapse: What Can We Learn from Integrating the History of Humans and the Rest of Nature?" Ambio, Vol. 36, No. 7, Royal Swedish Academy of Sciences, November 2007: 522.

2. Andy Merrifield, "Citizens' Agora: The New Urban Question," Radical Philosophy, No. 179, May/June 2013: 33.

3. Tim Arango, "Park Defender Helped Set Off Turkey's Crisis," New York Times, June 4, 2013, http://www.nytimes.com/2013/06/05/world/europe/istanbul-protests-started-over-trees.html.

4. Merrifield, "Citizens' Agora," 33.

5. Ibid., 32–3.

6. Ibid., 33.

7. Ibid.

8. Timothy Morton, The Ecological Thought (Cambridge: Harvard University Press, 2010), 4.

9. Robert Neuwirth, Stealth of Nations: The Global Rise of the Informal Economy (New York: Pantheon, 2011).

10. Ibid., 17.

11. Robert Neuwirth, "Toward That Better City," in Timothy Mennel, Jo Steffins, and Christopher Klemek (eds.), Block by Block: Jane Jacobs and the Future of New York (New York: Princeton Architectural Press, 2008), 30.

12. Neuwirth, Stealth of Nations, 18–19.

13. Ibid., 27–28.

14. Daniel Kemmis, Community and the Politics of Place (Norman: University of Oklahoma Press, 1990), 6.

15. Angela Sanchez, "Social Urbanism: The Metamorphosis of Medellín," Barcelona Metropolis, Winter 2010, http://w2.bcn.cat/bcnmetropolis/arxiu/en/page6dde.html.

16. Ibid.

17. Michael Kimmelman, "Who Rules the Street in Cairo? The Residents Who Build It," New York Times, April 27, 2013.

18. Cisco Systems, www.cisco.com.

19. William Cronon, Nature's Metropolis: Chicago and the Great West (New York: W.W. Norton, 1992), 268.

20. Carl Smith, City Water, City Life: Water and the Infrastructure of Ideas in Urbanizing Philadelphia, Boston, and Chicago (Chicago: University of Chicago Press, 2013), 162.

21. Stephen Graham and Simon Marvin, Splintering Urbanism: Networked Infrastructures, Technological Mobilities and the Urban Condition (London: Routledge, 2001).

22. Rob Van Kranenberg, The Internet of Things: A Critique of Ambient Technology and the All-Seeing Network of RFID (Amsterdam: Network Notebooks, 2008), 15.

23. Lewis Hyde, Common as Air: Revolution, Art and Ownership (New York: Farrar, Strauss and Giroux, 2010), 77.

The Trans/Local Geography of Olympic Dissent: Activism, Design, Affect

1. According to Article 53, "no kind of demonstration or political, religious or racial propaganda is permitted in any Olympic sites, venues or other areas,"

http://www.olympic.org/Documents/olympic_charter_en.pdf.

2. Monroe E. Price, "On Seizing the Olympic Platform," in Monroe E. Price and Daniel Dayan, Owning the Olympics: Narratives of the New China (Ann Arbor: University of Michigan Press, 2008), 86–116.

3. Daniel Dayan, "Beyond Media Events: Disenchantment, Derailment, Disruption," in Price and Dayan, Owning the Olympics, 391–402.

4. For a discussion on a wide range of criticism of Olympic design in relation to the Athens 2004 Olympics, see Jilly Traganou, "Mobile Architects, Static Ideas: Santiago Calatrava in 2004 Athens Olympics," in Jilly Traganou and M. Mitrasinovic (eds.), Travel, Space, Architecture, (Aldershot: Ashgate, 2009).

5. Kristine Toohey and A. J. Veal, The Olympic Games: A Social Science Perspective (Wallingford: CAB International), 88.

6. http://www.nytimes.com/1993/11/21/us/plan-for-olympic-park-spurs-atlanta-protest.html.

7. http://www.guardian.co.uk/sydney/story/0,7369,367879,00.html.

8. http://chronicle.augusta.com/stories/2004/05/01/oly_414177.shtml.

9. As Luis Rodriguez Morales (head of the Design Theory and Processes Department. Universidad Autónoma Metropolitana Cuajimalpa in México) discussed in the conference Design/History/Revolution at Parsons The New School for Design in 2011, the Mexico 1968 graphic design program represented "the need to reject the idea of 'modern,'" in contrast to "the government's aspiration to establish a modern image of the country. . . . The graphics for the Olympic Games gave birth to Graphic Design as a profession in Mexico."

10. Lance Wyman and Milton F. Curry, "Branding a Cityscape: Mexico City 1968 Lance Wyman," interview in Productive Critical, Journal of Architecture, Urbanism and Critical Theory 1, 2011, Theoretical Action, 92.

11. Grupo Mira, La gráfica del 68: homenaje al movimiento estudiantil (Mexico "City: Ediciones Zurda,1982

12 http://www.wolffolins.com/work/london-2012.

13. Interview with Jilly Traganou, July 5, 2012, and included in "Because," an event presentation at Wolff Olins office, London, July 4, 2012.

14. See for example, http://www.telegraph.co.uk/news/1553851/Your-2012-logo-alternatives.html.

15. For more information on the London Inspire Program see http://www.london2012.com/get-involved/inspire-programme/inspire-programme-case-studies.php.

16. Jilly Traganou, "Understanding Olympic Design," in OUP Blog, Oxford University Press's Academic Insights for the Thinking World, http://blog.oup.com/2012/08/understanding-olympic-design/, 2012.

17. Jules Boykoff, "The Anti-Olympics," New Left Review 67, January-February 2011: 41–59.

18. See following sites: http://takethesquare.net/2012/08/05/international-newsletter-5a-occupynewsletter/ and http://www.guardian.co.uk/environment/bike-blog/2013/mar/18/police-activism.

19. Emily Graham, "The Regeneration Games: Development and

Displacement in London, 2012" (Undergraduate Thesis, Yale University, Sociology, 2013), 27–28, 32–40.

20. Hilary Powell and Isaac Marrero-Guilamon, Art of Dissent: Adventures in London's Olympic State (London: Marshgate, 2012), 68.

21. The platform remained in place from 6:00 a.m. on June 12, 2008, to June 14, when it was removed by the Olympic Delivery Authority. See http://www.dezeen.com/2008/08/12/point-of-view-by-office-for-subversive-architecture/.

22. Powell and Guilamon, Art of Dissent, 35–39.

23. A good example of this would be the campaign led by Jane Jacobs against Robert Moses's plans to build the Lower Manhattan Expressway.

24. Victoria Hattam, "The Color of Identification," (Unpublished paper, 2011).

25. Susan Yelavich, introduction to Design as Future-Making (New York: Bloomsbury, 2014)., 15.

26. Hattam.

27. Yelavich, 15.

28. Some of these design acts are directly related to how the Olympics function, and others serve representational needs. The implementation of the Olympics requires building new athletic venues and athlete housing as well as providing infrastructure for the smooth circulation of attendees. The Olympics also necessitate the printing of large volumes of promotional and supporting material, while in today's commodified world they are supplemented by the production of all sorts of paraphernalia, from mascots to pins and collectors' items. Last, participating nations pay great attention to the fashioning of their athletes' bodies during the opening and closing ceremonies and place marketing campaigns that are intended to reinvigorate their national perception by the global public.

Garments as Agents of Change: Lucia Cuba

1. David Gilbert, "From Paris to Shanghai: The Changing Geographies of Fashion's World Cities," in Christopher Breward and David Gilbert (eds.), Fashion's World Cities (Oxford and New York: Berg, 2006), 3.

2. Barbara Vinken, Fashion Zeitgeist: Trends and Cycles in the Fashion System (Oxford and New York: Berg, 2005), 35.

3. Ibid., 143.

4. Hazel Clark, "Conceptual Fashion," in Adam Geczy and Vicki Karaminas, Fashion and Art (London and New York: Berg, 2012), 67–75.

5. www.articulo6.pe [accessed June 19, 2013].

6. "We Have Woken Up," an interview by Lucia Cuba with Aurelia Paccohuanca and Micaela Flores, videotaped by Mauricio Delfin, January, 2012, accessed June 19, 2013, http://vimeo.com/422817777.

7. "Lucia Cuba on Strength and Politics," Pas un Autre, June 22, 2013, http://www.pasunautre.com/2012/06/22/interview-lucia-cuba-on-gender-strength-and-politics/.

8. www.luco.com, accessed June 19, 2013.

9. www.proyectogamarra.pe, accessed June 19, 2013.

10. Clark, "Conceptual Fashion," 70–72.

11. Amanda Cohen, "Fashioning a Political Case," The Genteel, posted October 5, 2012, accessed February 25, 2013, http://www.thegenteel.com/articles/society/fashioning-a-political-case.

12. Eric Wilson, "The New Masters of Parsons," New York Times, May 23, 2012, accessed April 6, 2013. http://www.nytimes.com/2012/05/24/fashion/the-new-masters-of-parsons.html?_r=0.

13. Still shots at http://on.mtv.com/TSQ4a4 and access to the complete interview http://youtu.be/bePV30_aExk.

14. http://www.motherjones.com/politics/2012/04/north-carolina-sterilization-eugenics-photos, accessed June 18, 2013.

15. Wilson, 2012.

Up-Ending Systems

1. Zygmunt Bauman, Liquid Modernity (Malden: Polity Press, 2000), 14.

2. Michael Taussig, The Nervous System (New York: Routledge, 1992).

3. Fredric Jameson, The Geopolitical Aesthetic: Cinema and Space in the World System (Bloomington: Indiana University Press, 1992), 2.

4. Ulrich Beck discusses this at length in his work, including his 2006 lecture, "Living in the World Risk Society," published in Economy and Society 35(3): 329–45.

5. Do Tank, http://dotank.nyls.edu/about-the-do-tank/.

6. Ezio Manzini (February 6, 2013) "Small, Local, Open, and Connected: Resilient Systems and Sustainable Qualities," Design Observer: Change Observer, accessed August 29, 2013. http://changeobserver.designobserver.com/feature/small-local-open-and-connected-resilient-systems-and-sustainable-qualities/37670/ See also DESIS, http://www.desis-network.org/content/thematic-clusters-page.

7. Bel Reed, "Design for Public Good—A Report for the European Commission," SEE Bulletin, Issue 9, June 2013: 13.

8. Peter Hall, "IDEO Takes on the Government: The Nimble Consultancy Brings Design Thinking to Political Structures in Desperate Need of Reinvention," Metropolis, June 2011.

9. Jaron Lanier, You Are Not a Gadget: A Manifesto (New York: Vintage, 2010). Lanier particularly objects to systems like Web 2.0 or MIDI, the musical trigger system, which routinizes music production and eliminates improvisational play. Both are examples of systems that block alternative ways of doing and making things.

10. As Brian Massumi notes, "Possibility is a variation implicit in what a thing can be said to be when it is on target. Potential is the immanence of a thing to its still indeterminate variation, under way." Parables for the Virtual: Movement, Affect, Sensation (Durham: Duke University Press, 2002), 9. It should also be noted that "potential" has its origin in "power," something "which is not actualized until put into activity." Aristotle, Poetics, trans. Richard Janko (Indianapolis: Hackett Publishing, 1987), 218.

11. See Walter Benjamin's ninth thesis on history from "Theses on the

Philosophy of History" in *Illuminations* (New York: Schocken, 1969), 257–8.
12. Peter-Paul Verbeek, *What Things Do: Philosophical Reflections on Technology, Agency, and Design*. (University Park: Pennsylvania State University Press, 2005), 218.
13. Otto von Busch, "Research Navigations," *The Journal of Artistic Research*, 2011, accessed September 28, 2012. http://www.researchcatalogue.net/view/7967/7968.
14. Jacques Rancière, *The Politics of Aesthetics: The Distribution of the Sensible* (Continuum: New York, 2007).
15. Jacques Rancière, "Contemporary Art and the Politics of Aesthetics," in Beth Hinderliter, William Kaizen, Vered Maimon, Jaleh Mansoor, and Seth McCormick (eds.), *Communities of Sense: Rethinking Aesthetics and Politics* (Durham: Duke University Press, 2009), 49.
16. Ibid.
17. See the chapter, "*Vita Activa* and the Modern Age," in Hannah Arendt, *The Human Condition* (Chicago: University of Chicago, [1958] 1998).
18. Arendt, *The Human Condition*, 246.

Reasons to Be Cheerful

1. Roland Barthes, trans. Stephen Heath, "From Work to Text," in *Image/Music/Text* (Glasgow: Collins, 1971).
2. Francis Fukuyama, *The End of History and the Last Man* (New York: Free Press, 1992). Fukayama was substantively wrong—"What we may be witnessing is not just the end of the Cold War, or the passing of a particular period of postwar history, but the end of history as such. . . . That is, the end point of mankind's ideological evolution and the universalization of Western liberal democracy as the final form of human government"—yet correct in that as the notion of progress except in quantitative economic and technological forms disappeared so to have real notions of the future. The end of history therefore means, the end of the future.
3. I use the term "affirmative" in a particular sense that is the opposite in many ways of how Marcuse used it in in his 1937 essay "Culture as Affirmation." Marcuse was concerned to define the ways in which bourgeois culture more or less directly (and critically) affirmed bourgeois society. After a long period in which affirmation in Marcuse's sense has been transmuted into varieties of what I name as prosaic nihilisms, it becomes possible to use the concept again in a critical manner. This is the mode in which it is used in this essay, i.e., as the counter to nihilism or resignation and in something of the sense that Adorno and Horkheimer intended when they wrote in the preface to *Dialectic of Enlightenment*, "today critical thought (which does abandon its commitment even in the face of progress) demands support for the residues of freedom, and for tendencies towards true humanism, even if these seem powerless in regard to the main course of history," (London, Verso, 1979), ix–x. The term is used actively, too, in the sense too that Badiou deploys it in his lecture published as *Philosophy in the Present* (London: Verso, 2009). The latter is discussed in the body of the essay. See the concluding section to chapter one.
4. Heidegger's savage post-war comment, "even the immense suffering that surrounds the earth is unable to awaken transformation," applies today not only to the suffering of others but to the future suffering of ourselves. Not even this motivates our beginning to act otherwise.
5. As the architect Peter Eisenman said of this period, today we live within "a new sensibility born in the rupture of 1945. This sensibility was neither predicated in the tenets of modernism nor brought about by their failure to achieve the utopias of the present. Rather, it emerged from something unforeseen to modernism, in the fact that not since the advent of modern science, technology and medicine has a generation faced, as it does today, the potential extinction of an entire civilization The Futility of Objects." *Harvard Architectural Review* 3, Winter 1984, 65.
6. "This week it is announced that the concentration of carbon dioxide in the atmosphere has passed 400 parts per million for the first time in 4.5m years. Since it is continuing to rise at a rate of about 2 parts per million every year this means that, on present course, it could be 800 parts per million by the end of the century. At that point talk of 'mitigating' the catastrophic risks of climate change would be moot." "We will watch the rise in greenhouse gases until it is too late to do anything about it." Martin Wolf, *Financial Times*, May 14, 2103, and "The Climate Change Skeptics Have Won," May 21, 2013.
7. "Arctic melt is 'economic time bomb,'" *Financial Times*, July 25, 2013, 4. A recent report puts the economic cost of Arctic melt through higher methane emissions "at up to $60tn." However, 80 percent of the damage will occur in the developing countries. This means that the developing world will be left to itself. A safe prediction of this century is ethnocide on scales that will make the last (murderous) century appear relatively benign.
8. It is entirely typical in this respect that the only concentrated international action in the last decade was the brief moments of dealing with the banking crisis in 2008.
9. By the late 1930s, Heidegger was already disinclined to see technology purely as such. "This name includes all the areas of beings which equip the whole of beings: objectified nature, the business of culture, manufactured politics, and the gloss of ideals overlying everything. Thus 'technology' does not signify here the separate areas of the production and equipment of machines." Martin Heidegger, *Overcoming Metaphysics* (Chicago: University Chicago Press, 1977), 93.
10. Herbert Simon, in the late 1960s, understood it this way: "The world we live in today is much more a man-made, or artificial, world than it is a natural world. Almost every element in our environment shows evidence of human artifice. The temperature in which we spend most of our hours is kept artificially at 20 degrees Celsius; the humidity is added to or taken from the air we breathe; and the impurities we inhale are largely produced (and filtered) by man. Moreover for most of us—the white-collared ones—the significant part of the environment consists mostly of strings of artifacts called 'symbols' that we receive through eyes and ears in the form of written and spoken language and that we pour out into the environment—as I am now doing—by mouth or hand. The laws that govern these strings of symbols, the laws that govern the occasions on which we emit and receive them, the determinants of their content are all consequences of our collective artifice. One may object that I exaggerate the artificiality of our world. Man must obey the law of gravity as surely as does a stone, and as a living organism man must depend for food, and in many other ways, on the world of biological phenomena. I shall plead guilty to overstatement, while protesting that the exaggeration is slight. To say that an astronaut, or even an airplane pilot, is obeying the law of gravity, hence is a perfectly natural phenomenon, is true, but its truth calls for some sophistication in what we mean by 'obeying' a natural law. Aristotle did not think it natural for heavy things to rise or light ones to fall (Physics, Book IV); but presumably we have a deeper understanding of 'natural' than he did. So too we must be careful about equating 'biological' with 'natural.' A forest may be a phenomenon of nature; a farm certainly is not. The very species upon which we depend for our food—our corn and our cattle—are artifacts of our ingenuity. A plowed field is no more part of nature than an asphalted street—and no less. These examples set the terms of our problem, for those things we call artifacts are not apart from nature. They have no dispensation to ignore or violate natural law." And Simon adds, in a point we need to consider deeply: "At the same time they are adapted to human goals and purposes. They are what they are in order to satisfy our desire to fly or to eat well. As our aims change, so too do our artifacts—and vice versa." Herbert Simon, *Sciences of the Artificial*, (Cambridge: MIT Press, 1996), 2–3
11. In the same way, technology, which begins in the factory gradually moves ever closer to the subject (the home, consciousness, the body) to the point where today the distinction exists only artificially, for heuristic convenience, not by nature. Though we dislike acknowledging its implications, the human being is today fundamentally made.
12. Which means also that we cannot think past that which historically determines how we act. A culture that prides itself on dissembling history is in fact in thrall to it: all the more so that it pretends to despise it.
13. Simon, *Sciences*, 131.
14. Ibid., 3.
15. In turn, we now see the universe revealed as less determinate and law-like, more radically contingent than we imagined (in the sense that the configuration of the universe itself—and its laws—are not immune to the law of the configuration of all things; that they are not simply law determined but are the outcome of the contingent negotiation of forces).
16. Culture was what made people willingly do what they must do (that was called "ethos," "values," or "standards"—cognitive or cathectic) or rendered their actions regular independently of their will (that was called "learning" or "acculturation"). Zygmunt Bauman in Z. Bauman and Keith Tester, *Conversations with Zygmunt Bauman* (Cambridge: Polity, 2001), 31–32.
17. Ibid. We can add an earlier formulation of the same concepts: Culture pushes at human experience in that it brings into relief the discord between ideal and real . . . it exposes the limitations and imperfections of reality . . . it conjoins and blends knowledge and interests . . . culture stands and falls on the assumption that accomplished reality is not the most authoritative much less is it the only object of interested knowledge. The unfinishedness, incompleteness, imperfectness of the real, its infirmity and frailty, undergirds the status of culture in the same way as the authority of the real buttresses science. Zygmunt Bauman, *Culture as Praxis* (London: Sage, 1982).
18. Ibid.
19. Simon, *Sciences*, 6.
20. If the artificial is a mediation between the "inner" environment of the artifact itself (its configuration) and the "outer" environments to which it refers and in relation to which (on behalf of which) it must act then, once we see these environments not in the singular and as matter of physical law (Simon) but in their existential, social and ecological pluralities then it is obvious that the relations between an any artifact or system (physical or political) and (i) human subjects in social relations; (ii) existing artifacts likewise in complex social, technical, and economic relations (and operating within complex and irreducible systems of power; and (iii) natural laws and conditions, is *necessarily* a matter of complex negotiation between irreconcilable or incommensurable moments and demands.
21. This is Elaine Scarry's argument. See especially chapter 5 of Scarry, *The Body in Pain* (Oxford: Oxford University Press, 1985).
22. Technology seeks to dissolve incommensurability or negotiation by thinking technologies on the basis of their putative operation in a law-determined, and (ideally) in socially and environmentally null (abstracted) world. Just so can one create systems of "bounded rationality"—which are in many ways the pre-requisite for successful action. At extreme this allows for the technology to be determined, as far as possible, on the basis of single ideal representation—a mathematical equation that establishes performative certainty *before* it is configuratively codified.
23. Nuclear technology is the obvious instance.
24. The last place where such distinctions are still institutionalized are the universities whose litany of major subjects taught has barely altered over the last century.
25. The designer Jamer Hunt offers some acute observations on this condition.
Beginning by noting that science historian and theorist Donna Haraway, exploring the dissolution of this boundary as far back as 1985, prophetically declared, "Late twentieth-century machines have made thoroughly ambiguous the difference between natural and

artificial, mind and body, self-developing and externally designed ... our machines are disturbingly lively, and we ourselves frighteningly inert." He continues: "The designed, artificial world that envelops us is coming alive with communicative possibilities. There was a time when our tools of communication were distinct from our bodies: we spoke into a telephone wired into the walls of our home, or we hunted and pecked and clicked at a keyboard to type data into a personal computer. That era is vanishing as quickly as it arrived. Instead we are drifting into a new alignment, in both mind and body, with technology that is far more immersive, encompassing, and confounding. Surrounded by synthetic voices that talk to us and near-invisible sensors that observe and learn us, we are entering an age of uncanny technologies. These animated electronic encounters sketch the contours of an evolving landscape, illuminating the psychological and political implications of our warm, wet embrace of technology. We believe we are deft at negotiating the thinning boundary between human and machine, but in the thrumming traffic we are often left grasping at electronic shadows. Jamer Hunt, "Nervous Systems and Anxious Infrastructures," in Paola Antonelli (ed.), Talk to Me (New York: MOMA, 2011), 48.
26. Kevin Kelly, What Technology Wants (New York: Penguin, 2010), 270.
27. The continuing, even increasing, relevance of Simon's The Sciences of the Artificial is that his interests in programming and psychology lead him early to this understanding, hence his emphasis on the artificiality of (for example) economic rationality, the logic of thought processes, procedures of memory, and learning.
28. A quotation from Philip Rawson may suffice. "To their makers and users pots have always been a kind of two-way revelation, first of man to himself as a creative and independently working agent, and second of the world to man as a medium, imbued with 'reality', which he is able to transform." Ceramics (Oxford: OUP, 1971). In other words, artifice is the realm of revealing to humans the character of themselves as acting-agents and of the world as that which is capable of transformation and adaptation.
29. Simon, Sciences, 111.
30. Alain Badiou, Ethics (London: Verso, 2001), p. 15. Adapted quotation.
31. Alain Badiou, Philosophy in the Present (London, Verso, 2009), 81.

Design Away
1. Republished in Richard Buchanan & Victor Margolin (eds.), Discovering Design, (Chicago: University of Chicago Press, 1995).
2. Tony Fry, Design Futuring: Sustainability, Ethics, and New Practice (Oxford: Berg, 2010).3. According to Aristotle, despite the fact that materials have agency enough to be considered one of the four causes of any product of techne, the key difference between a tree and table is that the tree can (re)produce itself and so keeps becoming what it is, whereas a table must be produced by some thing (the efficient cause, the human) other than itself, and

stops becoming once the final form has been "finished." In other words, killing natural resources is essential to making things that stay as we designers intend them to (which of course they do not, because being dead is still an entropic process of decay and dispersement).
4. This is somewhat exaggerated. In the case of lumber, branches and leaves can be composted to assist the growing of other plants; sawdust from mills is often combusted to generate the heat used to season timber.
5. "MIPS and Ecological Rucksacks in Designing the Future," Environmentally Conscious Design and Inverse Manufacturing, 2001. Proceedings EcoDesign 2001: Second International Symposium.
6. This is the famous claim in the opening paragraph of Design for the Real World (New York, Pantheon, 1971).
7. "Disposability, Graphic Design, Waste, and Style" in Michael Bierut (ed.), Looking Closer: Critical Writings on Graphic Design—Volume 1 (New York: Skyhorse, 1994).
8. This point is also made by Pantzar cited in the previous note, but related is Jodi Forlizzi's notion of a "product ecology." See "Product Ecology: Understanding Social Product Use and Supporting Design Culture," Interaction Institute Paper 35 (2007), http://repository.cmu.edu/hcii/35), and Erik Stolterman and colleagues' notion of a "device landscape." See Erik Stolterman, Heekyoung Jung, Will Ryan, and Marty Siegel, "Device Landscapes: A New Challenge to Interaction Design and HCI Research," Journal of Korean Society of Design Research, Vol.26, No.2 (2013).
9. In fact, designing affordances is itself a matter of creative reinforcement or destructive innovation: should an interaction make use of existing conventions, whether habitual actions, symbol conventions, expected feedback, or perceptual saliences; or can the designer boldly create new types of interactions, thereby destroying existing ones?
10. This opposition between attending-toward as always also an attending-from is in Michael Polanyi, The Tacit Dimension (London: Routledge, 1966).
11. The opposition between ready-to-hand—the hammer withdrawn into the act of hammering—and present-at-hand—the broken hammer now manifest as wood and stone—is in Division of I of Being and Time (1927), but particularly see Graham Harman, Tool Being (Chicago, Open Court, 2002).
12. Don Ihde, Technics and Praxis (Dordrecht: D. Reidel Publishing Company, 1979).
13. See for example Rob Hopkins The Transition Handbook: From Oil Dependence to Local Resilience (London, Chelsea Green Publishing, 2008).
14. In addition to Design Futuring cited in note 2, see also the earlier account of the way the history of twentieth-century design as destruction of possible futures as result of what those modernist designs designed: Tony Fry, A New Design Philosophy: An Introduction to Defuturing (Sydney: UNSW Press, 1999).

15. See for instance Nicola Morelli, "Technical Innovation and Resource Efficiency: A Model for Australian Household Appliances," Journal of Sustainable Product Design Vol.1 (2001). However, Tim Cooper notes in his introduction to Longer Lasting Products: Alternatives to the Throwaway Society (Burlington: Ashgate, 2010) that the latest appliances, while more energy efficient in core components, often are not overall more energy efficient due to increased features, size, etc; in addition newer appliances, as we have discussed, tend to also require other newer products in their "device landscape," so the embodied energy involved is not just that of the product itself.
16. Though carpeting a well-oriented thermal mass can destroy its passive solar capacities.
17. "Is Your Innovation Really an Unnovation?" Harvard Business Review Blog Network May 27, 2009, http://blogs.hbr.org/haque/2009/05/unnovation.html.
18. James Pierce "Undesigning Technology: Considering the Negation of Design by Design," Proceedings of the 2012 ACM annual conference on Human Factors in Computing Systems (CHI '12). Pierce's schema is more complex than I have indicated; it aims to capture not quantities of restriction, but qualities, whether in relation to perceptions (inhibition), practices (displacement) or possibilities (foreclosure). It also aims to be less deterministically materialistic in its account of the undesigning that design can do.
19. The following is based on an unpublished paper on "Prefigurative Criticism" from the early 1990s by Tony Fry and Anne-Marie Willis. That paper extracted a generalizable method from a critical project entitled Towers of Torture, in which a series of artists were commissioned to create sculptures that would associate models of a building an Australian multimillionaire planned to build in Sydney with his investments in Argentinian telecommunications companies known at the time to be assisting the government with police state activities. When it was exposed that the multimillionaire had asked the University of Sydney, where the exhibition was being held, to be shut down, the project received widespread media attention. The multimillionaire never built that building and was later jailed for corruption.
20. Everett Rogers, Diffusion of Innovations, 5th Edition (New York: Free Press, 2003).
21. Donald Norman The Design of Everyday Things (New York: Basic Books, 2002), 32.
22. For a survey with some reference to sustainable design see Elizabeth Shove, Mika Pantzar, and Matt Watson, The Dynamics of Social Practice (London: Sage, 2012).
23. Theodore Schatzki, The Timespace of Human Activity: On Performance, Society and History as Indeterminate Teleological Events (New York: Rowman & Littlefield, 2010).
24. See the publications associated with the Eternally Yours project: Time in Design: Product Value Sustenance (Rotterdam, 010 Publishers, 2004).
25. See the account of the FRIA concept in Ursula Tischner and

Martin Charter's chapter "Sustainable Product Design," in Martin Charter and Ursula Tischner (eds.), Sustainable Solutions: Developing Products and Services for the Future (Sheffield: Greenleaf, 2001).
26. Dolores Hayden, The Grand Domestic Revolution: A History of Feminist Designs for Homes, Neighborhoods, and Cities (Cambridge: MIT, 1982).
27. Anique Hommels, Unbuilding Cities: Obduracy in Urban Sociotechnical Change (Cambridge: MIT, 2008).
28. Arnold Tukker and Ursula Tischner (eds.), New Business for Old Europe: Product-Service Development, Competitiveness and Sustainability (Sheffield: Greenleaf, 2006).

"When we understand that slide, we'll have won the war." Systemic Complexity and the Irregularities of Scale
1. Sarah Lyall, "Missing Micrograms Set a Standard on Edge," New York Times, February 13, 2011.
2. Elisabeth Bumiller, "We Have Met the Enemy and He Is PowerPoint," New York Times, April 27, 2010.
3. Paul Virilio, "The Lost Dimension" (New York: Semiotext(e), 1991): 30.
4. Frits Went, "The Size of Man" American Scientist 56 (1968): 400–13.
5. For complete audio book, see http://www.longtail.com/the_long_tail/2009/07/free-for-free-first-ebook-and-audiobook-versions-released.html.
6. Carolyn Kellogg, "Chris Anderson's Almost-'Free', Kindle Price Drop and More Book News," Los Angeles Times, July 9, 2009, http://latimesblogs.latimes.com/jacketcopy/2009/07/chris-andersons-almost-free-and-more-book-news.html [accessed January 31, 2013].
7. Gilles Duranton and Matthew A. Turner, "The Fundamental Law of Road Congestion: Evidence from US Cities," American Economic Review 101(6) (2011): 2616–52.
8. Lance Gunderson, C.S. Holling, Lowell Pritchard Jr., and Garry D. Peterson, "Resilience of Large-Scale Resource Systems," in Lance Gunderson and Lowell Pritchard, Jr. (eds.), Resilience and the Behavior of Large-Scale Systems, (Washington: Island Press, 2002), 13.
9. Tom McNichol, "Roads Gone Wild," Wired 12.12, December 2004, accessed January 31, 2013, http://www.wired.com/wired/archive/12.12/traffic.html

ENDNOTES

249

BIBLIOGRAPHY

Antonelli, Paola (ed.). *Talk to Me.* New York: MOMA, 2011.

Appadurai, Arjun. *Modernity at Large: Cultural Dimensions of Globalization,* "Public Worlds," Vol. 1. Minneapolis: University of Minneapolis Press, 1996.

Appiah, Kwame Anthony. *Cosmopolitanism.* New Jersey: Princeton University Press, 2006.

Arendt, Hannah. *The Human Condition.* Chicago: University of Chicago, [1958] 1998.

Badiou, Alain. *Ethics.* London: Verso, 2001.

———. *Philosophy in the Present.* London: Verso, 2009.

Balsamo, Anne. *Designing Culture: The Technological Imagination at Work.* Durham: Duke University Press, 2011.

Barthes, Roland, trans. Stephen Heath. *Image/Music/Text.* Glasgow: Collins, 1971.

Bauman, Zygmunt, and Keith Tester. *Conversations with Zygmunt Bauman.* Cambridge: Polity, 2001.

Bauman, Zygmunt. *Culture as Praxis.* London: Sage, 1982.

———. *Liquid Modernity.* Malden: Polity Press, 2000.

Benjamin, Walter. *Illuminations.* New York: Schocken, 1969.

Beylerian, George, and A. Dent. *UltraMaterials: How Material Innovation Is Changing the World.* London, Thames and Hudson, 2007.

Bierut, Michael (ed.). *Looking Closer: Critical Writings on Graphic Design—Volume 1.* New York: Skyhorse, 1994.

Bourriaud, Nicolas. *The Radicant.* New York: Lukas & Sternberg, 2009.

Breward, Christopher, and David Gilbert (eds.). *Fashion's World Cities.* Oxford and New York: Berg, 2006.

Buchanan, Richard, and Victor Margolin (eds.). *Discovering Design.* Chicago: University of Chicago Press, 1995.

Burman, Barbara (ed.). *The Culture of Sewing.* Oxford: Berg, 1999.

Calasso, Roberto. *The Marriage of Cadmus and Harmony.* New York: Alfred A. Knopf, 1988.

Charter, Martin, and Ursula Tischner (eds.). *Sustainable Solutions: Developing Products and Services for the Future.* Sheffield: Greenleaf, 2001.

Cooper, Tim. *Longer Lasting Products: Alternatives to the Throwaway Society.* Burlington: Ashgate, 2010.

Crary, Jonathan, and Sanford Kwinter (eds.). *Incorporations.* New York: Zone, 1992.

Cronon, William. *Nature's Metropolis: Chicago and the Great West.* New York: W.W. Norton, 1992.

Dilnot, Clive. *Ethics? Design?* Chicago: The Archeworks Papers, Vol. 1, No. 2, 2005.

DiSalvo, Carl. *Adversarial Design.* Cambridge: MIT Press, 2012.

Frayling, Christopher. *On Craftsmanship.* London: Oberon, 2011.

Fry, Tony. *Design Futuring: Sustainability, Ethics, and New Practice.* Oxford: Berg, 2010.

———. *A New Design Philosophy: An Introduction to Defuturing.* Sydney: UNSW Press, 1999.

Fukuyama, Francis. *The End of History and the Last Man .* New York: Free Press, 1992.

Galloway, Alexander. *Protocol.* Cambridge: MIT Press, 2004.

Geczy, Adam, and Vicki Karaminas. *Fashion and Art.* London and New York: Berg, 2012.

Gerstel, Sharon E. J. *Thresholds of the Sacred: Architectural, Art Historical, Liturgical, and Theological Perspectives on Religious Screens.* Washington, DC: Dunbarton Oaks, distributed by Harvard University Press, 2006.

Goodman, Nelson. *Ways of World-Making.* Cambridge, Mass: Hackett Publishing Company, 1978.

Graham, Stephen, and Simon Marvin. *Splintering Urbanism: Networked Infrastructures, Technological Mobilities and the Urban Condition.* London: Routledge, 2001.

Harman, Graham. *Tool Being.* Chicago: Open Court, 2002.

Hayden, Dolores. *The Grand Domestic Revolution: A History of Feminist Designs for Homes, Neighborhoods and Cities.* Cambridge: MIT, 1982.

Heidegger, Martin. *Overcoming Metaphysics.* Chicago: University of Chicago Press, 1977.

Hinderliter, Beth, William Kaizen, Vered Maimon, Jaleh Mansoor, and Seth McCormick (eds.). *Communities of Sense: Rethinking Aesthetics and Politics.* Durham: Duke University Press, 2009.

Hommles, Anique. *Unbuilding Cities: Obduracy in Urban Sociotechnical Change,* Cambridge: MIT, 2008.

Hopkins, Rob. *The Transition Handbook: From Oil Dependence to Local Resilience.* London: Chelsea Green Publishing, 2008.

Hyde, Lewis. *Common as Air: Revolution, Art, and Ownership.* New York: Farrar, Strauss and Giroux, 2010.

Ihde, Don. *Technics and Praxis.* Dordrecht: D. Reidel Publishing Company, 1979.

Jameson, Frederic. *The Geopolitical Aesthetic: Cinema and Space in the World System.* Bloomington: Indiana University Press, 1992.

Kelly, Kevin. *What Technology Wants.* New York: Penguin, 2010.

Kelly, Christopher. *Two Bits: The Cultural Significance of Free Software.* Durham: Duke University Press, 2008.

Kemmis, Daniel. *Community and the Politics of Place.* Norman: University of Oklahoma Press, 1990.

Kolarevic, Branko, and Kevin Klinger (eds.). *Manufacturing Material Effects: Rethinking Design and Making in Architecture.* New York: Routledge, 2008.

Lanier, Jaron. *You Are Not a Gadget: A Manifesto.* New York: Vintage, 2010.

Massumi, Brian. *Parables for the Virtual: Movement, Affect, Sensation.* Durham: Duke University Press, 2002.

Mennel, Timothy, Jo Steffins, and Christopher Klemek (eds.). *Block by Block: Jane Jacobs and the Future of New York.* New York: Princeton Architectural Press, 2008.

Mills, Č. Wright. *The Politics of Truth: The Writings of C. Wright Mills.* New York: Oxford University Press, [1958] 2008.

———. *The Sociological Imagination.* New York: Oxford University Press, [1959] 2000.

Mitchell, William J. *Placing Words.* Cambridge: MIT Press, 2005.

Morton, Timothy. *The Ecological Thought.* Cambridge: Harvard University Press, 2010.

Neuwirth, Robert. *Stealth of Nations: The Global Rise of the Informal Economy.* New York: Pantheon, 2011.

Norman, Donald. *The Design of Everyday Things.* New York: Basic Books, 2002.

Nussbaum, Martha. *Creating Capabilities.* Cambridge: Belknap Press, 2011.

Polanyi, Michael. *The Tacit Dimension.* London: Routledge, 1966.

Powell, Hilary, and Isaac Marrero-Guilamon. *Art of Dissent: Adventures in London's Olympic State.* London: Marshgate, 2012.

Price, Monroe E., and Daniel Dayan. *Owning the Olympics: Narratives of the New China.* Ann Arbor: University of Michigan Press, 2008.

Rancière, Jacques. *The Politics of Aesthetics: The Distribution of the Sensible.* New York: Continuum, 2007.

Rawson, Philip. *Ceramics.* Oxford: Oxford University Press, 1971.

Rogers, Everett. *Diffusion of Innovations* 5th Edition. New York: Free Press, 2003.

Rossi, Corinna. *Architecture and Mathematics in Ancient Egypt.* Cambridge: Cambridge University Press, 2004.

Scarry, Elaine. *The Body in Pain.* Oxford: Oxford University Press, 1985.

Semper, Gottfried, trans. Harry Francis Mallgrave and Wolfgang Herrmann. *The Four Elements of Architecture.* Cambridge: Cambridge University Press, 1989.

Sen, Amarty. *Commodities and Capabilities.* Amsterdam: Elsevier, 1985.

Sennett, Richard. *The Craftsman.* New Haven: Yale University Press, 2009.

Schatzki, Theodore. *The Timespace of Human Activity: On Performance, Society and History as Indeterminate Teleological Events.* New York: Rowman & Littlefield, 2010.

Shove, Elizabeth, Matthew Watson, Martin Hand, and Jack Ingram. The Design of Everyday Life. Oxford: Berg, 2007.

Shove, Elizabeth, Mika Pantzar, and Matt Watson. *The Dynamics of Social Practice.* London: Sage, 2012.

Simon, Herbert. *Sciences of the Artificial.* Cambridge: MIT Press, 1996.

Smith, Carl. *City Water, City Life: Water and the Infrastructure of Ideas in Urbanizing Philadelphia, Boston, and Chicago.* Chicago: University of Chicago Press, 2013.

Stone, Alison. *Luce Irigaray and the Philosophy of Sexual Difference.* New York: Cambridge University Press, 2006.

Taussig, Michael. *The Nervous System.* New York: Routledge, 1992.

Toohey, Kristine, and A. J. Veal. *The Olympic Games: A Social Science Perspective.* Wallingford: CAB International, 2007.

Traganou, Jilly, and M. Mitrasinovic (eds.). *Travel, Space, Architecture.* Aldershot: Ashgate, 2009.

Tukker, Arnold, and Ursula Tischner (eds.). *New Business for Old Europe: Product-Service Development, Competitiveness and Sustainability.* Sheffield: Greenleaf, 2006.

Van Kranenberg, Rob. *The Internet of Things: A Critique of Ambient Technology and the All-Seeing Network of RFID.* Amsterdam: Network Notebooks, 2008.

Verbeek, Peter-Paul. *What Things Do: Philosophical Reflections on Technology, Agency, and Design.* University Park: Pennsylvania State University Press, 2005.

Vinken, Barbara. *Fashion Zeitgeist: Trends and Cycles in the Fashion System.* Oxford and New York: Berg, 2005.

Von Busch, Otto. *Fashion-able: Hacktivism and Engaged Fashion Design.* Göteborg: ArtMonitor, 2008.

Von Busch, Otto and Karl Palmas. *Abstract Hacktivism: The Making of a Hacker Culture.* London: OpenMute, 2006.

DESIGN AS FUTURE-MAKING

CONTRIBUTOR BIOGRAPHIES

Barbara Adams studies the creative practices of artists, curators, and social scientists. Her research considers what social scientists might learn from artists and designers in terms of developing and expanding their methodological dispositions. She has written for artists and art institutions and is contributing to the book *Designing Experience: Positions & Approaches* (edited by Peter Benz, Bloomsbury, 2014). She teaches at the New School, Eugene Lang, and Parsons The New School for Design.

Arjun Appadurai is the Paulette Goddard Professor of Media, Culture, and Communication at New York University. He is an internationally recognized scholar of globalization, cities, and material life, and he has held teaching positions at the University of Pennsylvania, the University of Chicago, and Yale University and was also the John Dewey Distinguished Professor in the Social Sciences at The New School, where he also served as provost. He is the author of numerous books and articles, including *The Future as Cultural Fact: Essays on the Global Condition* (London, Verso, 2013) and *Modernity at Large: Cultural Dimensions of Globalization* (University of Minnesota Press, 1996). He is a fellow of the American Academy of Arts and Sciences.

Anna Barbara graduated in architecture from the Politechnic of Milan and has been visiting professor at Kookmin University in South Korea. In 2000, she won the Canon Foundation Fellowship for research at Hosei University Faculty of Architecture and Town Planning in Tokyo. She has served as professor of sensorial design as a member of the Politechnic of Milan's Faculty of Design; as professor of senses and design at Università dell'Immagine; and as director of the fashion school and the director of the Textile Design and New Materials Masters program at NABA (Nuova Accademia di Belle Arti, Milan). She is currently a researcher in architecture at the Politechnic of Milan campus in Piacenza and has been a visiting lecturer at colleges and universities in United States, Korea, Japan, Philippines, Brazil, the United Arab Emirates, and Jordan. She is the author of *Storie di Architettura attraverso i sensi* (Bruno Mondadori, 2000); *Invisible Architectures. Experiencing Places through the Sense of Smell* (Skira, 2006); and *Sensi, tempo e architettura* (Postmedia Books, 2012). She has designed temporary, movable architecture, such as the Polycarbonate House in Tokyo (2000), and Dumia—Interreligeous Dome (2002) with Brigata Tognazzi and Monoloco (2013). She is co-founder with Luca Molinari of VIAPIRANESI srl.

Elio Caccavale is design studio leader in the Masters in Design Innovation and Service Design program at the Glasgow School of Art. In addition, he holds a visiting professorship at the Polytechnic of Milan and an honorary professorship at Hubei University of Technology. Prior to joining Glasgow School of Art, he was the founder and director of the MS in product design program at the University of Dundee. He has held teaching positions at the Royal College of Art, Staatliche Hochschule für Gestaltung Karlsruhe, Central Saint Martins College of Art and Design, the Architectural Association, and research positions at Newcastle University in the Policy, Ethics, and Life Sciences Research Centre, Reading University in the School of System Engineering (Cybernetics), and the Imperial College in the Institute of Biomedical Engineering. He is the co-author of *Creative Encounters*, a book that explores the opportunities provided by collaborations of artists, designers, educators, and scientists. His work has been exhibited extensively in America, Europe, Asia, and the Middle East and is held in the permanent collection of the Museum of Modern Art in New York. He is the founder of Elio Caccavale Design Studio, a design practice that includes product design, interaction design, and ethnography research.

Hazel Clark is research chair of fashion at Parsons The New School for Design in New York, where she teaches principally in the MA in Fashion Studies program. She is a design historian and theorist specializing in fashion and textiles and design studies, including issues of design and cultural identity, and fashion and design in China. She has taught internationally, in the United States, the UK, Hong Kong, China, Australia, and Europe. Her publications include *The Cheongsam* (Oxford University Press, 2000), the co-edited *Old Clothes, New Looks: Second-Hand Fashion* (Bloomsbury, 2005), *The Fabric of Cultures: Fashion, Identity, and Globalization* (Routledge, 2009), *Design Studies: A Reader* (Bloomsbury, 2009) and the forthcoming, co-authored, *Fashion and Everyday Life: Britain and America, 1890–2010* (Bloomsbury, 2015).

Teddy Cruz earned a Master in Design Studies at Harvard University and established his research-based architecture practice in San Diego, California. He has been recognized internationally for his urban research of the Tijuana-San Diego border. In 1991, he received the Rome Prize in Architecture, and in 2005 he was the first recipient of the James Stirling Memorial Lecture on the City prize by the Canadian Centre for Architecture. His work has been profiled in important publications, including *The New York Times*, *Domus*, and *Harvard Design Magazine*. In 2008, he represented the United States in the Venice Architecture Biennial, and this year his work will be included *Small Scale, Big Change*, an exhibition at the Museum of Modern Art, New York. He is currently a professor in public culture and urbanism in the Visual Arts Department at University of California, San Diego, where he co-founded the Center for Urban Ecologies.

Clive Dilnot is professor of design studies in the School of Art and Design History and Theory at Parsons The New School for Design. Previously, he was professor of design studies and director of design initiatives at the School of the Art Institute of Chicago. He has also taught at Harvard University, in Hong Kong,

and the United Kingdom, and has been a visiting professor at the University of Technology, Sydney, the University of Illinois in Chicago, and Rhode Island School of Design. His writing appears in numerous scholarly journals and recent publications, including *Ethics? Design?* (Archeworks, 2005) and a forthcoming study with Tony Fry and Susan Stewart, *Design and the Question of History*.

Sean Donahue is principal of ResearchCenteredDesign (RCD/LA), a Los Angeles-based design practice. The former director of research for the humanities and sciences at Art Center College of Design, he is now co-launching MDP+Field, a graduate-degree track within Art Center's Graduate Media Design Practices program. The track's mission is to host a platform for critical dialogue and contributions around design and social practice. He has lectured and held workshops at Harvard University, Cal Arts, IDEO, and North Carolina State University, where he was designer-in-residence. He is currently the scholar in residence at the Helen Hamlyn Centre, Royal College of Art. His recent work has been included in the Cooper-Hewitt, National Design Triennial *Why Design Now?* (2010); the California Design Biennial *Action/Reaction* (2011); the AIGA Design Educators Conference *New Practices/New Contexts* (2011). His work has also been published in *Archis Magazine*, *Expanding Architecture: Design as Activism* (Metropolis Books, 2008); *The Journal of Biomedical Informatics*; *Idea Magazine*; and he served as co-editor of *Beyond Progressive Design* (Design Philosophy Papers, 2011)

Jamer Hunt is the director of the MFA program in Transdisciplinary Design at Parsons The New School for Design. He was previously the director of the master's program in Industrial Design, a graduate laboratory for postindustrial design, at the University of the Arts in Philadelphia. His practice, Big + Tall Design, combines conceptual, collaborative, and communication design. Hunt is a co-founder of DesignPhiladelphia and has served on the board of directors of the American Center for Design and the editorial board of the forthcoming journal *Design and Culture*. His written work explores the poetics and politics of the built environment in various books, journals, and magazines, and he is now writing a graphic design textbook entitled *Form Follows Context* (Thames & Hudson).

Ivan Kucina is an assistant professor at the School of Architecture, University of Belgrade, Serbia, and a visiting professor at the School of Design Strategies, Parsons The New School for Design, New York; Polis University, Tirana, Albania; KTH School of Architecture, Stockholm, Sweden; Dessau International School of Architecture, Dessau, Germany; and the Faculty of Media and Communication, Singidunum University, Belgrade. In bridging his research pursuits with his teaching, he has established collaborations with informal educational and research groups such as School of Missing Studies, New York, and STEALTH group, Rotterdam. He published *15/3* (Univerzitet u Beogradu, Arhitektonski Fakultet, 2008), a textbook on innovative methods of learning space-form dialectics. He is also a practicing architect and runs an interdisciplinary architectural and design practice together with architect Nenad Katic. In 2006, he co-founded the Belgrade International Architecture Week and currently serves as its program director. Since 2012 he has been a program director of the Urban Transformations program at the Mikser Festival, Belgrade, and, from 2013, the program director of the Balkan Architecture Conference.

Sze Tsung Leong is an artist based in New York. His work is included in the permanent collections of the Metropolitan Museum of Art and Museum of Modern Art in New York; the San Francisco Museum of Modern Art; the National Galleries of Scotland; the National Gallery of Canada; the Museum of Fine Arts, Houston; the Deutsche Börse Art Collection; and the Yale University Art Gallery, among others. His work has been exhibited internationally, including a solo exhibition at the Museo de Arte Contemporáneo de Monterrey, Mexico; and group exhibitions, including

An Atlas of Events at the Calouste Gulbenkian Foundation in Lisbon, the 2006 Havana Biennial, *New Photography* at the High Museum of Art, the 2004 Taipei Biennial, and *Painting as Paradox* at Artists Space in New York. After attending Art Center College of Design, receiving a BA and the Eisner Prize in Photography from University of California at Berkeley, and a masters degree from Harvard University, he was awarded a Guggenheim Fellowship in 2005. His books include *History Images* (Steidl, 2006), and *Horizons* (Hatje Cantz, 2014).

Tim Marshall, The New School's provost since 2009, oversees the development of the university's academic profile as manifested through its faculty, programs and curricula, pedagogy, and research. He has led new initiatives to connect the university's strengths in design, social research, liberal and performing arts, media, and professional programs, and an increased emphasis on interdisciplinary, project-based, and thematic learning. Marshall has also advanced the university's approach to distributed and global education through new partnerships in important urban centers, including Paris, Mumbai, and Shanghai. Prior to his appointment as provost, Tim was dean of Parsons The New School for Design, where he is also a tenured associate professor. At Parsons, he led a major restructuring effort, organizing a dozen disparate departments into five thematic schools, overhauling the undergraduate curriculum, and launching a range of new graduate degrees. He has held academic leadership positions at the University of Western Sydney in Australia and served as a consultant to academic institutions in Australia, Germany, Hong Kong, China, and Singapore, and has written and lectured internationally on design research and education.

William Morrish is an architect, urban designer, and professor of urban ecologies at Parsons The New School of Design in New York City. He holds a Bachelor of Architecture from the University of California, Berkeley, and a Masters of Urban Design in Architecture from the Harvard

Graduate School of Design. Collaborating with a network of interdisciplinary city actors, he has been leading an effort to identify constructive aspects of existing urban practice and theory to generate new design knowledge for the next generation of infrastructure. These ideas have been tested in such urban research programs as *THINK Rebuilding the World Trade Center*, the winning competition proposal; *Rebuilding New Orleans*, a handbook of policy and design options; and *Cambodian Living Arts City*, a public forum on arts and cultural development of post-conflict cities. He is an active contributor in a number of design and policy network collectives such as the Council on the Internet of Things, Fredrick P. Rose Architectural Fellowship Network, and the Political Equator Collective. He has also authored and co-authored an extensive list of publications on urban history, community planning, architecture and urban ecology, including *Civilizing Terrains, The Earth in the City* (William K. Stout, 1989, 2005); and *Building for the Arts: A Guidebook for the Planning and Design of Cultural Facilities* (Western States Arts Foundation, 1984).

Tom Shakespeare is a sociologist and bioethicist who has worked at the Universities of Sunderland, Leeds, and Newcastle and at the World Health Organization. He is currently senior lecturer in medical sociology at University of East Anglia Medical School. His best-known book is *Disability Rights and Wrongs* (Routledge, 2006). In addition to his own creative practice, he has worked as a critic and curator in the field of Sci-Art. His media work includes three television documentaries and regular contributions to print and broadcast media.

Bruce Sterling, an author, journalist, editor, and critic, is best known for his ten science fiction novels. He also writes short stories, book reviews, design criticism, opinion columns, and introductions for books ranging from Ernst Juenger to Jules Verne. His nonfiction works include *The Hacker Crackdown: Law and Disorder on the Electronic Frontier* (Bantam, 1993), *Tomorrow Now: Envisioning the Next Fifty*

Years (Random House, 2002), and *Shaping Things* (The MIT Press, 2005). He is a contributing editor of *WIRED* magazine and writes a blog. In 2005, he was the Visionary in Residence at Art Center College of Design in Pasadena, and in 2008 he was the guest curator for the Share Festival of Digital Art and Culture in Turin, Italy, and the Visionary in Residence at the Sandberg Instituut in Amsterdam. In 2011, he returned to Art Center as Visionary in Residence to run a special project on augmented reality.

Mette Ramsgard Thomsen's research centers on the intersection between architecture and computer science. During the last fifteen years, her focus has been on the profound changes that digital technologies instigate in the way architecture is thought, designed, and built. In 2005 she founded the Centre for IT and Architecture research group (CITA) at the Royal Academy of Fine Arts, School of Architecture, Design and Conservation in Copenhagen, and in 2010 she became full professor in architecture and digital technologies. At CITA she has piloted a special research focus on the new digital-material relations that digital technologies bring forth. Investigating advanced computer modeling, digital fabrication, and material specification, CITA has been central in the forming of an international research field examining the changes to material practice in architecture. This has been led by a series of research investigations developing concepts and technologies as well as strategic projects, such as the international Digital Crafting Network that fosters interdisciplinary sharing and dissemination of expertise and supports new collaborations in the fields of architecture, engineering, and design.

Cameron Tonkinwise is associate professor and director of design studies at the School of Design at Carnegie Mellon University. He was previously at Parsons The New School for Design in New York, where he was the associate dean for sustainability and before that the co-chair of the Tishman Environment and Design Center and chair of design thinking and sustainability in the

School of Design Strategies. He has also been director of design studies at the University of Technology, Sydney, and executive director of Change Design, formerly known as the EcoDesign Foundation. He has published a range of articles on the role of design and, in particular, service design in the promotion of the sharing economy and collaborative consumption. He is currently editing *The Sustainable Design Reader* (Bloomsbury) and is writing a book about transition design.

Jilly Traganou is an architect and associate professor in spatial design studies at the School of Art and Design History and Theory at Parsons The New School for Design. She is the author of *The Tokaido Road: Traveling and Representation in Edo And Meiji Japan* (RoutledgeCurzon, 2004) and a co-editor with Miodrag Mitrasinovic of *Travel, Space, Architecture* (Ashgate, 2009). She has contributed to *Design and Culture*, *Design Issues*, *Journal of Design History*, *Journal of Sport and Social Issues*, *Journal of Modern Greek Studies*, *L'architecture d'aujourd'hui*, *Journal for Architecture Building Science of the Architectural Institute Japan*, as well as *Critical Cities* Vol. 02 (Myrdle Court Press, 2010), *Global Design History* (Routledge, 2011), and the forthcoming *Iconic Designs* (Bloomsbury). In 2012, she was guest-editor of a special issue in the *Journal of Design History* titled "Design Histories of the Olympic Games," and she is the book reviews editor of the *Journal of Design History*. She has also co-organized and participated in practice-based collaborative research projects in critical design pedagogy.

Grace Vetrocq Tuttle is a Brooklyn-based communication design specialist with a transdisciplinary practice that is investigative, strategic, and collaborative. Using her skills as an anthropologist, writer, and visual designer, she works with individuals, organizations, and communities to articulate objectives, analyze challenges, and mobilize ideas and resources for change. She has a BA in anthropology from Bard College and an MFA from the transdisciplinary design program at Parsons The New School for Design.

Otto von Busch is an assistant professor of integrated design at Parsons The New School for Design, New York, and a professor at Konstfack, University College of Arts, Crafts, and Design, Stockholm. He earned his PhD in critical fashion design at Göteborg University and is an artist, activist, fashion theorist, and designer. His work explores the emergence of a new "hacktivist" designer role in fashion, and his current projects take a critical and political look at design, fashion systems and its networks.

Susan Yelavich is an associate professor and director of the MA Design Studies program in the School of Art and Design History and Theory at Parsons The New School for Design. Her research explores the dynamics of global culture and design, the relationship between textiles and architecture, and the parallels between design and literature. She is the author of numerous articles and books, including *Contemporary World Interiors* (Phaidon, 2007), *Pentagram/Profile* (Phaidon, 2004), *Inside Design Now* (Smithsonian's Cooper-Hewitt, National Design Museum, 2003), *Design for Life* (Whitney Library of Design, 1997), and *The Edge of the Millennium: An International Critique of Architecture, Urban Planning, Product and Communication Design* (Smithsonian's Cooper-Hewitt, National Design Museum, 1993). A fellow of the American Academy in Rome, she was awarded the Academy's Rolland Prize in Design in 2003. Previously, she was the assistant director for public programs at the Smithsonian's Cooper-Hewitt, National Design Museum in New York.

INDEX